D1082636

WEST'S LAW SCHOOL
ADVISORY BOARD

JESSE H. CHOPER
Professor of Law and Dean Emeritus,
University of California, Berkeley

JOSHUA DRESSLER
Professor of Law, Michael E. Moritz College of Law,
The Ohio State University

YALE KAMISAR
Professor of Law Emeritus, University of San Diego
Professor of Law Emeritus, University of Michigan

MARY KAY KANE
Professor of Law, Chancellor and Dean Emeritus,
University of California,
Hastings College of the Law

LARRY D. KRAMER
President, William and Flora Hewlett Foundation

JONATHAN R. MACEY
Professor of Law, Yale Law School

ARTHUR R. MILLER
University Professor, New York University
Formerly Bruce Bromley Professor of Law, Harvard University

GRANT S. NELSON
Professor of Law, Pepperdine University
Professor of Law Emeritus, University of California, Los Angeles

A. BENJAMIN SPENCER
Professor of Law,
Washington & Lee University School of Law

JAMES J. WHITE
Professor of Law, University of Michigan

JUVENILE JUSTICE ADMINISTRATION

IN A NUTSHELL

THIRD EDITION

by

BARRY C. FELD
Centennial Professor of Law
University of Minnesota

WEST
ACADEMIC
PUBLISHING

Mat #41459007

The publisher is not engaged in rendering legal or other professional advice, and this publication is not a substitute for the advice of an attorney. If you require legal or other expert advice, you should seek the services of a competent attorney or other professional.

Nutshell Series, In a Nutshell and the Nutshell Logo are trademarks registered in the U.S. Patent and Trademark Office.

© West, a Thomson business, 2003
© 2009 Thomson/Reuters
© 2014 LEG, Inc. d/b/a West Academic

        444 Cedar Street, Suite 700
        St. Paul, MN 55101
        1–877–888–1330

West, West Academic Publishing, and West Academic are trademarks of West Publishing Corporation, used under license.

Printed in the United States of America

ISBN: 978–0–314–28821–9

To Patricia,
with love and gratitude

PREFACE

Young offenders constitute a significant part of the "crime problem." They pose difficult and interesting problems for youth policy and criminal justice policy—how do we respond when the child is a criminal and the criminal is a child? This Nutshell on Juvenile Justice Administration focuses exclusively on the criminal and non-criminal misconduct of children that bring them within the jurisdiction of juvenile courts and examines the school, law enforcement, judicial, and administrative responses to it. It does not address child abuse, dependency and neglect, or juvenile or family courts' dependency processes. It deals with issues of children's rights only insofar as they relate to the processes of investigating and prosecuting juvenile offenders for delinquency and status-offenses. Like all Nutshells, it strives to provide a succinct exposition of the law for students studying juvenile justice, for lawyers who do not regularly practice in juvenile court and who find themselves appointed or retained to represent a child, and for legislators and policy officials involved in juvenile justice law reform efforts.

In the field of juvenile justice, states truly constitute "laboratories of experimentation." No single source of law governs juvenile courts. Rather, a combination of United States Supreme Court constitutional decisions, state court constitutional and non-constitutional decisions, statutes, juvenile court procedural rules, and administrative procedures govern different aspects of juvenile justice administration. As a consequence, states' laws and policies toward young offenders vary considerably. This Nutshell will provide students and practitioners with the background necessary to understand the policy issues that state statutes, court procedural rules, and federal and state judicial opinions address.

Three contending policy themes affect variations in juvenile justice administration—the legal and administrative consequences of regulating *children* rather than *adults*, the procedural and substantive implications of a justice system that nominally emphasizes *treatment* rather than *punishment*, and the tensions between *discretion* and *rules* that occur in a system that *treats children* rather than *punishes adults*. Where states' policies diverge, the Nutshell identifies different responses to the same problem to enable readers unfamiliar with the field to understand the range of legal options. The Nutshell examines central doctrines but without extended citations or discussion of court opinions, legislation, or academic commentary. Readers also may wish to refer to the cases and notes in my casebook, *Cases and Materials on Juvenile Justice Administration* (4th Ed. West Group 2013). To facilitate learning and interchangeability, the Nutshell follows the organization of the casebook.

The organization of the Nutshell reviews the origin of juvenile courts and then follows the typical flow of a delinquency case. Chapter 1 addresses the origins and contemporary history of the juvenile court. Chapter 2 focuses on the delinquency and status offense jurisdiction of the juvenile court. Chapter 3 analyzes law enforcement and selected issues of criminal procedure—search and seizure, interrogation, and the like—in the context of juveniles. It examines procedural variations that occur because the offender is a child or located in youth-specific institutions like schools. Chapter 4 analyzes case screening, diversion, and other informal methods to resolve delinquency referrals without formal juvenile court intervention. Chapter 5 examines pretrial detention and the use of methods other than bail to protect children or to secure their presence at trial. Chapter 6 examines how and when states try youths in criminal court rather than in juvenile court. It examines the principle statutory mechanisms—judicial waiver, legislative offense exclusion, and prosecutorial direct file—and the criteria and procedures used to make "adulthood" determinations. It also describes the criminal court consequences for youths tried as adults. In a recent trilogy of cases—Roper, Graham, and Miller/Jackson—the Supreme Court recognized the diminished criminal responsibility of young offenders, required states to consider youthfulness as a mitigating factor in sentencing, and reaffirmed that "children are different." Chapter 7 analyzes juveniles' procedural rights at trial in a delinquency and status offense hearing. Chapter 8 explores the dispositional process and the alternative sentencing options available to juvenile courts.

I have dedicated this book to my wife, Patricia Feld, my life partner of more than four decades and the mother of my two wonderful children, Ari and Julia. I am grateful to Patricia beyond the capacity of words to express for the life that we share. Her support, encouragement, and patience have enabled me to grow professionally and personally and make every day of my life a joy and pleasure.

October, 2013
Effie, MN

OUTLINE

TABLE OF CASES

References are to Pages

Cases

TABLE OF STATUTES

References are to Pages

UNITED STATES CONSTITUTION

UNITED STATES CODE ANNOTATED

TABLE OF BOOKS AND ARTICLES

References are to Pages

JUVENILE JUSTICE ADMINISTRATION

IN A NUTSHELL

THIRD EDITION

CHAPTER 1
INTRODUCTION

Until the early nineteenth century, the American legal system treated young people who violated the criminal law much as it did adult offenders. The classical criminal law recognized that the threat of sanctions could not deter those who did not know "right from wrong," and it excused from criminal liability the severely mentally ill and young children. Sanford J. Fox, *Responsibility in the Juvenile Court*, 11 Wm. & Mary L. Rev. 659 (1970). The common law's infancy defense provided the only formal doctrinal protection for youths. It conclusively presumed that children less than seven years of age lacked criminal capacity, treated those fourteen years of age and older as fully responsible adults, and created a rebuttable presumption that those between seven and fourteen years of age lacked criminal capacity. If courts found children criminally responsible, then they imposed the same sentences—including capital punishment—and committed them to the same penal facilities as they did adult criminals.

At the end of the nineteenth century, punishing juveniles just like adults appalled Progressive reformers. They created the juvenile court as an informal welfare system and a diversionary alternative to the criminal process. Rather than punishing young offenders for their crimes, juvenile court judges made dispositions in the child's "best interests" and the state functioned as *parens patriae*, as a surrogate parent. In 1967, the Supreme Court in In re Gault, 387 U.S. 1 (1967), granted juveniles some constitutional procedural rights in delinquency hearings. In turn, Gault and subsequent due process decisions provided the impetus for states to modify juvenile courts' procedures, jurisdiction, and jurisprudence. Over the next three decades, judicial decisions and legislative amendments transformed the juvenile court from a nominally rehabilitative social welfare agency into a more criminal-like and punitive system for young offenders. The "baby boom" increase in youth crime that began in the 1960s and a sharp rise in urban youth homicide in the early 1990s provided political impetus to "get tough" on youth crime and led to harsher juvenile justice sentencing and transfer policies. More recently, research by developmental psychologists has demonstrated that children think and act differently from adults and reminded policy makers why states require a different type of justice system for juveniles than adults. Within the past decade, a trilogy of Supreme Court decisions—Roper v. Simmons, 543 U.S. 551 (2005), Graham v. Florida, 130 S.Ct. 2011 (2010), and Miller v. Alabama, 132 S.Ct. 2455 (2012)—relied on that developmental research, reaffirmed the reduced criminal responsibility of adolescents, and emphasized that "children are different." This Chapter briefly examines juvenile courts' historical origins, "constitutional domestication," "get tough" era policies, and more recent, evidence-based focus on how children differ from adults.

A. ORIGINS OF THE JUVENILE COURT

Historians trace many features of the first juvenile courts to the earlier Houses of Refuge that emerged in eastern cities during the middle-third of the nineteenth century. David J. Rothman, *Conscience and Convenience: The Asylum and Its Alternative in Progressive America* (1980). The Houses of Refuge provided the first specialized institutions for the formal social control of youth and juveniles' correctional segregation preceded their judicial separation. John Sutton, *Stubborn Children: Controlling Delinquency in the United States* (1988). Refuges initially appeared in New York and Boston in 1825 in conjunction with America's first burst of industrialization, immigration, and urbanization. Many legal features later incorporated into the juvenile court first appeared in the laws creating the Houses of Refuge. Refuge legislation embodied three legal innovations: a formal, age-based differentiation between juvenile and adults offenders and their institutional separation, the use of indeterminate commitments, and a broadened *parens patriae* legal authority that encompassed both juvenile criminal offenders and neglected and incorrigible children. Sanford J. Fox, *Juvenile Justice Reform: An Historical Perspective*, 22 Stan. L. Rev. 1187 (1970). In the mid-nineteenth century, penal reformers constructed a second type of youth institution—the reformatory—to shelter and reform young deviants. Unlike urban Houses of Refuge, sponsors of reform schools located them in rural settings to provide a wholesome agrarian environment in which to train children.

Progressive reformers established the first juvenile court in Cook County, Illinois on July 1, 1899, and the idea of a separate court for children spread rapidly to other states during the first quarter of the twentieth century. The creation of a separate juvenile justice system reflected a marked change in thinking about youthful misconduct and the state's role in responding to it. Changes in two cultural ideas—*childhood* and *social control*—accompanied modernization and industrialization over a century ago and provided impetus for a separate juvenile court. Between 1870 and World War I, railroads transformed America from a rural, agrarian society into an urban industrial society and fostered rapid economic modernization. New immigrants, including many Catholics from southern and eastern Europe, flooded into the growing cities and crowded into ethnic enclaves and urban slums. These immigrants differed in language, religion, and culture from the dominant Anglo–Protestant Americans who had preceded them a few generations earlier. From its inception, the juvenile court sought to assimilate, integrate, "Americanize," and control the children of immigrants pouring into the industrial centers of the East and Midwest. Anthony Platt, *The Child Savers: The Invention of Delinquency* (1977); Steven Schlossman, *Love and the American Delinquent: The Theory and Practice of Progressive Juvenile Justice* (1977); David S. Tanenhaus, *Juvenile Justice in the Making* (2004).

The dislocations associated with modernization, industrialization, urbanization, and immigration posed many social problems and the Progressive reform movement emerged to address them. Progressives believed that benevolent state action guided by experts could alleviate social ills. They created a variety of public agencies to inculcate their Anglo–Protestant middle-class values and to assimilate and "Americanize" immigrants, Catholics, and the poor to become virtuous citizens like themselves.

Changes in family structure and functions accompanied the economic transformation. Economic activities shifted from the family household to other work environments like the industrial factory and substantially modified the roles of women and children. Family life became more private, women's roles more domestic, and, particularly within the upper and middle classes, a newer view emerged of childhood and adolescence as distinct developmental stages. Before the past two or three centuries, age provided neither the basis for a separate legal status nor for social segregation. People generally regarded young people as miniature adults, small versions of their parents. Phillipe Aries, *Centuries of Childhood* (1962). Children were not separated from adult activities and by age fourteen were integrated into the economy through apprenticeships and the like. By the end of the nineteenth century, however, people increasingly viewed children as vulnerable, innocent, passive, and dependent beings who needed extended preparation for life. The newer vision of children altered traditional child-rearing practices and imposed a greater responsibility on parents to supervise their children's moral and social development. Many Progressive reform programs—the juvenile court, child labor and welfare laws, and compulsory school attendance laws—shared a child-centered theme that reflected and advanced the changing imagery of childhood.

Changes in ideological assumptions about the causes of crime inspired many Progressive criminal justice reforms. The classical criminal law attributed crime to free-willed actors who chose to offend. By contrast, positivist criminology regarded crime as determined rather than chosen and the product of prior causes rather than free will. Criminology's deterministic explanation of criminal behavior reduced offenders' moral responsibility and focused on reforming them rather than punishing them for their offenses. Applying medical analogies to the treatment of offenders, a growing class of social science professionals fostered the "Rehabilitative Ideal." Although historians debate whether the Progressive movement was exclusively a humanitarian one to save poor and immigrant children or also an "elitist" effort to expand social control over them, e.g. Platt, *Childsavers*, Progressive "child-savers" described juvenile courts as benign, non-punitive, and therapeutic. The juvenile court combined the new conception of children with the new strategies of social control to create a judicial-welfare alternative to the criminal justice system, to remove children from the adult criminal process, and to enforce the newer conceptions of children's dependency. See e.g., Barry C. Feld, *Bad Kids: Race and the Transformation of the Juvenile Court* (1999); David Tanenhaus, *Juvenile Justice in the Making* (2004); Elizabeth Scott and Laurence Steinberg, *Rethinking Juvenile Justice* (2008); Thomas J. Bernard and Megan C. Kurlycheck, *The Cycle of Juvenile Justice* (2nd Ed. 2010).

Reflecting the changing social construction of adolescence, Progressive reformers viewed youthful autonomy as malign. Juvenile courts exercised jurisdiction over unruly children, reinforced parental authority and control, and allowed the state to intervene when parents proved inadequate to the task. The legal doctrine of *parens patriae*—the right and responsibility of the State to substitute its own control for that of the natural parents when the latter appeared unable or unwilling to meet their responsibilities or when the child posed a problem for the community—provided the formal justification to intervene. The doctrine of *parens patriae* originated in the English chancery courts to protect the Crown's interests in feudal succession and established royal authority to administer the estates of orphaned minors with property. In the American colonies, local poor laws authorized the State to act *in loco parentis* to separate children from their destitute or neglectful parents. In 1838, in Ex parte Crouse, 4 Whart. 9 (Pa. 1838), the Pennsylvania Supreme Court invoked *parens patriae* to justify a juvenile's commitment to a House of Refuge, rejected legal challenges to incarceration of troublesome youths, and uncritically accepted the Refuge managers' humanitarian claims.

Juvenile court personnel used informal, discretionary procedures to diagnose the causes of and prescribe the cures for delinquency. By separating children from adults and providing a rehabilitative alternative to punishment, juvenile courts rejected the jurisprudence of criminal law and its procedural safeguards. See e.g., Feld, *Bad Kids*; Tanenhaus, *Juvenile Justice in the Making*. Juvenile courts conducted confidential hearings, used informal procedures, and excluded lawyers and juries. To avoid the stigma of a criminal prosecution, they employed a euphemistic vocabulary and initiated proceedings by "petitions" rather than indictments or complaints, "adjudicated" youths for delinquency rather than conducted criminal trials and convicted them, and imposed "dispositions" that could include commitment to training schools rather holding sentencing hearings that could result in confinement in prison.

Juvenile courts' jurisdiction encompassed youths suffering from abuse, dependency, or neglect, as well as those charged with criminal offenses and non-criminal status offenses such as waywardness, stubbornness, incorrigibility, and disobedience. As a result, reformers characterized juvenile court proceedings as civil rather than criminal. Theoretically, a child's "best interests" background, and welfare guided dispositions. Because judges viewed a youth's offense only as a symptom of her "real needs," they imposed indeterminate and non-proportional dispositions that potentially continued for the duration of minority.

The juvenile court's rehabilitative ideal envisioned a specialized judge trained in the social sciences and child development whose empathic qualities and insight would aid in making individualized dispositions. Julian Mack, *The Juvenile Court*, 23 Harv.L.Rev. 104 (1909). Reformers anticipated that social service personnel, clinicians, and probation officers would assist the judge to decide what to do to secure the child's "best interests." Progressives assumed that a scientific analysis of the child's social circumstances would reveal the proper diagnosis and prescribe the cure. The juvenile court maximized discretion to diagnose and to treat and focused on the child's character and lifestyle rather than on the particular crime. Other analysts contend that regardless of juvenile courts' ability to intervene effectively and to rehabilitate youths, a central objective was simply to protect young delinquents from the punishments of criminal courts. Franklin E. Zimring, *The Common Thread: Diversion in Juvenile Justice*, 88 Cal. L. Rev. 2477 (2000). Providing a diversionary alternative to processing in criminal courts would enable juvenile courts to achieve a social good regardless of the success or failure of rehabilitative intervention.

Early juvenile court law and practice varied considerably from jurisdiction to jurisdiction and depended significantly on the personality of the presiding judges. However, a number of common features marked the Progressive conception of the juvenile court: informal procedures and confidential, non-stigmatic hearings; individualized treatment and rehabilitation; and correctional facilities to separate youths from adults. Despite those good intentions, a substantial gap existed between juvenile courts' benevolent rhetoric and reality.

B. CONSTITUTIONAL DOMESTICATION OF THE JUVENILE COURT

For the first half-century of its existence, the juvenile justice system brushed aside occasional legal challenges and criticisms. No sustained or systematic examinations occurred until the 1960s. The Supreme Court fired its first constitutional salvo in Kent v. United States, 383 U.S. 541 (1966), in which it required some procedural due process in judicial waiver hearings to transfer youths to criminal court for prosecution as adults. See Chapter 6 A. The Court's juvenile justice decisions were part of its broader "due process revolution" in the 1960s to regulate states' power, reform criminal procedures and expand civil rights for minorities. Feld, *Bad Kids*.

In 1967, the Supreme Court in In re Gault, 387 U.S. 1 (1967), substantially transformed the juvenile court from a social welfare agency into a more formal and legalistic institution. This "constitutional domestication" marked the first step in the procedural and substantive convergence between the juvenile and adult criminal justice systems. Gault involved the delinquency adjudication and institutional commitment of a youth who allegedly made a lewd telephone call to a neighbor of the "irritatingly offensive, adolescent, sex variety." Fifteen-year-old Gerald Gault was taken into custody, detained overnight without notice to his parents, and appeared at a hearing the following day. A probation officer filed a petition which alleged simply that he was a delinquent minor in need of the care and custody of the court. No complaining witness appeared and the judge did not hear any sworn testimony or prepare a transcript or record of the proceedings. At the hearing, the judge questioned Gault about the phone call, and he apparently made some incriminating responses. The judge neither advised Gault nor his parents of the right to remain silent, the right to counsel, nor provided him with an attorney. Following his hearing, the judge returned Gault to a detention cell. At his dispositional hearing a week later, the judge committed Gault to the State Industrial School "for the period of his minority [that is, until 21], unless sooner discharged by due process of law." If Gault had been an adult, his sentence could have resulted in no more than a $50 fine or two months' imprisonment; as a juvenile, however, he was subject to incarceration for up to six years, the duration of his minority.

Rather than accepting uncritically the rehabilitative rhetoric of Progressive juvenile reformers, the Court examined the punitive realities of the juvenile justice system. In reviewing the history of the juvenile court, the Court noted that the traditional rationales for denying procedural safeguards to juveniles rested on the belief that the proceedings were neither adversarial nor criminal and that because the State acted as *parens patriae*, the child was entitled to custody rather than to liberty. The Court rejected these assertions, however, because denial of procedures frequently resulted in arbitrariness rather than "careful, compassionate, individualized treatment." Although the Court hoped to retain the potential benefits of the juvenile process, it insisted that it would candidly appraise the claims of the juvenile court process in light of the realities of recidivism, the failures of rehabilitation, the stigma of a delinquency label, the breaches of confidentiality, and the arbitrariness of the process. The Court noted that a juvenile process free of constitutional safeguards had not abated recidivism or lowered the high crime rates among juvenile offenders. It also emphasized the harsh realities of juvenile institutional confinement. However, the Court did not simply equate delinquency sanctions with criminal punishment and extend to delinquents all of the rights of adult criminal defendants. Rather, the Court mandated some elementary procedural safeguards necessary for "fair treatment" and avoided completely criminalizing the juvenile process. These "fundamental" rights included advance notice of charges, a fair and impartial hearing, assistance of counsel, the opportunity to confront and cross-examine witnesses, and the Fifth Amendment privilege against self-incrimination.

Although the Court discussed the realities of the juvenile system and required some procedural safeguards, it limited the scope of its holding to the adjudicatory hearing or trial at which a judge decided whether a child committed a delinquent act. It asserted that providing some procedures would not impair juvenile courts' ability to process and treat juveniles. However, Gault insisted that procedural safeguards at the trial were essential both to determine the truth—accurate fact-finding— and to preserve individual freedom by limiting the power of the state—prevent governmental oppression.

In contrast to its narrow holding, the Court relied on the Fourteenth Amendment Due Process Clause and broad notions of "fundamental fairness" to grant delinquents the rights to notice, counsel, and confrontation, rather than the specific provisions of the Sixth Amendment to grant those rights. The Court explicitly incorporated the Fifth Amendment to grant juveniles the privilege against self-incrimination in delinquency proceedings. The Court's extension of the Fifth Amendment provides the clearest example of the dual function of procedural safeguards in delinquency adjudications: assuring accurate fact finding *and* protecting against government oppression. In so doing, the Court recognized that the juvenile system functioned equivalently to the adversarial criminal justice system. Gault reflected the Court's ambivalence about juvenile courts. On the one hand, the Court recognized that involuntary confinement for criminal conduct was at least implicitly punitive, but it declined to extend to delinquents all adult criminal procedural safeguards.

In subsequent decisions, the Supreme Court further elaborated upon the criminal nature of delinquency proceedings. In In re Winship, 397 U.S.

358 (1970), the Court decided that the state must prove delinquency "beyond a reasonable doubt," rather than by lower civil standards of proof by a preponderance of the evidence. Because the Bill of Rights contains no explicit provision for the standard of proof in criminal cases, Winship first held that the constitution required proof beyond a reasonable doubt in adult criminal proceedings. The Court then extended the same standard of proof to delinquency proceedings because of the criminal standard's equally vital role there. The Court concluded that the need to prevent factually unwarranted convictions and to guard against abuses of government power was sufficiently important to outweigh concerns that it would thwart the court's therapeutic mission or erode the differences between juvenile and criminal courts.

One year after Winship, however, the Court in McKeiver v. Pennsylvania, 403 U.S. 528 (1971), declined to extend all of the procedural safeguards of adult criminal prosecutions to delinquency proceedings. The Court in Duncan v. Louisiana, 391 U.S. 145 (1968), granted adult defendants a Sixth Amendment constitutional right to a jury trial in state criminal prosecutions. However, the Court decided McKeiver under the Fourteenth Amendment due process standard, rather than the Sixth Amendment, and held that a jury is not constitutionally essential in delinquency proceedings because the only requirement for "fundamental fairness" in such proceedings is "accurate fact finding," which a judge can satisfy as well as a jury. By emphasizing only accurate fact finding, the Court departed significantly from its prior analyses in Gault, which relied on the *dual* rationales of accurate fact finding *and* protection against governmental oppression. Indeed, Gault held that delinquents required the Fifth Amendment privilege against self-incrimination to protect against governmental oppression even though it might impede accurate fact finding. However, the McKeiver Court denied that juveniles required protection from the state, invoked the mythology of the paternalistic juvenile court judge, and rejected the argument that the inbred, closed nature of the court could prejudice the accuracy of fact finding. In part, the Court denied juries because it perceived that juvenile courts *treated* juveniles rather than *punished* them, although the Court did not analyze the differences. The distinction between treatment and punishment remains one of the fundamental justifications for a separate juvenile court and for its procedural differences. Barry C. Feld, *The Juvenile Court Meets the Principle of Offense: Punishment, Treatment, and the Difference It Makes*, 68 B.U.L.Rev. 821 (1988). In denying juveniles the constitutional right to jury trials, McKeiver emphasized the adverse impact that they would have on the informality, flexibility, and confidentiality of juvenile court proceedings. Although McKeiver found faults with the juvenile process, the Court asserted that imposing jury trials would not correct those deficiencies but would make the juvenile process unduly formal and adversarial. Ultimately, the Court feared that granting juveniles all of the adult criminal procedural safeguards would erode the rationale for a separate juvenile justice system. Some states grant juveniles the right to a jury as a matter of state law. See Chapter 7 A. 3. b.

Five years later, the Court in Breed v. Jones, 421 U.S. 519 (1975), held that the double jeopardy clause of the Fifth Amendment prohibited the adult criminal prosecution of a youth after he was adjudicated delinquent in juvenile court for the same offense. Although the Court framed the issue in terms of the applicability of a specific provision of the Bill of Rights to state proceedings, it resolved the question by recognizing the functional equivalence and identical interests of defendants in a delinquency proceeding and an adult criminal trial.

C. "GET TOUGH" POLICIES— 1970s TO 1990s

The Supreme Court's "Due Process Revolution" coincided with a synergy of campus disorders, escalating baby-boom crime rates, and urban racial rebellions in the mid–1960s. National Republican politicians characterized these events as a crisis of "law and order," appealed to white southern voters' racial antipathy and resistance to school integration, and engineered a conservative backlash to foster a political realignment around issues of race and public policy. Barry C. Feld, Race, *Politics and Juvenile Justice: The Warren Court and the Conservative "Backlash"*, 87 Minn. L. Rev. 1447 (2003). From the 1970s to the 1990s, conservative politicians used crime as a code word for race for electoral advantage, and advocated harsher, "get tough" crime policies that affected juvenile justice administration throughout the nation. In the mid–1980s, crack cocaine markets exploded in the inner cities, young drug dealers armed themselves, and rates of homicide among black youths escalated sharply. Increased urban violence accompanied the deindustrialization of the urban core and the emergence of the black underclass and provided political incentive to toughen responses to youth crime. Misgivings about the ability of juvenile courts either to rehabilitate violent offenders or to protect public safety bolstered policies to prosecute larger numbers of youths as adults.

Culminating in the late 1980s and early 1990s, almost every state enacted laws to simplify the transfer of youths to criminal courts or to require juvenile court judges to impose determinate or mandatory minimum sentences on those who remained within a more punitive juvenile system. Patricia Torbet, et al., *State Responses to Serious and Violent Juvenile Crime* (1996). Statutory changes in waiver laws used offense criteria as dispositional guidelines to structure and limit judicial discretion, to guide prosecutorial charging decisions, or automatically to exclude certain offenses from the jurisdiction of the juvenile court. See Chapter 6 B and C. Politicians' sound bites—"adult crime, adult time" or "old enough to do the crime, old enough to do the time"—exemplify the reformulation of adolescence and represent policies on crime that provide no formal recognition of youthfulness as a mitigating factor in sentencing. Similar legislative changes affected the sentences judges imposed on delinquent offenders as well. See Chapter 8 B 2. Other get tough reforms included erosion of juvenile courts' traditional confidentiality in favor of more open proceedings and access to records. Both waiver and sentencing strategies de-emphasized rehabilitation and the needs of offenders, stressed personal and justice-system accountability and punishment, and based disposition on the seriousness of the offense and prior record. These changes inverted juvenile justice jurisprudence and sentencing policies—from rehabilitation to retribution, from an emphasis on the offender to the seriousness of the offense, from a concern with "amenability to treatment" and a child's "best interests" to public safety and punishment—and shifted discretion from the judicial to the legislative or executive branches. Once youths made the transition to criminal court, judges sentenced them just like adults, confined them in the same prisons and, until Roper v. Simmons (2005), some states executed them for the crimes they committed as juveniles.

D. REASSESSING ADOLESCENT COMPETENCE AND CULPABILITY

Nearly a century after its creation, widespread public, policy-maker, and political dissatisfaction with the juvenile justice system produced contradictory impulses. Some politicians advocated "get tough" policies and criticized juvenile courts for failing to adopt harsher, retributive strategies to hold young offenders accountable and to treat them just like adults. Supporters of juvenile courts criticized them for failing to meet the needs of their clientele, many of whom suffered from psychological problems, educational deficits, poverty and abuse. They condemned the racial disparities in juvenile justice administration that produced disproportionate minority confinement. The general public perceived the juvenile justice system as incapable of rehabilitating offenders, reducing youth crime, or protecting the public safety.

Beginning in the mid–1990s, the John D. and Catherine T. MacArthur Foundation sponsored a Network on Adolescent Development and Juvenile Justice (ADJJ) to provide an evidence-based rationale for juvenile justice policy. http://www.adjj. org. The ADJJ Network conducted interdisciplinary research to examine developmental differences between children and adults and to consider the implications of immaturity for structuring the juvenile justice system. The research program focused on three broad themes: adolescents' competence; culpability; and potential for change. Research on competence focused on how adolescents think and their decision-making capacities and how those limitations affect their ability to exercise legal rights and to participate in the criminal or juvenile justice systems. Research on culpability focused on adolescents' criminal responsibility and their degree of deserved punishment and provides a rationale for categorical mitigation of sanctions for adolescents. Research on capacity to change examines the etiology of delinquency and the factors that promote youths' desistance from crime. Developmental psychologists distinguish between youths' cognitive abilities and their judgment and self-control. Although mid-adolescents' cognitive abilities are comparable with adults, their judgment and impulse control do not emerge for several more years. Youths' immature judgment reflects differences in risk perception, appreciation of future consequences, experience with autonomy, and susceptibility to peer influences. The differences that social scientists observe between youths' and adults' thinking and behavior correspond with human brain development. The ADJJ Network has published a series of edited books and monographs and its research is encouraging a re-examination and amelioration of some of the harsher "get tough" policies enacted previously. See Scott and Steinberg, *Rethinking Juvenile Justice*. The MacArthur Foundation is collaborating with policy makers in several states to implement developmentally appropriate juvenile justice policies.

E. CONCLUSION

Despite their benevolent rhetoric and aspirations, Progressive "child-savers" designed the juvenile court to discriminate—to "Americanize" immigrants, to control the poor, and to provide a coercive mechanism to distinguish between "our children" and "other people's children." Rothman, *Conscience and Convenience*. And, a century later, racial disparities and disproportionate minority confinement remains a characteristic feature of juvenile justice administration. Feld, *Bad Kids*. In their pursuit of the rehabilitative ideal, the Progressives situated the juvenile court on several legal and cultural fault-lines. They created binary conceptions for the juvenile and criminal justice systems: either child or adult; either determinism or freewill; either dependent or responsible; either treatment or punishment; either procedural informality or formality; either discretion or the rule of law.

The past four decades have witnessed a significant shift from the former to the latter of each of these pairs as a result of Gault and its progeny. Gault precipitated a procedural revolution in the juvenile court system that unintentionally but inevitably transformed its original Progressive conception. Progressive reformers envisioned the commission of an offense as essentially secondary to a determination of the "real needs" of a child. They premised intervention on the need for rehabilitation rather than the crime committed. Although McKeiver refused to extend the right to a jury trial to juveniles, Gault and Winship imported the adversarial model, the privilege against self-incrimination, the right to an attorney, the criminal standard of proof, and the primacy of factual and legal guilt as a constitutional prerequisite to intervention. By emphasizing criminal procedural regularity in delinquency hearings, Gault shifted the focus of delinquency hearings from a child's "real needs" to proof of legal guilt and formalized the connection between criminal conduct and coercive intervention. Providing a modicum of procedural justice also legitimated greater punitiveness in juvenile courts.

Over the next three decades, court decisions, statutory amendments, and administrative changes transformed the juvenile court from a social welfare agency into a scaled-down, second-class criminal court for young offenders. These trends included procedural, jurisdictional, and jurisprudential modifications of the juvenile court. In addition to the procedural convergence between juvenile and criminal courts, jurisdictional reforms diverted many noncriminal status offenders away from the juvenile court and transferred increasing numbers of serious young offenders to criminal court. Jurisprudential changes in juvenile court sentencing policies de-emphasize rehabilitation and focus increasingly on punishment of ordinary delinquents.

Two competing cultural and legal conceptions of young people facilitated juvenile courts' transformation from a social welfare agency into a penal organization. On the one hand, the law and culture view young people as innocent, vulnerable, fragile, and dependent *children* whom their parents and the state should protect and nurture. On the other hand, the law and culture perceive young people as vigorous, autonomous and responsible almost *adult-like* people from whose criminal behavior the public needs protection. The ambivalent and conflicted "jurisprudence of youth" enables policy makers selectively to manipulate the competing social constructs of *innocence* and *responsibility* to maximize the social control of young people. Over the past three decades, the intersections of race and crime have provided the impetus for juvenile justice policies to use these alternative constructs of youth to conduct a form of "criminological triage." At the "soft-end," juvenile court reforms have shifted non-criminal status offenders, primarily female and white, out of the juvenile justice system into a "hidden system" of social control in the private-sector mental health and chemical dependency industries. See Chapter 8. Diversion, deinstitutionalization, and "decriminalization" of status offenders have altered the role of juvenile courts as states removed status jurisdiction from their juvenile codes entirely, redefined it to avoid the stigma of crime/delinquency adjudications, and limited the dispositions noncriminal offenders can receive. At the "hard end," states transfer increasing numbers of youths, disproportionately minority, into the criminal justice system for prosecution as adults. See Chapter 6. As states narrow their jurisdiction at the "hard end" and at the "soft-end," the dispositions the remaining delinquents receive increasingly reflect the impact of the "justice model" and doctrines of criminal law in which principles of proportionality and determinacy based on the present offense and prior record, rather than the "best interests" of the child, dictate the length, location, and intensity of intervention. Finally, as the dispositions by the juvenile court increasingly subordinate the needs of the offender to the nature of the offense and traditional justifications for punishment, the formal procedural safeguards of the juvenile court increasingly resemble those of the adult criminal process.

Although Gault transformed the juvenile court from a social welfare agency into a more legalistic one, a substantial gulf remains between the "law on the books" and the "law in action." States continue to manipulate the fluid concepts of children and adults, or treatment and punishment to maximize the social control of young people. On the one hand, almost all states use the adult standard of "knowing, intelligent, and voluntary waiver" under the "totality of the circumstances" to gauge juveniles' waivers of *Miranda* rights and their right to counsel, even though juveniles may lack the legal competence of adults. See Chapters 3 and 7; Barry C. Feld, *Kids, Cops, and Confessions: Inside the Interrogation Room* (2013); Barry C. Feld, *Justice For Children: The Right To Counsel and the Juvenile Courts* (1993). On the other hand, even as juvenile courts have become more punitive, most states continue to deny juveniles access to jury trials and to other procedural rights guaranteed to adults. See Chapter 7; Barry C. Feld, *The Constitutional Tension Between Apprendi and McKeiver: Sentence Enhancements Based on Delinquency Convictions and the Quality of Justice in Juvenile Courts,* 38 Wake Forest L. Rev. 1111 (2003). The recent developmental psychological research on adolescents' legal competence and criminal responsibility raises troubling questions about the structure and administration of the juvenile justice system which the following chapters will explore.

CHAPTER 2

JUVENILE COURT JURISDICTION OVER DELINQUENT AND STATUS OFFENDERS

A. INTRODUCTION

Juvenile courts are exclusively statutory entities. Legislatures create them and their policy judgments determine courts' jurisdiction and practices. State laws, judicial opinions, court rules of procedure, and bureaucratic practices define the details of juvenile justice administration. Every state has a court which exercises jurisdiction over matters involving juveniles that may include delinquency, status offenses, abuse and neglect, adoption, and termination of parental rights. The names of these courts and their subject matter jurisdiction vary from state to state—for example, Superior, Circuit, District, County, Probate, or Family Court. In some states, the trial court of general jurisdiction handles juvenile matters, whereas in others, the juvenile court may be a separate division of a specialized court, for example, "the juvenile division of the probate court." In a growing number of jurisdiction, a unified family court has jurisdiction over traditional juvenile court matters—delinquency, status offenses, abuse and neglect—as well as divorce, paternity, criminal prosecutions of abuse and domestic violence, and the like. Sarah H. Ramsey and Douglas E. Abrams, *Children and the Law in a Nutshell 3rd Ed.* (2008). The federal government exercises limited delinquency jurisdiction and conducts about 250 delinquency proceedings annually. 18 U.S.C. § 5031 et seq. The federal delinquency authority applies to children under eighteen years of age who commit federal crimes on military bases, federal lands, national parks, or Indian reservations. Because most federal crimes have parallel state provisions, states process virtually all delinquency matters unless the Attorney General certifies that there is a substantial federal interest in the case.

Young offenders do not have a constitutional right to be tried in a juvenile court. However, once a state creates a juvenile court, various constitutional limitations and requirements structure their administration. In re Gault, 387 U.S. 1 (S.Ct.1967). Because juvenile courts are legislative creations, states' regulation of children's misconduct may vary considerably. As a matter of state policy, juvenile courts differ in their maximum age of jurisdiction, for example, seventeen, sixteen, or fifteen years of age, the types of offenses over which they exercise jurisdiction, some of the procedural safeguards they provide such as the right to a jury trial, and the lengths and types of dispositions they impose. Howard Snyder and Melissa Sickmund, *Juvenile Offenders and Victims: 2006 National Report* (2006).

Delinquency Jurisdiction: Age and Conduct States define juvenile courts' delinquency jurisdiction based on a youth's age and criminal misconduct. The maximum age of jurisdiction varies from state to state. Typically, the maximum age of juvenile court jurisdiction is seventeen years of age, i.e. an eighteen year old offender is an adult. Some states set the maximum jurisdictional age at sixteen or even fifteen years of age. Youths below the statutory maximum age normally will be treated as "juveniles." Most states define juvenile court jurisdiction in terms of a youth's age at the time of offense or misconduct. Juvenile courts in most states may impose a disposition on a youth adjudicated a delinquent that can continue beyond the maximum age jurisdiction until age nineteen, twenty, twenty-one, or older. Snyder and Sickmund, *National Report 2006*.

In addition to age, states base juvenile court jurisdiction on conduct by children or toward children by their care-takers. "Delinquency" jurisdiction subsumes conduct by a child that would be a crime, offense, or violation if committed by an adult. In most states, juvenile courts have original and exclusive jurisdiction over crimes committed by children. However, many states *exclude* some serious *offenses* from juvenile court jurisdiction. In several states, juvenile and criminal courts share *concurrent jurisdiction* over certain crimes which gives prosecutors discretion to decide in which forum to try the case. See Chapter 6; Snyder and Sickmund, *National Report 2006*.

Non–Criminal Status Offenses Juvenile courts also exercise jurisdiction over non-criminal misconduct by juveniles, the so-called "status offenses." These non-criminal violations are based on the status of being a child—i.e. someone under the jurisdictional age—and engaging in prohibited behavior such as truancy, incorrigibility, disobedience, running away from home, curfew violations, and consumption of alcohol and tobacco. Status offenses regulate some conduct of juveniles that would not be a crime if engaged in by adults. " 'Status offense' means an act prohibited by law which would not be an offense if committed by an adult." Va. Code Ann. § 16.1–228 (Michie 1998). The existence of status jurisdiction, in whatever form, is an instance of regulating children under circumstances in which adults remain free from state controls. Until reforms in the 1970s, status offenses comprised a form of "delinquency" and juvenile court judges could impose the same dispositions on youth adjudicated delinquent for criminal or for non-criminal misconduct. Feld, *Bad Kids*. Recent changes have "decriminalized" status offenses by relabeling juveniles who engage in such conduct as Persons in Need of Services (PINS), or Children in Need of Protection and Services (CHIPS). D.C. Code § 16–2301(8)(1989); N.Y. Fam. Ct. Act § 712(1)(McKinney 1983); S.D. Codified Laws § 26–8B–22 (Michie 1992). Apart from restrictions on pre-trial detention and secure institutional confinement, juvenile courts may impose most of the same dispositions on both delinquents and status offenders.

Dependency, Neglect, and Abuse Juvenile courts also exercise jurisdiction on behalf of children to protect them from the conduct of others. Typically, legal definitions of abuse focus on physical, emotional, or moral harm inflicted upon children by their caretakers. For example, states define "child abuse" as "physical injury, mental or emotional injury, sexual abuse, sexual exploitation, sale or attempted sale or negligent treatment or maltreatment of a child by a parent, guardian or custodian who is responsible for the child's welfare, under circumstances which harm or threaten the health or welfare of the child." W. Va. Code § 49–1–3(c) (1998). Abuse or neglect jurisdiction typically entails "fault" on the part of a child's caretaker. By contrast, dependency jurisdiction suggests "no fault" and a child's welfare suffers as a result of circumstances or conditions beyond the control of the caretaker. E.g., Ramsey and Abrams, *Children and the Law.* In some states, authorities may proceed against very young children who commit crimes under juvenile courts' dependency jurisdiction rather than as delinquents.

B.   DELINQUENCY JURISDICTION FOR CRIMINAL CONDUCT

1.   JUVENILE CRIME

The Federal Bureau of Investigation's *Uniform Crime Report* records the numbers of reported violent crimes—murder, rape, robbery, and aggravated assaults—and serious property crimes—burglary, larceny, auto theft, and arson—in its Violent and Property Crime Indexes as well as the numbers of arrests and the characteristics of arrestees by age, sex, and race. In 2011, police arrested juveniles—persons under the age of eighteen—for 12.7% of all index violent crimes.

Juveniles accounted for 7.8% of homicide, 10.2% of aggravated assault arrests, 14.1% of rape arrests, and 22.3% of robbery arrests. Police arrested juveniles for 20.4% of all index property crimes, including 20.9% of burglaries, 20.1% of larceny, 21.1% of auto theft, and 41.3% of arson. F.B.I., *Uniform Crime Reports 2011, Table 41.* Juvenile arrest statistics overstate somewhat juveniles' actual contribution to the overall volume of crime. Juveniles commit their crimes in groups to a greater extent than do adults and police may arrest several juveniles in conjunction with single criminal incident which inflates their apparent rate of criminal involvement. When measured by clearance rates, juveniles account for 12% of index violent crime and 19% of index property crime arrests.

The F.B.I. arrest rates for serious crime overall, juvenile crime, and violent juvenile crime have followed roughly similar patterns—increasing from the mid–1960s until 1980, declining during the mid–1980s, and then increasing to another peak in the early–1990s, since which time the rates have fallen sharply again. Between 1965 and 1980, the overall rates of juvenile violent crime and homicide doubled, followed by a second, sharp upsurge between 1986 and 1994. Snyder and Sickmund, *National Report 2006.* Between 1994 and 2003, juvenile arrests for all crimes declined 18%, and the juvenile arrest rate for violent crimes dropped 32%. Snyder and Sickmund, *National Report 2006.* Between 2002 and 2011, juvenile violent index crimes declined 28.5%, and property index crime decreased by 29.4% to the lowest level in decades.

F.B.I., *Uniform Crime Reports 2011, Table 32.* Despite the recent precipitous decline, the earlier increases in juvenile violence and homicide in the late–1970s and again in the late–1980s and early–1990s provided the impetus for many "get tough" and punitive changes in juvenile transfer and sentencing laws. See Chapters 6 and 8. These harsh laws remain in place despite dramatically lower current levels of youth crime.

In 2009, police arrested 1.9 million juveniles for felonies, misdemeanors, and status offenses. Charles Puzzanchera and Benjamin Adams, *Juvenile Arrests 2009* (2011). Female juveniles accounted for nearly one-third (30%) of all juvenile arrests, 18% of all juvenile arrests for violent index crimes, and 38% of arrests for property index crimes. Although black juveniles constitute about 16% of the youth population aged 10–17, police arrested black juveniles for 32% of all juvenile offenses, 51.4% of all violent index crimes, and 35% of all property index crimes committed by juveniles. F.B.I., *Uniform Crime Reports 2011, Table 43B.* Analysts attribute some minority over-representation in arrests to real differences in rates of offending by race. However, discretionary decisions by justice system personnel—arrest, intake, court referral, charge, detention, and sentence—amplify racial disparities and contribute to disproportionate minority over-confinement. Joan McCord, Cathy Spatz Widom, and Nancy A. Crowell, *Juvenile Crime, Juvenile Justice* (2001).

2.   AGE AND JUVENILE COURT JURISDICTION

In most states, juvenile courts exercise original and exclusive jurisdiction over a youth below the age of eighteen and charged with a violation of a criminal law or local ordinance. Original and exclusive jurisdiction means that the state initially must file all charges of criminal violations against a child below the maximum age of jurisdiction in juvenile court, although the judge may *waive* the juvenile court's jurisdiction through a *transfer hearing*. See Chapter 6. A number of states *exclude* youths of a certain age and charged with a serious *offense* from juvenile court jurisdiction, for example, cases of youths sixteen years of age or older and charged with murder originate in the criminal court. By legislative definition, these youths are adults for purposes of criminal responsibility. If either a juvenile *or* a criminal court may hear cases involving youths of certain ages and charged with certain serious crimes, then the juvenile and criminal courts exercise *concurrent jurisdiction*. See Chapter 6. In those states, the prosecutor's decision to charge a case in juvenile or criminal court determines the judicial forum and the sentencing consequences. Thus, juvenile court jurisdiction takes several different forms that define its boundaries and its interaction with the criminal justice system.

The maximum age for original juvenile court jurisdiction is seventeen years of age in 38 states and the District of Columbia, sixteen years of age in ten states, and fifteen years old in two states—New York and North Carolina. Snyder and Sickmund, *National Report 2006*. During the "get tough" era, in 1993, Wyoming lowered its upper age jurisdiction from eighteen to seventeen and in 1996, New Hampshire and Wisconsin lowered theirs from seventeen to sixteen years of age. Reflecting more recent awareness of differences between children and adults, in 2010, Connecticut joined the majority of states and raised its age of delinquency jurisdiction from fifteen to seventeen years of age, CT.G.S.A. § 46b–120, and North Carolina is considering a similar proposal.

Sixteen states also establish a minimum age of delinquency jurisdiction which is six years of age in North Carolina, seven of age in Maryland, Massachusetts, and New York, eight years of age in Arizona, and ten years of age in eleven states. Snyder and Sickmund, *National Report 2006*. In the remaining states, prosecutors theoretically may file a delinquency petition against a child of any age.

Because states define juvenile courts' jurisdiction on the basis of a youth's age, states confront the question whether the age at the time of the offense or at the time of the filing of charges determines the court's jurisdictional authority. If a child commits an offense while below the age of juvenile court jurisdiction, but evidence implicating the child is not found or the prosecutor does not file a delinquency petition until after the youth exceeds the jurisdictional age limit, then should the case be heard in a juvenile or criminal court? Because juvenile court jurisdiction reflects the idea of diminished responsibility, most states provide that the age at the time of offense determines jurisdiction. Samuel Davis, *Rights of Juveniles § 2.3* (1994) [hereinafter Davis, *Rights of Juveniles*]. While jurisdiction based on the child's age at the time of the offense reflects her criminal capacity at that time, a youth who has "aged-out" of jurisdiction by the time the state files charges may not be as responsive to treatment as a younger juvenile. If a youth is older than the juvenile court's maximum age jurisdiction, but younger than its dispositional authority, then a juvenile court may hold a waiver hearing to determine whether to try and sentence the youth as a juvenile or to transfer the case to criminal court. If a prosecutor deliberately delays filing charges in order to allow a youth to "age-out" of juvenile court, courts have held that the proper remedy is for the criminal court to transfer the case back to juvenile court to conduct a waiver hearing to determine whether the youth should be tried as a juvenile or adult. State v. Scurlock, 286 Or. 277, 593 P.2d 1159 (Or.1979). In other states, if the adult demonstrates that the prosecutor deliberately delayed filing a delinquency petition in order to gain an unfair advantage, the court may not certify the matter. Minn. Stat. § 260B.125(2); Minn. Stat. § 260B.193, Subd. 5 (2002). When the legislature confers original and exclusive jurisdiction based on age, then the decision whether the youth should be treated as a juvenile or adult should be made through the waiver process and, absent bona fide reasons for delay such as the need to try an accomplice or obtain testimony of a witness, prosecutorial manipulation of the jurisdictional boundary may defeat criminal court jurisdiction. State v. Montgomery, 148 Wis.2d 593, 436 N.W.2d 303 (Wis.1989); State v. Dixon, 114 Wash.2d 857, 792 P.2d 137 (Wash.1990). By contrast, a few states base juvenile courts' jurisdiction on a youth's age at the time the prosecutor files the charge rather than the age when she committed the crime. Wis. Stat. § 938.12 (2002); State v. Annala, 484 N.W.2d 138 (Wis.1992) (age at the time defendant is charged determines juvenile court jurisdiction).

3. CRIMINAL CONDUCT AND DELINQUENCY JURISDICTION

Delinquency matters comprise the largest portion of juvenile courts' dockets. Snyder and Sickmund, *National Report 2006*. While some states *exclude* either minor traffic or fish and game violations, or the most serious offenses from juvenile court jurisdiction, a judge may find a child below the jurisdictional maximum age limit "delinquent" if she violates any federal or state criminal law or local ordinance. Statutes typically define a "delinquent child" as one "who has violated any state or local law . . . [or] who has violated a federal law or a law of another state and whose case have been referred to the juvenile court . . ." Minn. Stat. § 260B.015, Subd. 5 (2001); Cal. Welf. & Inst. Code § 602 (West 2000).

Traffic Violations Although delinquency subsumes violations of criminal statutes and local ordinances, many jurisdictions exclude routine traffic offenses from their juvenile codes and leave their enforcement to the adult traffic process or to a separate juvenile traffic court. E.g. Ark. Code Ann. § 16–17–133(a)(1)(Michie 2000) (municipal court has jurisdiction over juveniles charged with fish and game violations and traffic offenses); N.D. Cent. Code § 27–20–02(3) (2000); N.C. Gen. Stat. § 15–11–73 (2001) (juvenile court has exclusive jurisdiction over juvenile traffic offenses which are *not* handled as delinquency matters). In part, this policy reflects the sheer volume of traffic cases, the fact that states license teen-aged drivers like adults, and the relative absence of "diagnostic significance" of most minor traffic violations. On the other hand, juvenile courts typically retain delinquency jurisdiction over juveniles under the age of sixteen, i.e. unlicensed drivers, and over those who commit the most serious traffic offenses which also suggest a need for rehabilitative services, for example automobile theft or vehicular homicide. E.g. Ga. Code Ann. § 15–11–73 (2000) (excepts from juvenile traffic offenses and treats as delinquency homicide by vehicle, any felony in which the juvenile uses a motor vehicle, hit and run or leaving the scene of an accident, driving under the influence of alcohol or drugs); Utah Code Ann. § 78–3a–104(2) (2000) (auto homicide, driving under the influence, reckless driving, fleeing an officer); N.D. Cent. Code § 27–20–02(9) (2000). In the absence of statutory enumeration, the principle controversy surrounds which traffic violations constitute serious offenses that belong within juvenile courts' delinquency jurisdiction. Robinson

v. Sutterfield, 302 Ark. 7 (Ark.1990) (driving under
the influence was a "traffic offense"); Zamora v.
State, 846 P.2d 194 (Idaho 1992) (felony traffic
offenses not excluded from juvenile court
jurisdiction).

Venue refers to which, among several courts that
have subject matter jurisdiction, will hear a case.
For adult criminal defendants, venue typically lies
in the county in which the offense occurs because
the availability of witnesses and evidence facilitates
prosecution and avoids hardship and unfairness to
the defendant. Wayne R. LaFave, Jerold H. Israel
and Nancy J. King, *Criminal Procedure Fourth Ed.*
(2000). Some juvenile court venue provisions follow
the adult criminal practice and conduct delinquency
trials in the county in which the crime occurred.
Ariz. Rev. Stat. § 8–206(B) (1999) (county where the
alleged delinquent act occurs). However, if a
juvenile commits an offense in one county, resides in
a second county, and is arrested or "found" in a
third county, many states give any of those three
juvenile courts the authority to try and sentence the
child. E.g. Wis. Stat. § 938.185 (2000) (county where
juvenile resides, is present, or in which violation
occurred). Courts typically determine the county in
which the child is found or present at the time of the
filing of the petition. In the Interest of Corey J.G.,
572 N.W.2d 845 (Wis.1998). The emphasis on venue
in the county where the child resides, rather than in
the county where the offense occurs, reflects the
belief that "in most cases it will be the county of his
residence where his roots will be found—parents,
school, church, friends and acquaintances—and

where will be the greatest interest in bringing about his rehabilitation and improvement, if it can be accomplished." In re J.D.H., 508 S.W.2d 497, 500 (Mo.1974). However, many states authorize the prosecutor to conduct the trial in the county in which the crime occurred for ease of proof and then, following adjudication, allow the juvenile court judge to transfer the case to the youth's county of residence for disposition. E.g. Ariz. Rev. Stat. § 8–206(E) (1999) (following adjudication, with agreement of judges in county of disposition and residence, supervise probationer in county of residence).

If states define delinquency jurisdiction based on conduct that would be a crime if committed by an adult, then how should juvenile courts resolve other criminal law doctrinal issues? For example, may a juvenile younger than fourteen years of age assert the common law's infancy defense to defeat juvenile court delinquency jurisdiction? May a delinquent seek acquittal on the grounds of insanity? May a juvenile court adjudicate a youth delinquent who lacks competence to stand trial? If the purpose of juvenile court is to treat young offenders, then should principles of criminal law developed to punish presumptively responsible actors even apply?

a. Infancy

Before the Progressives created the juvenile court, the common law infancy defense provided the only formal legal doctrine to protect younger offenders charged with crimes. Sanford Fox, "Responsibility in the Juvenile Court," 11 *Wm. & Mary L. Rev.* 659 (1970). The classical criminal law recognized that sanctions could not deter those who did not know "right from wrong," for example, the insane and the very young, and it excused them from criminal liability. Because the criminal law punished actors for conduct accompanied by blameworthy choices, the infancy defense affirmed that some younger people lack the capacity to appreciate the wrongfulness of their choices or the moral agency to be blamed for their actions. The common law infancy gradations conclusively presumed that children younger than seven years of age lacked criminal capacity, regarded those fourteen years of age and older as fully responsible adults, and created a rebuttable presumption of incapacity for those between seven and fourteen years of age. The presumption of incapacity was strongest at the age of seven and diminished gradually until it disappears entirely at the age of fourteen. The common law based the presumption of incapacity on chronological age and not some subjective "mental age." The presumption of incapacity for those under fourteen placed the burden on the prosecution to prove criminal responsibility. Andrew Walkover, "The Infancy Defense in the New Juvenile Court," 31 *U.C.L.A. L.Rev.* 503 (1984). The infancy defense focuses on cognitive capacity and moral responsibility and requires prosecutors to prove that the child had sufficient maturity to understand what she was doing, capacity to appreciate wrongfulness, and discretion to choose between good and evil. In short, if the child knew "right from wrong," then he could be criminally responsible. Historically, the onset of puberty marked the age at which most societies no longer excused criminal conduct by young people. Extending juvenile court jurisdiction to fifteen, sixteen, or seventeen years of age prolonged children's traditional immunity from criminal liability.

If children between the ages of seven and fourteen presumptively lack criminal capacity, then can a younger offender assert the common law infancy defense in juvenile court to defeat juvenile courts' delinquency jurisdiction. Andrew M. Carter, "Age Matters: The Case for a Constitutionalized Infancy Defense," 54 *Kan. L. Rev.* 687 (2006). If a younger juvenile may assert the infancy defense, then how would the prosecutor rebut the presumption that she lacked criminal responsibility? Although state courts divide on the question, the majority reject infancy as a defense that would preclude a juvenile court from finding delinquency jurisdiction.

In re Tyvonne J., 211 Conn. 151, 558 A.2d 661 (Conn.1989) represents the position of the vast majority of states and holds that juvenile court laws supersede and eliminate the need for an infancy defense. Lara A. Bazelon, "Exploding the Superpredator Myth: Why Infancy is the Preadolescent's Best Defense in Juvenile Court," 75 *N.Y.U.L.Rev.* 159 (2000). Because the infancy defense traditionally functioned to protect young children from criminal punishment, the juvenile court system itself provides even greater protection. Tyvonne J. emphasized the differences between a criminal prosecution and a delinquency proceeding and the rehabilitative nature of the juvenile justice system. Because juvenile courts diagnose and treat children based on assessments of their "real needs," rather than determine criminal responsibility and impose punishment, criminal law defenses like infancy simply have no applicability. Although Tyvonne J. recognized that juvenile courts sometimes fall short of their rehabilitative aspirations, the court saw no need to import criminal law doctrines that could thwart their mission.

In re Gladys R., 1 Cal.3d 855, 83 Cal. Rptr. 671, 464 P.2d 127 (Cal.1970), is the leading case to allow use of the infancy defense in delinquency trials. A criminal statute presumed that children under the age of fourteen lacked criminal capacity in the absence of "clear proof" that they knew the wrongfulness of their actions. The California Supreme Court required the prosecution to rebut the statutory presumption of incapacity to establish delinquency jurisdiction. If adjudication as a delinquent requires proof the child committed a crime—act and intent—then proof of criminal capacity is essential to establish delinquency jurisdiction. A child who lacked mens rea could not be guilty of a crime or found delinquent. Gladys R. recognized the infancy defense to avoid committing grossly immature youths to delinquency institutions and suggested that a juvenile court still might establish jurisdiction over such a child as a status offender.

A few states follow Gladys R., and recognize the infancy defense even if its successful assertion may defeat juvenile court jurisdiction. Those that find the infancy defense applicable to delinquency proceedings base their decisions on specific legislation adopting the defense. E.g. State v. Q.D., 102 Wash.2d 19, 685 P.2d 557 (Wash.1984). Others recognize the defense based on a judicial determination that the true purpose of juvenile courts is not only rehabilitation and treatment, but also accountability and punishment. E.g. In re William A., 313 Md. 690, 548 A.2d 130, 133 (Md.1988) ("[J]uvenile statutes typically require, for a delinquency adjudication, that the child commit an act which constitutes a crime if committed by an adult, and if the child lacks capacity to have the requisite mens rea for a particular crime, he has not committed an act amounting to a crime."). States that recognize the defense require prosecutors to prove and courts to weigh several factors bearing on a juvenile's awareness of the wrongfulness of the acts including: "(1) the nature of the crime; (2) the child's age and maturity; (3) whether the child showed a desire for secrecy; (4) whether the child admonished the victim not to tell; (5) prior conduct similar to that charged; (6) any consequences that attached to the conduct; and (7) acknowledgment that the behavior was wrong and could lead to detention." State v. J.P.S., 954 P.2d 894 (Wash.1998). The "clear proof" necessary to rebut the presumption of incapacity requires more substantial evidence than simply a child's acknowledgment that she knew right from wrong. In re Michael B., 44 Cal.App.3d 443, 118 Cal.Rptr. 685 (Cal.App. 1975).

Most appellate courts reject juveniles' assertion of the infancy defense and conclude that the juvenile court system supersedes it. In the absence of legislation adopting the defense, most states' delinquency proceedings do not recognize an immaturity or infancy defense because it could prevent a child who urgently needed treatment from receiving it. Jennings v. State, 384 So.2d 104 (Ala.1980); Gammons v. Berlat, 144 Ariz. 148, 696 P.2d 700 (Ariz.1985) (legislature did not intend to apply statutory infancy defense in juvenile court but only in criminal prosecutions of younger juveniles); In re Michael, 423 A.2d 1180, 1183 (R.I.1981) ("Once one accepts the principle that a finding of delinquency or waywardness in a juvenile proceeding is not the equivalent of finding that the juvenile has committed a crime, there is no necessity of a finding that the juvenile had such maturity that he or she knew what he or she was doing was wrong."). Because delinquency adjudications are not criminal convictions, courts find it unnecessary to determine whether the juvenile understood the moral implication of her behavior. Moreover, allowing the infancy defense to defeat jurisdiction would frustrate the remedial purposes of juvenile courts for those children most in need of intervention.

When a state tries a very young offender as an adult, the child may raise the infancy defense in a criminal proceeding. E.g. State v. Pittman, 373 S.C. 527, 647 S.E.2d 144 (S.C. 2007) (holding that a twelve-year-old defendant may raise infancy defense because persons between seven and fourteen years of age are rebuttably presumed to lack mental capacity to commit crime). However, the state need not present expert testimony to rebut the presumption of incapacity and may rely on lay testimony about the youth's action, behavior, and demeanor to sustain its burden.

b. Insanity

Youths' mental health and immaturity affects juvenile courts' dispositional options, transfer to criminal court, criminal responsibility for delinquent behavior—the insanity defense—and judges' ability to adjudicate delinquency—competency to stand trial. As with the infancy defense, juvenile courts confront the question whether a juvenile must be competent to stand trial and/or may plead not guilty by reason of insanity in delinquency proceedings. In the Interest of Causey, 363 So.2d 472 (La.1978); Golden v. State, 21 S.W.3d 8012 (Ark.2000); Commonwealth v. Chatman, 538 S.E.2d 304 (Va.2000); Thomas Grisso, *Double Jeopardy: Adolescent Offenders with Mental Disorders* (2004).

The Supreme Court in Medina v. California, 505 U.S. 437 (S.Ct.1992), held, as a matter of due process, that an adult criminal defendant has a constitutional right to a competency determination because it is "fundamentally unfair" to convict a defendant who cannot understand her trial, assist counsel, or participate in her defense. However, Medina held that the Constitution does not require states to recognize the insanity defense. Adult criminal defendants may assert an insanity defense only if the state legislature provides a statutory right or the state court grants it as a state constitutional right. Because the criminal law presumes blameworthy actors deserve punishment, the insanity defense recognizes that a severely mentally impaired actor may be unable to make responsible choices to engage in criminal behavior.

A few state courts have held that juveniles enjoy a state constitutional right to plead not guilty by reason of insanity. They reason that because the state bases delinquency jurisdiction on commission of a crime, then "fundamental fairness" requires some procedure to differentiate between youths who are culpable and responsible for their behavior and those whose acts are the result of a mental illness that prevents them from knowing "right from wrong." E.g. In the Interest of Causey, 363 So.2d 472 (La.1978); In re Carey, 615 N.W.2d 742 (Mich.Ct.App.2000); In re Stapelkempr, 562 P.2d 815 (Mont.1977). Legislation in other states provides juveniles with a statutory right to an insanity defense in delinquency proceedings. N.J. Stat. Ann. § 2A:4A–40 (West 1995); N.Y. Fam. Ct. §§ 335.1, 344.3 (McKinney 1999); Tex. Fam. Code Ann. § 55.15 (Vernon 1996).

Without explicit legislation, the majority of state courts have concluded that juveniles do not have a constitutional due process right to an insanity defense. The court in Matter of C.W.M., 407 A.2d 617 (D.C.Ct.App.1979), reasoned that because a delinquency adjudication does not involve a determination of criminal responsibility and judges make dispositions to rehabilitate a child, an insanity defense would be superfluous. Even where states provide a statutory insanity defense for adult criminal defendants, courts conclude that it does not violate equal protection to deny it to juveniles because the rehabilitative goals of the juvenile system provide a rational basis to treat delinquents differently than criminals. Golden v. State, 21 S.W.3d 801 (Ark.2000). Courts also emphasize that the juvenile system provides judges with more treatment options at disposition which obviates the needs for an involuntary civil commitment following a successful insanity defense as would be the case for an adult. Commonwealth v. Chatman, 538 S.E.2d 304 (Va.2000). Courts emphasize the civil and rehabilitative nature of delinquency proceedings to justify denying juveniles the procedural right available to adult criminal defendants. In re Chambers, 688 N.E.2d 25 (Ohio Ct.App.1996).

c. Competency

The Supreme Court has held that adult criminal defendants have a constitutional right to a competency determination. E.g. Drope v. Missouri, 420 U.S. 162 (S.Ct.1975); Medina v. California, 505

U.S. 437 (S.Ct.1992). An adult criminal defendant must have "sufficient present ability to consult with his lawyer with a reasonable degree of rational understanding [and have a] rational as well as factual understanding of the proceedings against him," Dusky v. United States, 362 U.S. 202, 402 (S.Ct.1960), and have the capacity "to assist in preparing his defense." Drope v. Missouri, 420 U.S. 162, 171 (S.Ct.1975). Recent research conducted by the MacArthur Foundation's Adolescent Development and Juvenile Justice Network reports significant age-related developmental differences in juveniles' adjudicative competence, understanding and judgment. Immaturity per se, rather than mental illness or mental retardation, compromises the adjudicative competence of youths. Most juveniles younger than fourteen years of age exhibited the same degree of impairment as severely mentally ill adult defendants and lacked even basic competence to understand or to participate in their defense. A significant proportion of juveniles younger than sixteen years of age lacked competence to stand trial, to make legal decisions, and to assist counsel, and many older youths exhibited substantial impairments. Thomas Grisso, et al., "Juveniles' Competence to Stand Trial: A Comparison of Adolescents' and Adults' Capacities as Trial Defendants," 27 *Law & Hum. Behav.* 333 (2003).

Most states give juveniles the right to a competency hearing. Emily S. Pollock, *Those Crazy Kids: Providing the Insanity Defense in Juvenile Courts,* 85 Minn. L. Rev. 2041 (2001). States address juveniles' competency in their statutes or case law and conclude that delinquents have a fundamental right not to be tried while incompetent. Fla.Stat.Ann. § 985.223 (West 1998) (incompetency in juvenile delinquency cases); Tate v. State, 864 So.2d 44 (Fla. App. 4 Dist. 2003) (holding trial court violated 12–year–old juvenile's due process rights by failing to order, sua sponte, pretrial and post-trial competence evaluations); Kan. Stat. Ann. § 38–1637 (1997) (proceedings to determine competency); In the Interest of S.H., 469 S.E.2d 810 (Ga.Ct.App.1996) (providing juveniles with procedural rights in delinquency proceedings would be meaningless if defendant was unable to exercise them); State v. E.C., 922 P.2d 152 (Wash.Ct.App.1996) (granting juvenile courts greater latitude in handling incompetent juveniles); Dandoy v. Superior Court, 127 Ariz. 184, 619 P.2d 12 (Ariz.1980) (procedure followed in adult prosecution must be applied to juvenile cases to determine mental competency). A few courts have held that because delinquency proceedings are rehabilitative and not criminal, the legislature intended for juvenile courts to adjudicate youths regardless of their mental state or ability to assist counsel. G.J.I. v. State, 778 P.2d 485 (Okla.Crim.App.1989).

States differ over the procedures and standards to use to determine juveniles' adjudicative competency. Some states use the same procedures for juveniles as for adults to determine who may be competent to stand trial. E.g. Matter of Welfare of D.D.N., 582 N.W.2d 278 (Mn. Ct. Ap. 1998). Other jurisdiction reason that juvenile courts' rehabilitative goals allow judges to use a more flexible process to determine youths' competency rather than the procedures used for adults. E.g. In re K.G., 808 N.E.2d 631 (Ind. 2004). Similarly, states differ over the appropriate standard to use to determine a juveniles' trial competency. Notwithstanding juvenile courts' rehabilitative goals, some states use the Drope and Dusky adult competency standard. They reasons that juvenile proceedings still may involve punishment and a substantial loss of liberty and require a child to be able to participate in the trial and sentencing proceedings in the same manner as an adult. E.g., In re Welfare of S.W.T., 277 N.W.2d 507 (Minn. 1979). Other states permit courts to use a more relaxed and less rigorous standard of competency in delinquency trials because of differences in the complexities in juvenile versus adult criminal proceedings. E.g. In re Bailey, 150 Ohio App. 3d 664, 782 N.E.2d 1177 (2 Dist. 2002). Trial courts recognize that developmental immaturity alone may produce deficits of understanding and adjudicative competence even without any underlying mental illness or abnormality. E.g. Timothy J. v. Superior Court, 150 Cal. App.4th 847, 58 Cal.Rptr.3d 746 (2007). Commentators favor using a relaxed juvenile, rather than adult, competency standard in delinquency proceedings because using the adult standard might preclude adjudication in any court and could prevent the juvenile court from providing an appropriate remedial disposition. Critically, to be constitutional, a relaxed competency standard would require real differences in the types of dispositions provided to developmentally immature youths found competent to stand trial under a relaxed standard. Elizabeth S. Scott & Thomas Grisso, "Developmental Incompetence, Due Process, and Juvenile Justice Policy," 83 *N. Car. L. Rev.* 793 (2005).

C.   JURISDICTION OVER NON–CRIMINAL MISCONDUCT: STATUS OFFENSES

Progressive reformers viewed childhood as a time of vulnerability and dependence and adolescence as a period to prepare for adulthood. They regarded "adult-like" activities and premature autonomy as inimical to children's long-term development. E.g., Platt, *Childsavers*. Families, communities, and schools bore primary responsibility to socialize, supervise, and control young people. Progressives re-enforced youths' dependency within these primary socializing agencies and regarded autonomy from them as a threat to themselves and the community. If a young person escaped from this overlapping network of supervision, then she literally was "out of control." The juvenile court provided a means to regulate children, to re-enforce the authority of other social institutions that controlled children, and to oversee the adequacy of their families' supervision. Feld, *Bad Kids*.

The Progressives conceived of the juvenile court as *parens patriae*—a benign substitute for parental inadequacy—and included status offenses in its definition of delinquency. E.g., Sutton, *Stubborn*

Children. Part of juvenile courts' mission included enforcing other peoples' rules about childhood, for example, parental discipline, compulsory school attendance regulations, or judges' normative sensibilities about child-rearing. Virtually all of the behaviors subsumed in the status jurisdiction represent efforts either to reinforce the authority of the primary socializing agencies, to reinstate controls over youths, or to enforce the norms of childhood. Because "incorrigible," "stubborn," or run-away children threatened parental control, juvenile courts intervened to reinforce parents' authority. When truant children were absent from or threatened the control of schools, juvenile courts reasserted the schools' dominion. Youthful behavior such as "waywardness," "immorality," alcohol consumption, or sexual experimentation posed a threat to a youth's long-term development, offended Progressives' sensibilities about the nature of children, violated the normative construction of childhood, and thus constituted adult activities forbidden to young people.

The essence of status offenses is non-criminal acts or omissions—for example, running away from home, incorrigibility, or failing to attend school—which the state prohibits for young people simply because of their age and status as children, but in which an adult freely may engage. Some status offenses are proscriptive and prohibit young people from engaging in certain conduct, for example, consuming alcohol, smoking, or being on the streets after a certain hour. Others are prescriptive and affirmatively require children to do something, for example, obey their parents or attend school. Still others are preventive and address generic concerns about child development, such as being "wayward" or "growing up in idleness or crime."

State statutes vary in the specificity with which they proscribe non-criminal misconduct. A juvenile court may declare a person under eighteen years of age a ward of the court "who persistently or habitually refuses to obey the reasonable and proper orders or directions of his or her parents, guardian, or custodian, or who is beyond the control of that person, or who is under the age of 18 years when he or she violated any ordinance of any city or county of this state establishing a curfew based solely on age . . ." Cal. Welf. & Inst. Code § 601 (West 1998). Other states define status offenses more broadly to include "any offense which would not be a misdemeanor or felony if committed by an adult, including, but not limited to, incorrigibility or beyond the control of parents, truancy, running away, playing or loitering in a billiard room, playing a pinball machine or gaining admission to a theater by false identification." S. C. Code Ann. § 20–7–6605(8) (Law. Co-op.1999). Some states grant juvenile courts even broader jurisdictional authority and define an "unruly child" as "Any child who so deports himself or herself as to injure or endanger his or her health or morals or the health or morals of others." Ohio Stat. § 2151.022 (West 1998).

Although juveniles have challenged these broad grants of discretion as unconstitutionally "void for vagueness," state appellate courts consistently reject vagueness objections to statutes that proscribe "incorrigibility," "immorality," or similar "misconduct." Blondheim v. State, 84 Wash.2d 874, 529 P.2d 1096 (Wash.1975). Courts emphasize that juveniles do not enjoy the same liberty interests as adults and therefore the state may regulate their conduct more extensively. E.g. S.S. and L.B. v. State, 299 A.2d 560 (Me.1973). Moreover, status jurisdiction is predictive and preventive and authorizes state intervention to forestall future criminality. Courts insist that statutes proscribing "incorrigibility" and "conduct endangering morals" provide juveniles with adequate notice as to the prohibited conduct. E.g., E.S.G. v. State, 447 S.W.2d 225 (Tex.Ct.Civ.App.1969). Although legislatures could adopt statutory language that specifies prohibited conduct more precisely, courts seldom require them to do so. In re Tina Marie Gras, 337 So.2nd 641 (La.Ct.App.1976) ("A cursory attempt to define all types of behavior injurious to a child with mathematical precision makes the reason for granting broad and general jurisdiction obvious. The state's interest in protecting the physical, moral or mental well-being of children . . . is at the heart of the juvenile act.")

Until the mid–1970s, most states included status offenses as one part of their definition of delinquency and detained and incarcerated status offenders in the same institutions as youth adjudicated for criminal behavior. At that time, status referrals comprised one-third or more of juvenile courts' dockets and parental referrals often involved intractable intra-family disputes. In the aftermath of Gault, juveniles charged with status offenses typically enjoyed fewer procedural rights than youths charged with criminal offenses, for example, the privilege against self-incrimination, the right to counsel, and the burden of proof. See Chapter 7; In re Spalding, 273 Md. 690, 332 A.2d 246 (Md.1975); In re Walker, 282 N.C. 28, 191 S.E.2d 702 (N.C.1972); Erin M. Smith, *In a Child's Best Interest: Juvenile Status Offenders Deserve Procedural Due Process*, 10 J. Law & Ineq. 253 (1992). As a result, courts may invoke the status jurisdiction when they could not establish delinquency jurisdiction over a child suspected of criminal behavior. E.g. In re Gladys R.

Because status offense legislation grants judges broad discretion to prevent unruliness or immorality from ripening into criminality, adjudication and intervention often reflected judges' personal values and prejudices. The exercise of standardless discretion to regulate noncriminal misconduct had a disproportionate impact on poor, minority, and female juveniles. Meda Chesney–Lind and Randall Shelden, *Girls, Delinquency, and Juvenile Justice* (2nd ed. 1997).

Legislative recognition that juvenile courts often failed to realize their benevolent purposes led to a strategic retrenchment of juvenile courts' jurisdiction over non-criminal misconduct such as "waywardness," "immorality," or "incorrigibility." In the 1970s, critics objected that juvenile courts' status jurisdiction treated non-criminal offenders like delinquents adjudicated for crimes, disabled families and other sources of referral through one-sided intervention, and posed insuperable legal issues for the court. H. Ted Rubin, *Juvenile Justice: Policy, Practice, and Law* (2nd ed. 1985). Many states removed status offenses from the statutory definition of delinquency and relabeled these children as Persons in Need of Supervision (PINS), Children in Need of Supervision (CHINS), or the like. D.C. Code § 16–2301(8) (1989); N.Y. Fam. Ct. Act § 712(a)(McKinney 1983); S.D. Comp. Laws Ann. § 26–8B–22 (1992). A few states have removed status offenses from their juvenile codes and deal with them as "dependent children." 42 Pa. Cons. Stat. § 6302 ("dependent child" includes one who is truant, incorrigible, or without proper parental care and control).

Legislative and judicial disillusionment with juvenile courts' responses to noncriminal youths also have led to diversion and de-institutionalization reforms. In 1974, the Federal Juvenile Justice and Delinquency Prevention Act (JJDPA) of 1974, 42 U.S.C. § 5633(a)(12)(A) (1995), required states to begin to remove noncriminal offenders from secure detention and correctional facilities and provided impetus to de-institutionalize status offenders. The number of status offenders in secure detention facilities and institutions declined by the mid–1980s. However, juvenile courts confined only a small proportion of status offenders in secure institutions and most remain eligible for commitment to forestry camps and other medium security facilities. E.g. Sutton, *Stubborn Children*.

Amendments to the JJDPA in 1980 weakened restrictions on secure confinement and allowed the state to charge status offenders who ran away from non-secure placements or who violated court orders with contempt of court, a delinquent act, for which a judge could incarcerate them. E.g. 42 U.S.C. § 5633(a)(12)(A) (1983); Chapter 8. The use of the contempt power to "bootstrap" status offenders into delinquents remains a continuing source of gender bias in juvenile justice administration. In addition, deinstitutionalization provided impetus to transfer many middle-class, white, and female status offenders into the private mental health and chemical dependency treatment systems to confine them there. See Chapter 8. Finally, juvenile justice administrators could relabel some status offenders as delinquents to circumvent the deinstitutionalization requirements. Coinciding with restrictions on placements of status offenders, policy makers and juvenile justice officials perceived a sharp increase in girls' violence. Police arrests of girls for violent offenses such as simple and aggravated assault either have increased more or decreased less than those of their male counterparts. Analysts attributed the supposed increase in girls' violence to changes in parental attitudes, police policies, and heightened surveillance of behaviors such as domestic violence and simple assaults which disproportionately affect girls. Barry C. Feld, "Violent Girls or Relabeled Status Offenders? An Alternative Interpretation of the Data," 55 Crime & Delinquency 241 (2009). They argue that the line between status offenses—

unruly or incorrigible—and delinquency—e.g. assault—is imprecise and manipulable. Many girls charged with assault are involved in non-serious altercations with parents and policies of mandatory arrest for domestic violence provide parents and police with another tool with which to control their unruly daughters by treating the same underlying behavior as delinquency.

Legislative and judicial reforms of status jurisdiction represent a strategic withdrawal from "child saving," an acknowledgment of the limited utility of coercive intervention to provide for child welfare, a reduced role in enforcing normative concepts of childhood, and a diminished prevention mission. Despite the decline of the broad "morality" status jurisdiction, efforts to regulate specific aspects of the non-criminal conduct of children persist in many guises, for example, run-away, truancy, curfew, and tobacco and alcohol consumption. Issues associated with non-criminal status offenses will arise when we consider diversion (Chapter 4), pre-trial detention (Chapter 5), procedural safeguards (Chapter 7), and dispositions (Chapter 8).

1.   CURFEW: AN OFFENSE FOR CHILDREN ONLY

Although juvenile curfew statutes have long lineage, many municipalities enacted curfew laws during the late–1980s and early–1990s in response to the rapid increase in youth violence and homicide. A 1997 survey of 347 cities with populations of 30,000 or more reported that 276 of the cities had curfew legislation. U.S. Conference of Mayors, *A Status Report on Youth Curfews in America's Cities* (Dec. 1997). Police arrested more than 136,500 juveniles for curfew and loitering violations in 2003, numbers essentially unchanged from a decade earlier. Snyder and Sickmund, *National Report 2006*. Municipalities enact curfew laws to protect children and to reduce juvenile crime by prohibiting youths from being out on the streets at night without a parent or a statutorily-defined valid reason. However, comparisons of when juveniles and adults offend indicate that most juvenile violent crimes occur between about 3 p.m. and 6 p.m., at the end of the school day, rather than later at night as is the case for adults.

Curfew ordinances typically prohibit persons younger than eighteen years of age from remaining in public places between 11 p.m. and 6 a.m. on week nights and from 12 midnight to 6 a.m. on weekends. E.g., Hutchins v. District of Columbia, 188 F.3d 531 (D.C.Cir. en banc 1999); Qutb v. Bartlett, 11 F.3d 488 (5th Cir.1993). To avoid constitutional infirmity, curfew ordinances also include exceptions for youths accompanied by a parent or guardian, on an errand at the parent's direction, traveling to or from a place of employment in a motor vehicle, or attending school, religious or civic organizational functions, or exercising First Amendment speech and associational rights.

Although the Supreme Court has not decided the constitutional validity of juvenile curfew laws,

Bykofsky v. Borough of Middletown, 401 F.Supp. 1242 (M.D.Pa.1975), cert. den'd, 429 U.S. 964 (1976), the majority of federal circuit and state courts have rejected juveniles' and their parents' due process, equal protection, First Amendment, and Fourth Amendment challenges to municipal curfew laws prohibiting children's presence on the streets "after hours." E.g., Hutchins v. District of Columbia, 188 F.3d 531 (D.C.Cir.1999); Schleifer v. City of Charlottesville, 159 F.3d 843 (4th Cir.1998); Treacy v. Municipality of Anchorage, 91 P.3d 252 (AK 2004). Because curfews create a classification that treats children differently from adults, the cases pose questions about young people's liberty interests and the level of scrutiny—rational basis, intermediate, or strict—to which courts will subject the classification. The level of scrutiny courts employ to review curfew ordinances depends, in part, on the way they frame the juveniles' interests at stake. While age-based classification per se does not create a suspect class, Gregory v. Ashcroft, 501 U.S. 452 (1991), some courts assume that the intrusion on juveniles' liberty interests requires strict scrutiny and seek a compelling governmental interest—e.g. juveniles' safety and decreasing crime—that trumps children's liberty interests. E.g., Qutb v. Bartlett, 11 F.3d 488 (5th Cir.1993). If courts find that curfew statutes affect juveniles' fundamental rights to privacy or freedom of movement and use a strict scrutiny analysis, then they require the curfew ordinance to be narrowly tailored to serve compelling governmental interests. State v. J.P., 907 So. 2d 1101 (Fla. 2004). Courts generally reject the claim that juveniles have a "fundamental right" to be on the streets at night without adult supervision. E.g., Sale ex rel. Sale v. Goldman, 539 S.E.2d 446 (W.Va.2000) (curfew requires only rational basis to protect health and welfare). Defining juveniles' interests as First Amendment activities more frequently elicits "strict scrutiny" and constitutional invalidation. E.g., Nunez v. City of San Diego, 114 F.3d 935 (9th Cir.1997); City of Maquoketa v. Russell, 484 N.W.2d 179 (Iowa 1992) (curfew prevented older minors from attending late church services or participating in political activities). By contrast, the courts in Schleifer and Hutchins used "intermediate scrutiny," found curfew restrictions "substantially related" to important governmental interests and upheld curfew statutes.

A plurality of the Supreme Court in Bellotti v. Baird, 443 U.S. 622 (S.Ct.1979), described a general framework for determining when states may give less deference to juveniles' constitutional claims than to those of adults. Belotti noted three factors which may justify different treatment of juveniles than adults: the special vulnerability of children; their inability to make crucial decision in an informed and mature manner; and parents' important role in child rearing. Courts have used the Belotti factors to analyze juvenile curfews and reached opposite conclusions. E.g., Matter of Appeal in Maricopa County, 181 Ariz. 69, 887 P.2d 599 (Ariz.Ct.App.1994) (plague of crime and drugs at which curfew is directed is more damaging to minors because they are more vulnerable); Waters

v. Barry, 711 F.Supp. 1125 (D.D.C.1989) (crime poses no peculiar danger to children but affects juveniles and adults equally).

Some ordinances also penalize parents for knowingly allowing their child to violate the curfew. E.g., Hutchins v. District of Columbia, 188 F.3d 531 (D.C.Cir.1999). Courts reject parents' claims that such curfew laws unconstitutionally abridge their child-rearing authority. While parents have a right, as against the state, to regulate their children in the home and to control their education, they do not have a right unilaterally to determine when and if their children may roam the streets at night despite the state's prohibition. E.g., Hutchins v. District of Columbia, 188 F.3d 531 (D.C.Cir.1999); Sale ex rel. Sale v. Goldman, 539 S.E.2d 446 (W.Va.2000) (curfew impact on parental rights minimal). However, courts may find the parental liability provisions of juvenile curfew statutes "void for vagueness" if they fail to precisely define the meaning of terms such as "remain" in a public place or what constitutes a constitutionally valid "errand." E.g. City of Sumner v. Walsh, 61 P.3d 1111 (Wash. 2003). Courts give short-shrift to juveniles' Fourth Amendment challenges to curfew ordinances. If a person in public "after hours" looks "young," then police have probable cause to investigate further to determine her age and reasons for being in a public place. E.g., Waters v. Barry, 711 F.Supp. 1125 (D.D.C.1989); Qutb v. Bartlett, 11 F.3d 488 (5th Cir.1993) ("The curfew ordinance provides an officer with reasonable suspicion to approach gangs to determine if any of them are juveniles.") Curfew statutes give police authority to intervene proactively and investigate those who appear "young" to forestall gang activity.

D. CONCLUSION

The Progressive creators of the juvenile court envisioned a social service agency in a judicial setting and attempted to fuse its welfare mission with the power of state coercion. Juvenile courts attempt to balance a social welfare mission with penal social control and these goals are reflected in the breadth of their criminal and non-criminal jurisdictional mandate. Defining delinquency jurisdiction on the basis of a criminal offense creates an impetus to subordinate social welfare concerns to penal considerations. It also requires courts and legislatures to reconcile criminal law doctrines with juvenile courts' rehabilitative mission. Over the past two decades, legal changes have emphasized punishment, accountability, and personal responsibility, reinforced juvenile courts' penal foundations, emphasized the criminal aspects of delinquency jurisdiction, and detracted from a compassionate response to young offenders. Despite the recent legislative emphases on punishment, the purposes of juvenile courts remain more rehabilitative and interventionist than those of the criminal justice system and courts use those differences to justify procedural differences.

CHAPTER 3

POLICE AND JUVENILES: PRE–TRIAL CRIMINAL PROCEDURE

The juvenile court is part of a larger system of youth social control and interacts with several other actors. Police encounter youths' criminal and non-criminal misbehavior in the community and may refer them to juvenile court. Parents may enlist the juvenile court to help them to control their children or refer them for criminal and non-criminal misconduct. School officials respond to students' truancy and misconduct in school and may refer them to the court. Probation officers informally and formally supervise youths referred to juvenile court and may invoke the court to sanction probation violations. And, juvenile courts, in turn, re-enforce the authority of and rely on these people to enforce their orders and supervise youth in the community. Because states define delinquency jurisdiction based on criminal law violations, police are the primary source of referrals to juvenile court. In 2002, law enforcement personnel referred 82 percent of the delinquency cases to court intake. Snyder and Sickmund, *National Report 2006*. Schools comprise the largest source of truancy referrals, parents the largest source of runaway and incorrigibility referrals, and court services personnel the largest source of probation violation referrals. Snyder and Sickmund, *National Report 2006*.

This chapter will not recapitulate standard criminal procedure principles, for example, Fourth Amendment search and seizure law or Fifth Amendment interrogation doctrines. Rather, it assumes that the adult constitutional criminal procedure framework generally applies to law enforcement practices involving juveniles. E.g. Wayne R. LaFave, Jerold H. Israel, Nancy J. King, Orin S. Kerr, *Criminal Procedure* (5th ed., 2000). Instead, it examines how statutes, court opinions, and schools modify ordinary criminal procedure policies when they apply them to children rather than to adults or because juvenile courts treat rather than punish young offenders. How do differences between children's and adults' competencies and judgment affect pre-trial police investigative procedures? How should juvenile courts' pursuit of rehabilitative goals rather than punishment affect police or court practices? If juveniles are less mature and competent than adults, then how should the legal system accommodate their developmental limitations when they deal with police? Questions of juveniles' legal competence occur, for example, when youths consent to a search or waive their *Miranda* rights and police interrogate them. Should legal doctrines treat children like adults, or should they provide them with greater protections to compensate for their immaturity and vulnerability? If children pose special problems of social control in certain contexts, for example, in schools, then how should states modify their criminal procedures to accommodate schools' "special needs"?

A. FOURTH AMENDMENT CRIMINAL PROCEDURE

Policing juveniles implicates both general police practices and the broader cultural assumptions that police and other adults make about children. Ordinary police practices involve enforcing criminal statutes, maintaining order and preserving the peace, and providing an array of public services. Law enforcement, order maintenance, and community service require police to make a host of discretionary, low-visibility decisions. When people call the police, they expect officers to respond immediately, to deal with the situation when and where it occurs, and to prevail in the face of any opposition. In the context of policing juveniles, officers share common cultural assumptions about children that further support adult controls. Like most adults, police assume that young people are accountable for their presence and activities in public places. Similarly, police like other adults assume that most of what young people do is non-productive, lacks any inherent significance, and therefore is subordinate to adult claims and interests. Despite the seriousness of the crime problem, much of what police do, especially involving juveniles, is not criminal law enforcement but rather order maintenance. In many non-felony cases involving juveniles—noise, public disorder, hanging out on street corners—police encounter groups of youths and cannot easily determine whether a criminal violation has occurred or individual responsibility. How police respond to these situations depends less on what happened in the past than what occurs during the interaction. In these encounters, police have several discretionary options—warn and release, write a field report, take the child into custody and release her to her parent, issue a citation to juvenile court, or arrest and/or detain the youth. Some jurisdictions formally authorize police officers to issue written warnings to juveniles in lieu of taking them into custody. E.g., Tex. Fam. Code § 52.01 (Vernon 2002) (written warning notice pursuant to guidelines approved by juvenile court, describing child's conduct, sent to parents, and filed with police agency). Most states allow officers to issue a citation—like a traffic ticket—in lieu of an arrest. In many non-felony situations, police responses often reflect the youth's demeanor, attitude, and reactions to the officer. Within a considerable range, police and juveniles' interaction will mediate substantive misconduct. A juvenile's diffidence can mitigate a situation while her arrogance may aggravate it.

Most juvenile disturbances occur in public places. Police address these problems *in situ* to maintain control of public spaces. Police often respond to citizen complaints about youths' activities, for example, store-owners' assertion that young people are making noise, hanging out, or harassing customers. Complainants' preferences also may constrain officers' discretion. When citizens call police, they monitor how the officer responds. Police perform a quasi-adjudicative function in which they indulge a presumption against juveniles. Police typically assume the validity of adult complainants' charges and do not give as much credence to youths' denials. Conversely, young people feel that police often wrongfully accuse them and impose arbitrary restrictions.

The mere conspicuous presence of young people poses a potential threat to police control of public spaces. Moreover, juvenile "trouble" is socially patterned because schools, shopping malls and stores, and recreation areas generate concentrations of youths in certain neighborhoods or locales. Especially in urban areas, police often find young people in places where adults do not feel they should be and where a contested relationship has emerged between police and youths. To forestall disorder, officers may engage in "proactive intervention" or "aggressive patrol" but which youths may experience as "hassling." Police officers' reliance on adult complainants, use of stereotypes and previous experiences with minority racial groups may create a self-fulfilling prophecy. Aggressive assertions of authority by police in certain areas may contribute to hostile reactions by youths which confirm stereotypes, inflate arrest statistics, and lead to more proactive intervention.

1. CUSTODY

The validity of an arrest affects the admissibility of evidence obtained through subsequent investigative activities such as searches incident to the arrest or interrogations. Juvenile court statutes, common law, and Fourth Amendment constitutional principles govern police behavior when they take juveniles into custody. Lourdes M. Rosado, "Minors and the Fourth Amendments: How Juvenile Status Should Invoke Different Standards for Searches and Seizures on the Street," 71 *N.Y.U.L.Rev.* 762 (1996). Juvenile codes typically provide that police may take a child into custody based on a court order or warrant, "in accordance with the laws relating to arrests," when an officer reasonably believes that a child has run away from home, is in circumstances which will endanger her health or welfare, or when she has violated terms of probation or parole. E.g. Wis. Stat. Ann. § 938.19 (West 2000) (officer reasonably believes juvenile has violated or is violating criminal law); Okla. Stat. Ann. tit. 10 § 7303–1.1 (West 1999) (peace officer may take a child into custody for any criminal offense for which the officer is authorized to arrest an adult without a warrant); Pa. Juv. Ct. Act § 6324 ("pursuant to law of arrest"). At the same time, however, juvenile codes provide that taking a child into custody "shall not be considered an arrest." Minn. Stat. Ann. § 260B.165 Subd. 2 (West 2000). This enables a juvenile truthfully to answer that she has not been arrested on employment applications or other forms. However, euphemistically calling a restraint of liberty "custody" rather than "arrest" does not avoid the constitutional requirements of probable cause. E.g. Lanes v. State, 767 S.W.2d 789 (Tex, Ct. Crim. App. 1989) (Fourth Amendment applies to juvenile arrests and requires probable cause). Some statutes make the Fourth Amendment's applicability to custody determinations explicit. Tex. Fam. Code Ann. § 52.01(b) (Vernon 2002) ("The taking of a child into custody is not an arrest except for the purpose of determining the validity of taking him into custody or the validity of a search under the laws and constitution of this state or of the United States."); Fla. Stat. Ann. § 985.207(3)(1997) (custody is not an arrest except for purposes of determining the legality of custody or evidence).

The Fourth Amendment provides that "[t]he right of the people to be secure in their persons, houses, papers, and effects, against unreasonable searches and seizures, shall not be violated, and no Warrants shall issue, but upon probable cause, supported by Oath or affirmation, and particularly describing the place to be searched, and the persons or things to be seized." U.S. Const. Amend. IV. Other than schools, courts generally apply Fourth Amendment principles to juveniles. New Jersey v. T.L.O., 469 U.S. 325 (S.Ct.1985); Florida v. J.L., 529 U.S. 266 (S.Ct.2000) (suppression of evidence obtained as a result of invalid "stop"); Lanes v. State, 767 S.W.2d 789 (Tex.Crim.App.1989) (applicability of Fourth Amendment probable cause requirement to juveniles).

An arrest, or Fourth Amendment seizure of the person, occurs when police deprive a person of his liberty. Whether or not a restraint of liberty constitutes an arrest is a fact-specific legal question. LaFave, *Criminal Procedure*. At common law and in most states, a police officer may arrest a person for a felony without an arrest warrant if the officer has probable cause to believe that the person committed a crime and the arrest occurs in a public place. United States v. Watson, 423 U.S. 411 (S.Ct.1976) (warrantless arrest in public); LaFave, *Criminal Procedure.* In addition, police may make a warrantless arrest for a misdemeanor that occurs in their presence and they may do so even if the underlying offense cannot result in any jail-time. Atwater v. City of Lago Vista, 532 U.S. 318 (S.Ct.2001). However, the admissibility of evidence hinges on the validity of the initial arrest and some courts suppress the evidence if the officer had no basis to take the youth into custody for a non-jailable offense. E.g. State v. Bauer, 36 P.3d 892 (Mont.2001) (search incident to arrest invalid because juvenile could not be arrested and detained for non-jailable offense of minor in possession of alcohol).

In the absence of "exigent circumstances," police ordinarily require an arrest warrant to enter private premises to arrest a suspect. Payton v. New York, 445 U.S. 573 (S.Ct.1980) (routine felony arrest in private home requires arrest warrant). When police validly arrest a suspect, with or without an arrest warrant, they may conduct a search incident to arrest to seize evidence on her person or within the area of her immediate control. Chimel v. California, 395 U.S. 752 (S.Ct.1969). Police may conduct a search incident to arrest regardless of whether or not they have reason to believe that they will find weapons or evidence as a result of the search and they may conduct the search either at the time of the arrest or later at the station-house. United States v. Robinson, 414 U.S. 218 (S.Ct.1973); United States v. Edwards, 415 U.S. 800 (S.Ct.1974). In addition, police may make brief investigative seizures of the person or "stops," which are less intrusive than arrests, when they have reasonable suspicion to believe that "criminal activity is afoot." Terry v. Ohio, 392 U.S. 1 (S.Ct.1968). Pursuant to an investigative detention, police also may pat-down or frisk a person whom they have objective reasonable grounds to believe is armed or poses a threat to their safety. LaFave, *Criminal Procedure*.

The Supreme Court has not explicitly addressed the applicability of the Fourth Amendment to arrests and searches of juveniles outside of the school context. Legislatures and courts consistently treat "custody" as the equivalent of arrest and use the adult constitutional criminal procedural framework to analyze the validity of juvenile arrests and searches in settings other than schools. "Being 'in custody' is a restraint of liberty. When a juvenile is taken into custody, whether it be shorter-termed or not, the juvenile is not free to leave. The taking into custody of a juvenile is analogous to the arrest of an adult." In the Interest of J.G., 547 A.2d 336 (N.J.Super.Ch.1988). Courts generally qualify the statutory language that custody is not an arrest to mean except for purposes of determining its constitutional validity. "While the term 'arrest' is not to be used to describe taking a juvenile into custody, it will be so used in this opinion for the purpose of evaluating the lawfulness of the search. . . . The criteria for the lawful arrest of a juvenile are those applicable to arrest for an adult offense . . . supplemented by criteria contained in rules of court pertaining to juvenile offenses." In re J.B., 131 N.J.Super. 6, 328 A.2d 46 (N.J.Juv. &

Dom. Rel. Ct., Union Co. 1974). In Lanes v. State, 767 S.W.2d 789 (Tex.Ct.Crim.App.1989), the court held that taking a juvenile into custody to take his fingerprints was the functional equivalent of an arrest which required probable cause. The absence of extensive decisions on this question reflects the consensus that the law of arrests for adults applies equally to juveniles. Samuel Davis, *Rights of Minors* (1994). A defendant only can challenge the validity of an arrest by objecting to the admissibility of evidence obtained as a result thereof. Wong Sun v. United States, 371 U.S. 471 (S.Ct.1963). An illegal arrest that does not produce any derivative evidence will not deprive a juvenile court of jurisdiction over the delinquent. Frisbie v. Collins, 342 U.S. 519 (S.Ct.1952); State v. E.T., 560 So.2d 1282 (Fla.Dist.Ct.App.1990).

Custody for Status Offenses Recall that juvenile court jurisdiction encompasses more than just criminal delinquency matters. The state's broader protective role and juvenile courts' status offense jurisdiction allow police to take juveniles into custody for non-criminal misconduct or when circumstances pose a threat to their health or welfare. For example, status jurisdiction encompasses children who are habitually truant, "unruly" or disobey the reasonable commands of parents, run away from home, violate curfew, commit other offenses applicable only to children, or who are in imminent danger from their surroundings. E.g., Ga. Code Ann. § 15–11–2(12) (2000); Pa. Juv. Ct. Act § 6324 (2000). The broad jurisdictional authority necessarily requires a correspondingly greater power to intervene with juveniles than adults. Thus, even if police lack probable cause to believe that a youth committed in crime, they still may take the youth into custody under the status or protective jurisdiction. For example, when officers reasonably believed that a school-aged minor was absent from school, they could stop him for a truancy violation and take him into custody. In re James D., 43 Cal.3d 903, 741 P.2d 161, 239 Cal.Rptr. 663 (Cal.1987), cert. den'd, 485 U.S. 959 (1988). When police received information that a juvenile ran away from home or was truant from school, they could take him into custody. In the Interest of J.G., 547 A.2d 336 (N.J.Super.Ch.1988); In the Matter of Z.M., 160 P.3d 490 (Mt. 2007). An officer must have a reasonable belief or probable cause to believe that a youth engaged in non-criminal misconduct to take her into custody for a status offense, rather than evidence that the youth committed a crime. Some states' laws specify the statutory criteria that provide an officer with reasonable belief that a juvenile is a status offender. E.g. N.Y. Fam. Ct. Act § 718(a)(McKinney 2002) (an officer may reasonably conclude that "a child has run away from home when the child refuses to give his or her name or the name and address of a parent or other person legally responsible for such child's care or when the officer has reason to doubt that the name or address given are the actual name and address of the parent or other person legally responsible for the child's care."); In re Mark Anthony G., 571 N.Y.S.2d 481 (N.Y.App.Div.1991) (youthful appearance, late hour, and presence alone at location, vague and inconsistent answers, and inability to produce identification provided basis for detention as a "runaway" and "pat down"). Ultimately, courts evaluate the validity of a status offense stop, custody, or arrest the same way as they do the validity of a Terry-stop or an arrest of an adult. E.g. Florida v. J.L., 529 U.S. 266 (S.Ct.2000) (sufficiency of anonymous tip to provide reasonable suspicion for investigative stop); In re D.J., 532 A.2d 138 (D.C.1987) (flight from police insufficient in itself to justify arrest).

2. SEARCH INCIDENT TO CUSTODY

The Supreme Court allows police to conduct a search incident to arrest to prevent destruction of evidence or danger to the officer. LaFave, *Criminal Procedure*. Courts do not require an officer to have search probable cause when she searches an arrestee. United States v. Robinson, 414 U.S. 218 (S.Ct.1973). Although the Court approved searches incident to arrest in the context of arrests for crimes, courts grant police the same authority to search youths taken into custody for non-criminal misconduct as well. Even if police initially took the youth into custody for a non-criminal status offense, courts admit evidence obtained as a result of a search incident to custody even if it leads to the filing of criminal delinquency charges. In the Interest of J.G., 547 A.2d 336 (N.J.Super.Ct. Ch.Div.1988) (delinquency drug charges based on evidence seized during search incident to custody for runaway); In re James D., 43 Cal.3d 903, 741 P.2d

161, 239 Cal.Rptr. 663 (Cal.1987) (delinquency drug charges based on evidence seized during search incident to custody for truancy); In re Terrence G., 492 N.Y.S.2d 365, 370 (N.Y.App.Div.1985) (gun discovered during pat down search of a juvenile detained as a runaway); In the Matter of Z.M., 160 P.3d 490 (Mt. 2007) (evidence of burglary admitted based on search accompanying a stop for truancy and drinking alcohol). Unlike the search incident to arrest of an adult, which courts justify for the protection of the officer and society, courts emphasize that police take juveniles into custody to protect their health, morals, and well-being. "Nothing in the noncriminal appellation of this detention serves to obliterate the dangers of the 'in-custody' situation. Here, the circumstances of respondent's detention, coupled with the particularly high duty of protection owed him and other detainees by the runaway statutes, were more than ample justification for the pat down. . . . The police officers who detained respondent . . . were clearly charged with effectuating the State's '*parens patriae* interest in preserving and promoting the welfare of the child.' " In re Terrence G., 492 N.Y.S.2d 365, 370 (N.Y.App.Div.1985)

States restrict the authority of the police to place in secure detention facilities youths whom they take into custody for non-criminal misconduct. See Chapter 5. For example, New York authorizes police to "take any child under the age of sixteen into custody without a warrant in cases in which he may arrest a person for a crime . . ." N.Y. Fam. Ct. Act § 305.2(2) (McKinney 2000). However, New York requires a police officer to return a PINS (Person In Need of Supervision) or run-away to her parents or to take her to a suitable youth facility or the Family Court. N.Y. Fam. Ct. Act § 718 (McKinney 2002); N.Y. Fam. Ct. Act § 724 (McKinney 2002). Even though these provisions do not allow police to hold a PINS youth in a secure detention facility, police still may conduct a pat-down of a runaway which may yield admissible evidence to support a delinquency charge. In re Jamel J., 246 A.D.2d 388, 667 N.Y.S.2d 732 (N.Y.App.Div.1998) (detention pursuant to runaway statute was custodial arrest that justified pat-down search of juvenile and warrantless search of bag that was within juvenile's immediate area); In re Sharon T., 248 A.D.2d 131, 669 N.Y.S.2d 535 (N.Y.App.Div.1998) leave to appeal denied 92 N.Y.2d 803, 677 N.Y.S.2d 73, 699 N.E.2d 433 (N.Y.1998) (detention of juvenile at bus terminal pursuant to runaway statute was a custodial arrest which justified officer's search of knapsack incident to her lawful arrest).

Courts apply the same principles to searches of juvenile probationers as to adults. For example, the California Supreme Court in In re Jaime P., 40 Cal.4th 128, 51 Cal.Rprt.3d 430, 146 P.3d 965 (2006), overruled its earlier decision in In re Tyrell J., 8 Cal.4th 68, 876 P.2d 519, 32 Cal.Rptr.2d 33 (Cal.1994), which gave police greater authority to search juvenile probationers than their adult counterparts. Tyrell J. allowed police to search juvenile probationers based on a condition of probation requiring the juvenile to "submit to a search of his person," even though the officer who conducted the search was unaware of Tyrell's probation status or search condition and acted without probable cause. Tyrell J. reasoned that the rehabilitative goals of juvenile courts required broader authority to deter probation violations than was the case for adults and juvenile probationers had a reduced expectation of privacy. Jaime P. rejected those rationales and held that neither juvenile court's "special needs" to treat or deter delinquents or juveniles' diminished expectations of privacy justified allowing police to search them randomly and without "reasonable suspicion."

3. POST–ARREST DUTIES: NOTICE AND DETENTION

When police take a child into custody, statutes typically require the officer to take the youth to a juvenile facility rather than to an adult jail and to attempt to notify the child's parents or probation officer. E.g. Fla. Stat. Ann. § 985.207(2) (1997); Idaho Code § 20–516 (Michie 2000); 705 Ill.Comp.Stat. Ann. § 405/5–405 (West 1999) (reasonable attempt to notify minor's parents when minor is taken into custody). For example, Tex. Fam. Code Ann. § 52.02(a) (Vernon 2002), requires that a person who takes a child into custody shall release the child to a parent or custodian upon that person's promise to return the child to the juvenile court, or bring the child before an official designated by the juvenile court, such as probation intake, if there is probable cause to believe that the child engaged in delinquent conduct or conduct indicating a need for supervision, or bring the child to a detention facility or, if delinquent, to a secure detention facility, or to a medical facility if the child's serious physical condition requires prompt treatment. When a person takes a child into custody, they must promptly notify the child's parent or guardian and a juvenile court official, such as a probation officer, of the reason for taking the child into custody. Similarly, the Federal Juvenile Delinquency Act requires an officer who takes a juvenile into custody to immediately advise the juvenile of his legal rights, to notify the juvenile's parents of the custody and the nature of the offense, and to take the juvenile "before a magistrate forthwith." 18 U.S.C. 5033 (2000). The federal notification statute envisions parental advice and assistance to their child and failure to comply with it may result in actual prejudice. E.g. United States v. Doe, 219 F.3d 1009 (9th Cir.2000) (confession suppressed because authorities unreasonably delayed presenting juvenile to magistrate and failed to notify parents). Under the federal delinquency provisions, after the police notify the parents, police must provide them with an opportunity to consult with their child before they may interrogate her. United States v. Wendy G., 255 F.3d 761 (9th Cir.2001). Courts have suppressed statements made by juveniles during custodial interrogation where law enforcement officers violate parental notification statutes. People v. Gardner, 257 A.D.2d 675, 683 N.Y.S.2d 351 (N.Y.App.Div.1999); Barrow v. State, 749 A.2d 1230 (Del.2000). However, courts generally do not treat the failure or inability to notify parents as a constitutional violation that renders the custody invalid. United States v. Watts, 513 F.2d 5 (10th Cir.1975) (parental notice is a prophylactic requirement to enable child to prepare defense); Gandy v. Panama City, 505 F.2d 630 (5th Cir.1974) (police violation of parental notification statute following arrest is not a federal constitutional violation); Palmer v. State, 626 A.2d 1358 (Del.1993) (failure to notify parents constitutes due process as well as statutory violation of rights). Ordinarily, police or probation officers release a juvenile to her parents unless the juvenile meet the statutory grounds for continued detention. E.g. Minn. Stat. § 260B.171 (West 2002); N.Y. Fam. Ct. Act § 305.2 (McKinney 2000). See Chapter 5.

4. CONSENT SEARCHES

The Supreme Court in Schneckloth v. Bustamonte, 412 U.S. 218 (S.Ct.1973), held that a valid consent to a search must be "voluntary" under the "totality of the circumstances." If police obtain a voluntary consent, then they do not require either a warrant or individualized suspicion to seize evidence. Schneckloth defined "voluntariness" as an uncoerced decision rather than as a knowing choice among alternatives, which would require proof of knowledge of the right to refuse. The Court emphasized that voluntariness is a question of fact that trial courts evaluate under the "totality of the circumstances" which include factors such as "the characteristics of the accused[,] . . . the youth of the accused, or his lack of education." However, unlike a waiver of "trial rights" which must be "knowing, intelligent, and voluntary," a consent to search only need be "voluntarily given, and not the result of duress or coercion, express or implied. Voluntariness is a question of fact to be determined from all of the circumstances, and while the subject's knowledge of a right to refuse is a factor to be taken into account, the prosecution is not required to demonstrate such knowledge as a prerequisite to establishing a voluntary consent."

How should "youthfulness" affect judges' evaluations of coercion or voluntariness when police obtain a juvenile's consent to a search or Miranda waiver and confession? Should the juvenile justice system treat juveniles like adults and use the same "totality of the circumstances" approach to assess children's decisions to relinquish legal rights or should it provide special procedural protections to protect them from their own immaturity and vulnerability? For most purposes, courts do not treat youthfulness as a categorical disability that precludes a voluntary consent nor do they require additional procedural safeguards. For example, in In re Jermaine, 399 Pa.Super. 503, 582 A.2d 1058, 1064 (Pa.Super.Ct.1990), the court noted that "The fact that the juvenile was sixteen and one-half years old at the time of the search, moreover, did not prevent her from giving voluntary consent to a search of her bag. 'Although age is one element to acknowledge in ascertaining when consent was given willingly, minority status alone does not prevent one from giving consent.' "

Most appellate courts treat voluntariness as a fact question within the discretion of the trial judge.

A few jurisdictions require judges to make explicit findings about the effects of a juvenile's age, immaturity, and lack of knowledge of a right to refuse on the voluntariness of consent to search. In In re J.M., 619 A.2d 497 (D.C.Ct.App.1992), drug-interdiction officers boarded a bus late at night and encountered 14–year–old J.M. riding alone. After J.M. expressly consented to a search of his carry-on bag which he knew contained no contraband, the officer asked to frisk J.M. After the youth raised his arms, the officer patted him down and found drugs taped to his body. The trial court admitted the drugs, but the appellate court remanded the case for explicit findings of fact about the effect of J.M.'s age on the voluntariness of his consent to the search. While the trial judge initially found that J.M. consented in order "to deflect suspicion from himself," the judge did not make express findings about "J.M.'s maturity or sophistication for his age, as shown by his conduct at the time of the search or his testimony and demeanor at the hearing." The court required explicit findings about J.M.'s youthfulness and inexperience because J.M. may have consented either to feign cooperation to deflect suspicion or because he succumbed to the inherent authority of the officer. However, the court declined to hold that "the special vulnerability of juveniles to intimidation by figures of authority . . . [requires] a presumptive rule invalidating consents by juveniles."

When police arrest a person, the more coercive pressures associated with custody may affect the voluntariness of a subsequent consent to search.

However, custody per se does not require additional safeguards, such as a warning of a right to refuse or invalidate consent to search. United States v. Watson, 423 U.S. 411 (S.Ct.1976). When police place juveniles in custody, a few states require that their parents also consent to the ensuing search. E.g. In re S.J., 778 P.2d 1384 (Colo.1989). However, these requirements of parental notice and concurrence constitute judicial extensions of statutes regulating police interrogation of juveniles that require parental presence. In the absence of such provisions, courts apply the "totality" analysis in which custody simply is one of the factors affecting voluntariness.

Unlike adults, who may control their own private living arrangements, children must live with their parent or other legal guardian. In United States v. Matlock, 415 U.S. 164 (1974), the Supreme Court upheld the authority of other people to give third-party consent to a search based on their "common authority" over the premises—their overlapping "expectations of privacy"—or their shared access to personal property. Parents may allow police to search the family home and their child's room based either on the parent's right to control their child or their exercise of control over the premises. E.g. In re Robert H., 78 Cal.App.3d 894, 144 Cal.Rptr. 565 (Cal.App.1978). In Georgia v. Randolph, 547 U.S. 103 (2006), the Court held that when one occupant objected to the search, another adult resident could not give a valid consent to a search that would override the objection. However, the Court distinguished that "equal authority" third-party consent search situation from "people living together . . . within some recognized hierarchy, like a household of parent and child . . ." Consent based on parents' authority normally will prevail when the child is absent and even if the child is present and objects to the search, if the parents also have a "reasonable expectation of privacy" in the place searched. The court in In re Tariq A–R–Y, 701 A.2d 691 (Md.1997), held that "a parent of an unemancipated minor can consent to a search of his or her child's personal belonging left in the common area of their home, over the child's objection." In In re C.M.B. v. State, 594 So.2d 695, 701 (Ala.Crim.App.1991), the court held that because the juvenile "had no legitimate expectation of privacy in his mother's bedroom where the gun was found," he lacked standing to challenge the search or to object to the validity of his mother's consent to the search. In In re Salyer, 44 Ill.App.3d 854, 859, 358 N.E.2d 1333, 1336–37 (Ill.App.Ct.1977), the court held that a mother may consent to the search of her 15–year–old son's room even though he locked his room with a combination lock on the outside and an inside lock and the mother had to knock to gain admittance. "We believe that there is implicit in the rights and duties imposed upon a parent, the right to exert parental authority and control over a minor son's surroundings and that such implied right to control obviously includes a room in the home of the mother. We also conclude that the mother had at least common authority as to the room occupied by her 15–year–old child." Where the child limits parental access and they have no proprietary interest in the object searched, some courts invalidate the search. E.g., In re Scott K., 595 P.2d 105 (Cal.1979), cert. denied, 444 U.S. 973 (1979) (where parents lacked property interest in child's locked toolbox or its contents, they lacked authority to consent to search).

B.   SEARCHING JUVENILES: SCHOOLS AND "SPECIAL NEEDS"

School officials' concern about maintaining order, promoting a suitable educational environment, and controlling guns and drugs sometimes may conflict with students' Fourth Amendment privacy interests. School officials, School Resource Officers, and police frequently search students, their purses, jackets, backpacks, or lockers as well as vehicle parked in a school parking lot. In addition, schools subject young people to rules and regulations—e.g. dress codes, prohibition of tobacco and alcohol, and the like—that do not apply to adults and create even greater potential for state infringement of young people's privacy interests. Because states regulate young people more extensively adults, courts do not ascribe to juveniles the same "reasonable expectation of privacy" as adults and are reluctant to recognize their privacy claims as "objectively reasonable" when balanced against schools' "special needs." Prior to New Jersey v. T.L.O., 469 U.S. 325 (S.Ct.1985), state courts used several rationales to justify school officials' searches of students, their possessions, desks and lockers: school administrators acted as private citizens, hence no state action occurred; school officials acted *in loco parentis* under delegated authority from the students' parents; the character and needs of public schools created a special relationship that justified special rules for searches of students' person and locker; students consented expressly or impliedly; or the school administrator provided third-party consent. E.g. In re Donaldson, 269 Cal.App.2d 509, 75 Cal.Rptr. 220 (Cal.App.1969); In re. J.A., 85 Ill.App.3d 567, 406 N.E.2d 958 (Ill.App.1980); Mercer v. State, 450 S.W.2d 715 (Tex.Civ.App.1970); Davis, *Rights of Juveniles*. The Supreme Court in T.L.O. brought school searches within the ambit of the Fourth Amendment but modified those doctrines to accommodate schools' "special needs."

1. SEARCHING JUVENILES IN SCHOOL

Although state statutes and court opinions treat juveniles and adults similarly for most Fourth Amendment law enforcement purposes, the Supreme Court has decided two school search cases—New Jersey v. T.L.O., 469 U.S. 325 (S.Ct.1985), and Vernonia School District 47J v. Acton, 515 U.S. 646 (S.Ct.1995)—that establish different legal standards for searching and drug-testing juveniles than adults.

In T.L.O., a high school teacher observed a fourteen-year-old female student smoking cigarettes in the restroom in violation of a school rule and reported her to vice principal Choplick. Choplick questioned T.L.O., searched her purse and found cigarettes, and confronted her with them for lying. While removing the cigarettes, he also observed cigarette wrapping papers which prompted a more extensive search that produced a small amount of marijuana, a pipe, and other evidence implicating T.L.O. in selling drugs. Choplick turned the evidence over to the police. Juvenile court authorities initiated delinquency proceedings against T.L.O. who moved to suppress the evidence. The parties originally briefed T.L.O. on the question whether the exclusionary rule applied in school disciplinary and/or delinquency proceedings. On re-argument, the Court found Choplick's search reasonable under the Fourth Amendment and did not reach decide whether the exclusionary rule applies either in delinquency hearings or schools.

The Court rejected the State's arguments that the Fourth Amendment only applied to searches conducted by law enforcement personnel and that school officials acted as private parties or *in loco parentis* when they searched. The Court also rejected the State's analogy of students to prison inmates who lacked any "legitimate expectation of privacy" under the Fourth Amendment. E.g. Hudson v. Palmer, 468 U.S. 517 (S.Ct.1984). Instead, the Court used its Fourth Amendment reasonableness balancing framework to assess the state's interests in searching students versus the nature of the intrusion on students' "reasonable expectation of privacy." The Court emphasized that the reasonableness of a search depended on its context and schools presented "special needs." The Court acknowledged that children in school have some reasonable expectations of privacy in their physical person, purses, wallets, personal effects, and backpacks. Against the juveniles' relatively minor privacy interests, the Court weighed school officials' interests in maintaining order, enforcing rules, and retaining a flexible and informal disciplinary process. The Court noted the prevalence of drugs, weapons, and violence in schools, the informality of student-teacher relationships, and schools' need for swift, uncomplicated responses.

The Court used the exigent circumstances rationale to dispense with requiring a search warrant. It found that a warrant process would impede school officials' ability to swiftly and informally investigate suspected violations and to maintain discipline. In addition, the Court dispensed with the Fourth Amendment requirement of "probable cause" and instead authorized school officials to act on the basis of the lower evidentiary standard of "reasonable suspicion." In approving the reasonableness of action based on less than probable cause, the Court invoked the stop-and-frisk rationale of Terry v. Ohio, 392 U.S. 1 (S.Ct.1968). In determining the validity of a search, the Court noted that

> the legality of a search of a student should depend simply on the reasonableness, under all the circumstances, of the search. Determining the reasonableness of any search involves a twofold inquiry: first, one must consider 'whether the . . . action was justified at its inception'; second, one must determine whether the search as actually conducted 'was reasonably related in scope to the circumstances which justified the interference

in the first place'. Under ordinary circumstances, a search of a student by a teacher or other school official will be 'justified at its inception' when there are reasonable grounds for suspecting that the search will turn up evidence that the student has violated or is violating either the law or the rules of the school. Such a search will be permissible in its scope when the measures adopted are reasonably related to the objectives of the search and not excessively intrusive in light of the age and sex of the student and the nature of the infraction.

Under these two prongs, the search must be justified at its inception and the scope of the search must be related to that justification. The Court denigrated the New Jersey Supreme Court's application of the reasonableness standard as "a somewhat crabbed notion of reasonableness," substituted its own views of the reasonableness of Choplick's actions, and upheld the search.

The T.L.O. majority rejected the argument that the seriousness of the law or school rule violated affected the justification for or reasonableness of a search. By contrast, Justice Stevens' dissent argued that the importance of the rule being enforced affected whether a search was reasonable; violations of some rules simply are too trivial to justify intruding on students' legitimate expectation of privacy. However, the majority declined to examine the reasonableness of school rules and instead deferred to school officials' assessment of the need for such regulations. The Court viewed Choplick's search for cigarettes as reasonable to enable him to impeach T.L.O.'s denial of smoking. Once Choplick searched in a place where he had right to be based on reasonable suspicion, he saw evidence of drugs in "plain view." Although the majority emphasized that a child's age, sex, and the nature of the infraction affected the scope and reasonableness of the search, Justice Stevens' dissent questioned what practical limitations those factors imposed if a male teacher could search a female student's purse and personal items for collateral impeachment evidence to enforce a trivial rule violation.

Justices Marshall and Brennan's dissent argued that the Court only employed reasonableness balancing and used a lower standard than probable cause when the police practice was qualitatively less intrusive than a search. They reasoned that because Choplick's search of T.L.O.'s purse constituted a full-blown search, it required probable cause. Moreover, they asserted that "totality of the circumstances" standard of probable cause announced in Illinois v. Gates, 462 U.S. 213 (S.Ct.1983), provided a perfectly workable, practical, nontechnical approach to school searches. The crucial issue in T.L.O. was whether adherence to a probable cause standard, rather than to a reasonable suspicion standard, would hamper school officials' ability to maintain order. The majority provided no reasons for its decision to apply the lower standard.

The T.L.O. decision explicitly identified a number of issues it did not decide in its initial juvenile Fourth Amendment foray. It did not decide whether the exclusionary rule applied either in juvenile delinquency hearings or school disciplinary proceedings. It did not decide whether students enjoyed a reasonable expectation of privacy in their lockers, desks, or other areas not immediately associated with their person. It did not decide whether "individualized suspicion" constituted a necessary prerequisite to the reasonableness of a search. It reserved the question whether the school "reasonableness" standard or the Fourth Amendment "probable cause" standard governed searches conducted by school personnel in conjunction with or at the behest of law enforcement officials for evidence to use in either school or delinquency proceedings. The Fourth Amendment issues associated with school searches, T.L.O.'s reserved questions, and the notes below are analyzed extensively in Barry C. Feld, "T.L.O. and Redding's Unanswered (Misanswered) Fourth Amendment Questions: Few Rights and Fewer Remedies," 80 Miss. L. J. 847 (2011).

a. Application of T.L.O.'s "Reasonableness" Standard

Since T.L.O., courts examining the reasonableness of school searches have applied the T.L.O. framework broadly to uphold most types of searches. See e.g. Williams v. Ellington, 936 F.2d 881 (6th Cir.1991); Cason v. Cook, 810 F.2d 188 (8th Cir.1987), cert. denied 482 U.S. 930 (1987);

Thompson v. Carthage School District, 87 F.3d 979 (8th Cir.1996). In assessing reasonableness, courts focus on the prohibited object sought and give school officials greater deference when they search for drugs or weapons than when they conduct a school-wide search for missing Magic Markers. People v. Alexander B., 270 Cal.Rptr. 342 (Cal.App.1990); Burnham v. West, 681 F.Supp. 1160 (E.D.Va.1987). A few courts have found school officials acted unreasonably when they lacked reasonable suspicion to believe that a youth committed a crime or violated a school rule. E.g. People v. William G., 40 Cal.3d 550, 709 P.2d 1287, 221 Cal.Rptr. 118 (Cal.1985). In assessing the quantity of information necessary to support reasonable suspicion, school officials may receive tips from teachers or school personnel, from students, from anonymous callers or note writers, from sniffer dogs, or from electronic detection devices. When they receive tips, "Absent information that a particular student informant may be untrustworthy, school officials may ordinarily accept at face value the information they supply." In re S.C. v. State, 583 So.2d 188 (Miss.1991). School officials also may rely on anonymous tips that provide specific details if the allegation is plausible because of conditions at the school. E.g. Martens v. District No. 220, 620 F.Supp. 29 (N.D.Il.1985).

b. "Reasonableness" of Strip Searches

Under T.L.O., a court must decide whether school officials conducted a search "reasonably related in scope to the circumstances which justified the interference in the first place." If school officials possess reasonable suspicion that a student possesses drugs, how intrusively may they search? May they conduct a strip search? Does reasonable suspicion support a nude search? Following T.L.O., courts have upheld strip-searches for drugs based on reasonable suspicion. E.g., Cornfield v. Consolidated High School District No. 230, 991 F.2d 1316 (7th Cir.1993) (school officials had strong reason to believe that plaintiff was hiding drugs in the crotch of his pants; he was taken to locker room, told to remove pants but allowed to put on gym uniform during search); Williams v. Ellington, 936 F.2d 881 (6th Cir.1991) (reason to believe female student was using drugs, student taken into private office where, in the presence of a female secretary, she removed her shirt, shoes and socks and lowered her jeans to her knees). On the other hand, when the object of the school officials' search is missing property or money, courts more frequently find strip-searches to be excessively intrusive. Courts look at three factors to assess reasonableness: 1) students' legitimate expectation of privacy; 2) the intrusiveness of the search; and 3) the school's need to conduct the search based on the severity of the problem presented. Beard v. Whitmore Lake School District, 402 F.3d 598 (6th Cir. 2005) (holding the strip search of groups of male and female students to locate missing prom money excessively intrusive); Galford v. Mark Anthony B., 189 W.Va. 538, 433 S.E.2d 41, 48–49 (W.Va.1993) (strip search of student to find money missing from teacher's purse was excessively intrusive and unreasonable in scope); Jenkins v. Talladega City Board of Education, 115 F.3d 821 (11th Cir.1997) (strip search of eight-year-old girls to find missing $7 invalid). In Konop v. Northwestern School District, 26 F.Supp.2d 1189 (D.S.D.1998), the court found a strip search of two eighth grade students unreasonable where officials had no reasonable basis to believe that either had stolen the $200 sought. Konop stated that "(1) a strip search is not justified absent individualized suspicion unless there is a legitimate safety concern (e.g. weapons); 2) school officials must be investigating allegations of violations of the law or school rules and only individual accusations justify a strip search; and (3) strip searches must be designed to be minimally intrusive taking into account the item for which the search is conducted."

The Supreme Court in Safford Unified School District #1 v. Redding, 129 S.Ct. 2633 (2009), applied *T.L.O.*'s principles to a strip search of a thirteen-year-old girl to find ibuprofen prohibited under the school's "zero tolerance" for drugs policy, and found that school officials acted unreasonably. Ultimately, *Redding* provided no additional guidance for school administrators confronting somewhat different factual situations and thereby provided no clarification of *T.L.O.*'s ambiguous reasonableness standard. A student-informant, Jordan, told assistant principal Wilson that students were bringing drugs to school. A week later, Jordan gave Wilson a white pill he received from Marissa and told him that students would take pills at lunch. Wilson called Marissa out of class, and her teacher gave Wilson a day-planner found within Marissa's reach that contained contraband items. A search of Marissa in Wilson's office produced a blue pill, white ones, and a razor blade. Marissa told Wilson that she received the blue pill from Savana Redding and denied any knowledge of the day-planner. Wilson did not ask Marissa when she received the pill from Savana, whether Savana presently had pills, or where she might be hiding them. Wilson called Savana to her office and showed her the planner. Savana admitted it was hers, said that she had loaned it to Marissa several days earlier, and denied knowledge of its contents. Wilson knew that Savana and Marissa were friends and members of a rowdy group of students who attended the school's opening dance at which staff found cigarettes and alcohol in the girls' bathroom.

The Court found these circumstances provided reasonable suspicion for Wilson to search Savana's backpack and outer clothes. After that search proved fruitless, Wilson subjected Savana to a strip search which produced no evidence of wrong-doing. Redding sought § 1983 relief for violation of her constitutional rights. Both the trial court and a panel of the Ninth Circuit concluded that Wilson's search did *not* violate her rights. After *en banc* reconsideration, the sharply divided Ninth Circuit bench concluded that the strip search violated the Fourth Amendment so egregiously that it denied the school officials qualified immunity.

The Supreme Court affirmed in part and reversed in part. It agreed with the Ninth Circuit's conclusion that the strip search was unreasonable and violated the Fourth Amendment, but it denied any relief. The Court distinguished between routine exposure when students change for gym and an accusatory and degrading body-search for evidence of wrong-doing. The Court invoked *T.L.O.*'s strictures that a search must be "reasonably related in scope to the circumstances which justified the interference in the first place . . . [and] not excessively intrusive in light of the age and sex of the student and the nature of the infraction." However, *Redding* did not discuss why Savana's age (thirteen years old) or her gender (female) rendered the strip search excessively intrusive nor did the Court indicate whether a similar search of an older youth or a boy or for another type of drug would have produced a different result. Although the Court did not prohibit strip searches, it characterized them as a uniquely intrusive type of search that required individualized suspicion to be justified. Despite the school's legitimate zero tolerance policy for drugs, *Redding* found that ibuprofen posed a limited threat and that without any reason to believe that Savana was hiding pills in her underwear, the search was unreasonable.

c. Exclusionary Rule in Delinquency and School Proceedings

Initially, the parties briefed T.L.O on the question whether the exclusionary rule applied either in school disciplinary proceedings or in delinquency hearings. Because the Court upheld the reasonableness of the search, it did not decide whether evidence illegally obtained during a school search must be excluded from school disciplinary proceedings or juvenile courts. Although the Court has not directly decided whether the exclusionary remedy is available to delinquents in juvenile court for violations of their Fourth Amendment rights, the Court in Florida v. J.L., 529 U.S. 266 (2000), unanimously held that an anonymous tip that a young black man wearing a plaid shirt who would be found in a particular location carrying a gun did not justify a stop-and-frisk. In holding that the information lacked sufficient "indicia of reliability" and failed to provide "reasonable suspicion," the Court reinstated the decision by the trial judge and the Florida Supreme Court to suppress the evidence against the juvenile. Irene Merker Rosenberg, "*Florida v. J.L.* and the Fourth Amendment Rights of Juvenile Delinquents: Peekaboo!," 69 *U. Cinn. L.Rev.* 289, 294–95 (2000) (interpreting the Court's decision in J.L. as implicitly finding that juveniles are entitled to the same Fourth Amendment protections as adults outside of the school context, including an exclusionary remedy). State courts consistently have applied the exclusionary rule in juvenile delinquency prosecutions. E.g., In re William G., 40 Cal.3d 550, 221 Cal.Rptr. 118, 709 P.2d 1287, 1298 (1985); In re Montrail M., 87 Md.App. 420, 434, 589 A.2d 1318 (Md.Ct.Spec.App.1991); Chapter 7.

Almost all state courts have rejected the exclusionary rule in school disciplinary proceedings, even when officials seized the evidence illegally. E.g., In re Lance W., 37 Cal.3d 873, 210 Cal.Rptr.

631, 694 P.2d 744 (Cal.1985); In the Matter of Juan C. v. Cortines, 89 N.Y.2d 659, 679 N.E.2d 1061, 657 N.Y.S.2d 581 (N.Y.Ct.App.1997) (juvenile court's decision to suppress evidence did not constitute collateral estoppel on the school officials who were not parties in the delinquency prosecution). The Court in Thompson v. Carthage School District, 87 F.3d 979 (8th Cir.1996), employed a cost-benefit analysis and declined to use the exclusionary rule in school proceedings. The Thompson court emphasized the need for flexibility, maintaining a non-adversarial relationship with students, and the societal costs of excluding probative evidence. "[W]e conclude that there is little need for the exclusionary rule's likely deterrent effect. Indeed, we see some risk that application of the rule would deter educators from undertaking disciplinary proceedings that are needed to keep the schools safe and to control student misbehavior. In any event, any deterrence benefit would not begin to outweigh the high societal costs of imposing the rule." A few courts have applied the exclusionary rule to illegally seized evidence in school disciplinary proceedings because it provides the only viable remedy for students whose rights school administrators have violated. E.g., Jones v. Latexo Indep. Sch. Dist., 499 F.Supp. 223 (E.D.Tex.1980). However, the Court in Pennsylvania Bd. Of Prob. and Parole v. Scott, 524 U.S. 357 (S.Ct.1998), declined to extend the exclusionary rule to proceedings other than criminal trials.

d. Reasonable Expectation of Privacy in Lockers and Desks

T.L.O. did not address whether students have a "reasonable expectation of privacy" in their "lockers, desks, or other school property provided for the storage of school supplies." In decisions prior to T.L.O., courts generally upheld searches of students' lockers because they were not under their exclusive control but controlled jointly with school officials. E.g. In re Donaldson, 269 Cal.App.2d 509, 75 Cal.Rptr. 220 (Cal.App.1969). Other earlier decisions held that schools retained a proprietary interest in the lockers they assigned to students and school rules authorized periodic inspections of the lockers. People v. Overton, 20 N.Y.2d 360, 229 N.E.2d 596, 283 N.Y.S.2d 22 (N.Y.1967); Zamora v. Pomeroy, 639 F.2d 662 (10th Cir.1981); In the Interest of Isiah B., 176 Wis.2d 639, 500 N.W.2d 637 (Wis.1993) (random search of locker was justified because school had policy allowing for searches of lockers for any reason).

Following T.L.O., some courts noted the Court's language that "school children may find it necessary to carry with them a variety of legitimate, non-contraband items, and there is no reason to conclude that they have necessarily waived all rights to privacy in such items merely by bringing them onto school grounds." These courts found that students have a reasonable expectation of privacy in their school lockers. See e.g. In re S.C. v. State, 583 So.2d 188 (Miss.1991); Commonwealth v. Cass, 446 Pa.Super. 66, 666 A.2d 313 (Pa.Super.1995) (expectation of privacy in school locker); Commonwealth v. Snyder, 597 N.E.2d 1363 (Mass.1992).

States have adopted school locker statutes that provide that "[s]chool lockers are the property of the school district. At no time does the school district relinquish its exclusive control of lockers provided for the convenience of students. Inspection of the interior of lockers may be conducted by school authorities for any reason at any time, without notice, without student consent, and without a search warrant. The personal possessions of students within a school locker may be searched only when school authorities have a reasonable suspicion that the search will uncover evidence of a violation of law or school rules. . . ." Minn. Stat. Ann. § 127.47 (West 1998). If state law provides that students have no reasonable expectation of privacy in their lockers, then the lockers remain subject to search without any requirement of "reasonable suspicion" or other justification. E.g. Alaska Stat. §§ 14.03.105, 14.45.190 (Michie 1998); Conn. Gen. Stat. § 54–33n (1997); N.J. Stat. Ann. § 18A:36–19.2 (West 1997); In re Patrick Y., 746 A.2d 405 (Md.2000). Although statutes authorize school officials to open students' lockers, they still need "reasonable suspicion" to feel coats, squeeze backpacks, or open briefcases or other closed containers within the locker. See e.g. Minnesota v. Dickerson, 508 U.S. 366 (S.Ct.1993) (officer's "squeezing, sliding and otherwise manipulating the outside of the defendant's pocket" after determining no weapon was present constituted a search in

violation of Terry); In the Interest of Dumas, 357
Pa.Super. 294, 515 A.2d 984, 985 (Pa.Super.1986)
("We are unable to conclude that a student would
have an expectation of privacy in a purse or jacket
which the student takes to school but would lose
that expectation of privacy merely by placing the
purse or jacket in school locker provided to the
student for storage of personal items.") Courts
sometimes fail to distinguish between inspections or
searches of school lockers in which students have no
reasonable   expectation   of   privacy   and
administrators' manipulation or search of students'
property in coats or backpacks within the locker.
E.g., State v. Jones, 666 N.W.2d 142 (Ia. 2003).

e. Schools Searches in Conjunction With or at the Behest of Law Enforcement

Cases since T.L.O. involving police officers and
School Resource Officers (SROs) in school settings
can be grouped into three categories: (1) those in
which school officials initiate the search or where
the police role is minimal, (2) those in which school
police liaison officers act on their own authority to
further educational goals, and (3) those in which
outside police officers initiate the search for law
enforcement purposes. The distinction is important
because school officials require only reasonable
suspicion whereas police require probable cause to
search. Where school officials initiate the search or
police involvement is minimal, most courts employ
T.L.O.'s reasonable suspicion standard rather than
the   Fourth   Amendment's   probable   cause
requirement. E.g., Cason v. Cook, 810 F.2d 188 (8th

Cir.1987) (applying reasonable suspicion standard where a school official acted in conjunction with a liaison officer); Coronado v. State, 835 S.W.2d 636 (Tex.Crim.App.1992) (applying reasonable suspicion standard where a school official and sheriff's officer assigned to the school searched a student); In re Alexander B., 220 Cal.App.3d 1572, 270 Cal.Rptr. 342 (Cal.App.1990) (applying reasonable suspicion where a school official initiated investigation and requested police assistance). Similarly, courts generally apply the reasonable suspicion standard when school police liaison officers act on their own authority to further educational goals. E.g., People v. Dilworth, 169 Ill.2d 195, 661 N.E.2d 310, 214 Ill.Dec. 456 (Ill.1996) (reasonable suspicion standard applied where liaison officer acting to maintain proper educational environment); In re S.F., 414 Pa.Super. 529, 607 A.2d 793 (Pa.Super.1992) (applying reasonable suspicion to a search by a plainclothes police officer assigned to school). But see A.J.M. v. State, 617 So.2d 1137 (Fla.App.1993) (holding that a school liaison officer employed by sheriff must have probable cause to search). Where outside police officers initiate a search, or where school officials act as an agent of law enforcement, courts apply the probable cause standard. E.g., F.P. v. State, 528 So.2d 1253 (Fla.App.1988) (probable cause standard where an outside police officer initiated the search of a student at school).

Some courts have reasoned that because the SRO is assigned to the school to assist school officials to maintain a safe and proper educational environment that reasonable suspicion is the appropriate standard *when* the officer conducts the search in conjunction with or at the behest of school officials. For example, if reasonable suspicion exists that a student has brought a weapon to school, it is better for a professional officer to conduct the search than an untrained teacher or school official. See e.g. *Ex Rel. Angelia D.B.*, 211 Wis.2d 140, 564 N.W.2d 682, 690 (1997). On the other hand, analysts observe that the increased and heightened presence of law enforcement officers in public schools and the convergence between school disciplinary practices and law enforcement strategies should require school liaison officers to adhere to traditional law enforcement and probable cause requirements. See Michael Pinard, "From the Classroom to the Courtroom: Reassessing Fourth Amendment Standards in Public School Searches Involving Law Enforcement Authorities," 45 *Arizona L. Rev.* 1067, 1079 (2003) (arguing that the increased interdependence between school officials and police has led to "increased use of the juvenile and criminal justice systems to monitor and punish a broadened array of student conduct. As a result, there is a widening gulf between the more expansive use of law enforcement personnel in school discipline, along with the broadened categories of behaviors that could potentially introduce students to the criminal justice system, and the narrow (and narrowing) protections afforded students under the Fourth Amendment.")

f. Individualized Suspicion

In any large groups of students, a statistical probability exists that someone will possess drugs or contraband. T.L.O. did not decide whether its "reasonable suspicion" standard required "individualized suspicion" or just a "generalized probability." "We do not decide whether individualized suspicion is an essential element of the reasonableness standard we adopt for searches by school authorities." Courts are divided on whether school officials must possess individualized reasonable suspicion. For example, teachers on previous extra-curricular band trips found that students had smuggled liquor along in their luggage. Could school officials reasonably search all students' luggage as a prerequisite to boarding the bus for a required concert? E.g. Desilets v. Clearview Regional Board of Education, 627 A.2d 667 (N.J.Super.A.D.1993) (nondiscretionary search of the hand luggage of all students participating in a field trip valid); Kuehn v. Renton School Dist. No. 403, 694 P.2d 1078 (Wash.1985) ("To meet the reasonable belief standard, it was necessary for the school officials to have some basis for believing that drugs or alcohol would be found in the luggage of each individual student searched."); Horton v. Goose Creek Indep. Sch. Dist., 690 F.2d 470 (5th Cir.1982) (requiring individualized suspicion under reasonableness standard); Thompson v. Carthage School District, 87 F.3d 979 (8th Cir.1996) (admitted evidence found in search of all male students in grades six to twelve despite lack of individualized suspicion). The issue may become more problematic when school officials conduct random, suspicionless drug tests of students. Infra.

g. Metal Detector Screening

Violence, the threat of violence, and weapons are a fact of life in many schools. Magnetometers, metal detectors, and x-rays already are standard fixtures in airports and other public buildings such as courthouses. Many schools install metal detectors to limit the presence of weapons. For most courts, requiring students to walk through a metal detector does not constitute a search and therefore does not require reasonable suspicion or individualized suspicion. E.g. In re F.B., 442 Pa.Super. 216, 658 A.2d 1378 (Pa.Super.1995) (individualized suspicion not required for metal detector screening because there was a high rate of violence and minimal intrusion); People v. Pruitt, 662 N.E.2d 540 (Ill.App.Ct.1996) (metal detector screening was reasonable under T.L.O. because justified at its inception by school violence and search conducted in a manner reasonably related in scope to that justification).

h. Individualized Suspicion Provided by Drug Detection Canines

In United States v. Place, 462 U.S. 696 (S.Ct.1983), the Supreme Court, in *dicta*, approved the use of canine partners in criminal investigations: "A 'canine sniff' by a well-trained narcotics detection dog, however, does not require opening the luggage. It does not expose non-contraband items that otherwise would remain hidden from public view, as does, for example, an officer's rummaging through the contents of the luggage. . . . [T]he particular course of investigation that the agents intended to pursue here—exposure of respondent's luggage, which was located in a public place, to a trained canine—did not constitute a 'search' within the meaning of the Fourth Amendment." The Court in Illinois v. Caballes, 543 U.S. 405 (2005), relied on Place and upheld the reasonableness of a canine sniff of a vehicle during a legitimate traffic stop without requiring any additional reasonable suspicion. The Court reasoned that as long as the stop was lawful at its inception and executed in a reasonable manner that did not prolong the detention, the additional use of a "well-trained narcotics-detection dog" that revealed only the presence of contraband did not constitute a search or unconstitutional intrusion on any legitimate expectation of privacy.

Courts generally uphold canine sniffs of luggage or vehicles as minimally intrusive investigative procedures if police conduct them pursuant to an otherwise valid detention or if reasonable suspicion exists. If police have some basis to suspect an individual's container—e.g., luggage, package, locker, trailer, car, or the like—holds contraband, police may use a dog to sniff the container because the inhalation does not constitute a search. A dog's sniff of the surrounding air does not open or enter personal property or violate a suspect's home or bodily integrity. Police may not prolong a lawful detention to accommodate a canine scan, but as long as the dog sniff occurs contemporaneously with an otherwise valid Fourth Amendment detention, the smelling itself does not raise additional search and seizure issues. E.g. Illinois v. Caballes, 543 U.S. 405 (2005); United States v. Colyer, 878 F.2d 469 (D.C.Cir.1989) (canine scan of sleeping compartment in train not a search); Commonwealth v. Cass, 709 A.2d 350 (Pa.1998) (canine sniff of locker provided reasonable suspicion for search that produced marijuana which resulted in school suspension and criminal charges.) Courts apply these principles to the use of drug-detection canines in the school parking lot. In Myers v. State, 839 N.E.2d 1154 (Ind. 2005), police conducted a canine sniff of students' cars in the parking lot at the request of school officials. The juvenile argued that police required reasonable suspicion of criminal activity before they could use a narcotics dog to sniff his car. The Indiana Supreme Court distinguished between searches initiated by school officials, those conducted by school resource officers to further educationally related goals, and those initiated by outside police for criminal investigative purposes. Even though police possessed no individualized suspicion, the Court relied on Caballes and upheld the search as reasonable because a dog sniff of an unoccupied vehicle did not constitute a search. The Court affirmed the admissibility of evidence seized from the student's car because a canine narcotics sniff of a car's exterior does not require reasonable suspicion, no detention of the person occurred, and the school initiated the search.

The reasonableness of canine sniffs to detect drugs becomes more problematic when police use them to smell children, rather than baggage or vehicles. Canine sniffs of people may involve significantly greater intrusions than sniffs of luggage or cars. Wayne LaFave, *Search and Seizure: A Treatise on the Fourth Amendment* (1987) (a canine sniff of a person "is embarrassing, overbearing and harassing, and thus should be subject to Fourth Amendment constraints."). The paucity of people-sniffing cases in conjunction with the abundance of cases challenging sniffs of luggage and cars, suggests that outside of the school context police rarely use dogs to smell people without reasonable suspicion. May school officials confine students in a classroom and expose them to a drug detection dog? Are the constitutional issues different between sniffing people and sniffing their effects, e.g. backpacks, purses, briefcases, lockers, or cars? If the dog signals the presence of contraband on the person, does that constitute reasonable suspicion for a more intrusive search of the person under T.L.O.? Does a canine sniff constitute probable cause for a complete search of the person? How intensely may authorities search without a warrant based on the information provided by a drug detection dog?

Prior to T.L.O., courts divided on whether the use of drug-sniffing canines in schools was reasonable. In Doe v. Renfrow, 475 F.Supp. 1012 (N.D.Ind.1979), aff'd in part, rev'd in part, 631 F.2d 91 (7th Cir.1980), the court upheld the use of canines to detect drugs in the classroom because the school confronted a serious drug problem, school officials already regulated students' movements in the building, the school conducted the investigation for internal disciplinary rather than for law enforcement purposes, and the court viewed the dog sniff as minimally intrusive and not a search. Once the dogs signaled the presence of contraband, the officials had reasonable suspicion to search further, emptying pockets, inspecting purses, and the like. However, the court found it unreasonable to strip search a student based solely on the dog's alert. The court in Horton v. Goose Creek Indep. School District, 690 F.2d 470 (5th Cir.1982), on facts similar to those in Doe v. Renfrow, observed that the intensive smelling by dogs is demeaning and intrusive, and held that it constituted a search and therefore required at least reasonable suspicion. E.g., Jones v. Latexo Independent School District, 499 F.Supp. 223 (E.D.Tex.1980). Since T.L.O., more courts have concluded that a canine sniff of a student constitutes a search for Fourth Amendment purposes and requires a substantial justification such as a serious school drug problem and individualized reasonable suspicion or even probable cause. E.g. Commonwealth v. Martin, 534 Pa. 136, 626 A.2d 556 (Pa.1993) (as a matter of state constitution, sniff of person requires probable cause and a search warrant); B.C. v. Plumas Unified School District, 192 F.3d 1260 (9th Cir.1999) (dogs sniffing students constitutes a search which required reasonable individualized suspicion, especially where no evidence of significant drug problem at school).

i. Students' Remedies for Fourth Amendment Violations and School Officials' Qualified Immunity

Although the Court asserts that students have Fourth Amendment protections against unreasonable searches, practical remedies for violations of their rights are illusory. Students do not have an exclusionary remedy for illegal searches in internal school disciplinary proceedings. They are subject to heightened surveillance and a lower search standard in their dealings with school officials. Parents may be reluctant to confront the school officials who search their children illegally. And the amorphousness of a "reasonableness" standard and "qualified good faith" immunity render any § 1983 civil remedy for violating constitutional rights illusory.

In Harlow v. Fitzgerald, 457 U.S. 800 (1982), the Supreme Court clarified the standard courts should use to assess the liability of public officials, such as school administrators, for violations of constitutional rights. "[T]he recognition of a qualified immunity defense for high executives reflected an attempt to balance competing values: not only the importance of a damages remedy to protect the rights of citizens, but also 'the need to protect officials who are required to exercise their discretion and the related public interest in encouraging the vigorous exercise of official authority.' . . . We therefore hold that government officials performing discretionary functions generally are shielded from liability for civil damages insofar as their conduct does not violate clearly established statutory or constitutional rights of which a reasonable person would have known." The qualified immunity doctrine protects school administrators performing discretionary functions from suit for damages under 42 U.S.C. § 1983 if their conduct did not violate clearly established rights of which a reasonable official would have known at the time of the conduct. *Burnham v. West*, 681 F.Supp. 1169, 1173 (E. D. Va. 1988) ("Liability for damages for every action which is found subsequently to have been violative of a student's constitutional rights and to have caused compensable injury would unfairly impose upon the school decision maker the burden of mistakes made in good faith in the course of exercising his discretion within the scope of his official duties."); B.C. v. Plumas Unified School District, 192 F.3d 1260 (9th Cir. 1999) (granting school officials qualified immunity defense if their conduct does not violate clearly established statutory or constitutional rights of which a reasonable person would have known).

Although eight of the nine Justice in Safford Unified School District #1 v. Redding agreed that her strip-search violated the Fourth Amendment, the majority granted the school administrators qualified immunity and denied any relief. The Safford majority reasoned that "A school official searching a student is 'entitled to qualified immunity where clearly established law does not show that the search violated the Fourth Amendment.' To be established clearly, however, there is no need that 'the very action in question [have] previously been held unlawful.' . . . *T.L.O.* directed school officials to limit the intrusiveness of a search, 'in light of the age and sex of the student and the nature of the infraction,' . . . [b]ut we realize that the lower courts have reached divergent conclusions regarding how the *T.L.O.* standard applies to such [strip] searches. . . . We think these differences of opinion from our own are substantial enough to require immunity for the school officials in this case. . . . [T]he cases viewing school strip searches differently from the way we see them are numerous enough, with well-reasoned majority and dissenting opinions, to counsel doubt that we were sufficiently clear in the prior statement of law. We conclude that qualified immunity is warranted."

Justices Stevens and Ginsburg dissented from the Safford majority's denial of relief. Applying T.L.O.'s reasonableness standard, they reasoned that "This is, in essence, a case in which clearly established law meets clearly outrageous conduct. I have long believed that " '[i]t does not require a constitutional scholar to conclude that a nude search of a 13–year–old child is an invasion of constitutional rights of some magnitude.' " The strip search of Savana Redding in this case was both more intrusive and less justified than the search of the student's purse in *T.L.O.*"

In light of the inherent imprecision of *T.L.O.*'s reasonable suspicion standard and the additional latitude provided by a good faith and objective reasonableness inquiry, how often will a school official who conducts an unreasonable search be found liable for violating students' constitutional rights? An analysis of students' remedies for school officials' violations of Fourth Amendment rights argues that the combination of several factors—e.g. *T.L.O.*'s nebulous reasonableness standard, school officials' good faith defense, the Court's reluctance to provide relief even when administrators violate students' rights as in Safford, fact-specific decisions that provide no precedential value in other cases, and practical impediments inherent in constitutional litigation—preclude recovery or substantial damages, provide no meaningful forms of redress, and reduce school administrators' incentives to learn or follow the law. Barry C. Feld, *T.L.O.* and *Redding*'s Unanswered (Misanswered) Fourth Amendment Questions: Few Rights and Fewer Remedies, 80 Miss. L. J. 847 (2011).

j. School-to-Prison Pipeline

The School-to-Prison Pipeline results from a confluence of federal, state, and school policies that have contributed to increased referrals of youths to juvenile courts for a variety of school-related misbehaviors. The interaction of seemingly unrelated laws like the Gun–Free Schools Act of 1994 and No Child Left Behind have created incentives for schools to suspend or expel "under-performing" students which has had a disproportionate impact on urban minority youth. Barry C. Feld, "*T.L.O.* and *Redding*'s Unanswered (Misanswered) Fourth Amendment Questions: Few Rights and Fewer Remedies," 80 Miss. L. J. 847,

884—895 (2011). The combinations of increased presence of police officers in schools—police liaison officers or school resources officers (SROs)—and heightened surveillance coupled with *T.L.O.*'s lower search standard, school "zero tolerance" policies that reduce discretion and reliance on internal discipline, and financial incentives to exclude under-performing students contribute to a school-to-prison pipeline and disproportionate referral of minority youths to juvenile courts.

In the 1980s, police departments began to assign sworn police officers—SROs—to schools to combat the scourge of drugs and in the 1990s to provide heightened security after high-profile school shootings. Local police agencies assign school resource officers (armed and uniformed police officers) to schools where they perform traditional law enforcement duties—patrolling campus, investigating crimes, and dealing with students who violate school rules or the law. Expanded use of metal detectors and canine partners to detect weapons and drugs accompanied the heightened police presence. The increased presence of police in schools heightens surveillance and increases opportunities for Fourth Amendment issues to arise. Simply by virtue of their presence, police observe violations, and school personnel report incidents that previously would not have come to law enforcement's attention. The increased police presence has led to a dramatic escalation in school referrals to juvenile courts for minor offenses such as simple assaults and disorderly conduct.

In response to escalating youth violence in the late 1980s, Congress passed the Gun–Free Schools Act of 1994, which required schools to expel students found on school property with firearms. States and schools responded by adopting laws and policies requiring suspension or expulsion of students who were found with any weapons or drugs or who committed violations on or near school grounds. These "zero tolerance" policies toward trivial infractions increasingly refer minor offenses—simple assaults, cursing as disorderly conduct, nail-clippers as knives—for delinquency proceedings that school officials previously handled internally and informally. Three decades of research report that these policies disproportionately contribute to over-representation of black youths in disciplinary suspensions and expulsions. Analyses of school disciplinary practices indicate that exclusionary practices cannot be attributed to socioeconomic class rather than race differences or to differences in types of behavior by race. Rather, school personnel perceive poor black males as "troublemakers" or "dangerous" and a threat to teachers' control in the classroom. Perceived threat of loss of control in the classroom leads to punitive responses that disproportionately affect black youths.

Many analysts have criticized the school-to-prison pipelines and recommended a variety of reform to reduce schools' reliance on law enforcement responses to student disciplinary matters and to address the disparate racial impact of referral decisions. See e.g. Lisa Thurau and Johanna Wald,

"Controlling Partners: When Law Enforcements Meets Discipline in Public Schools, 54 N.Y.L. Sch. Rev. 977 (2010(discussing emergence of "school-to-prison pipeline" as a result of increased law enforcement involvement in schools); Catherine Y. Kim, "Policing School Discipline," 77 *Brook. L. Rev.* 861 (2011) (advocating procedural safeguards in schools to protect against unnecessary juvenile court referrals); Aaron Sussman, "School Police, Race, and the Limits of the Law," 59 UCLA L.Rev. 788 (2012) (describing disparate racial impact); Amanda Petteruti, *Education Under Arrest: The Case Against Police in Schools* (2011) (available at http://www.justicepolicy.org/uploads/justicepolicy/documents/educationunderarrest_fullreport.pdf) (arguing that little evidence to indicate that SROs reduce school crime and noting that harsh disciplinary policies disproportionately consign students of color and those with disabilities to the juvenile justice system); American Psychological Association Zero Tolerance Task Force, "Are Zero Tolerance Policies Effective in the Schools? An Evidentiary Review and Recommendations," 63 *American Psychologist* 852 (2008) (concluding that "Zero tolerance has not been shown to improve school climate or school safety . . . and indeed may have exacerbated, minority overrepresentation in school punishments . . . By changing the relationship between education and juvenile justice, zero tolerance may shift the locus of discipline from relatively inexpensive actions in the school setting to the highly costly processes of arrest and incarceration.").

2.   DRUG–TESTING STUDENTS

In Skinner v. Railway Labor Executives'
Association, 489 U.S. 602 (S.Ct.1989), the Court
upheld Federal Railroad Administration regulations
that required drug and alcohol testing of railroad
employees involved in accidents without a warrant
or reasonable suspicion because of the compelling
governmental interest in "safety-sensitive tasks"
and the balance of public and private interests
involved. In National Treasury Employees Union v.
Von Raab, 489 U.S. 656 (S.Ct.1989), the Court
upheld the United States Customs Service employee
drug testing program which did not require a
warrant or individualized suspicion when employees
applied for promotion to positions involving
interdiction of illegal drugs or which required them
to carry firearms. Thus, the Court allowed
suspicionless drug-testing of adults under narrow
circumstances—following railroad accidents which
provided a form of *de facto* individualized suspicion
and for armed customs agents charged with
staunching the flow of illegal drugs.

T.L.O. did not decide whether the reasonableness
standard applicable to school searches required
individualized suspicion. In Vernonia School
District 47J v. Acton, 515 U.S. 646 (S.Ct.1995), the
Court confronted a school district policy requiring
students to submit to random drug tests as a
precondition to participate in extra-curricular
athletic activities. The District's random,
suspicionless testing policy purported to protect
students from themselves, to prevent injuries, and

to deter student-athletes who served as school role models. The policy required parents and students who wished to play a sport to sign a consent form, to submit to an initial test, and to receive random drug-tests during the season. The District policy excluded students who refused to consent from participating in extra-curricular sports. The parents of James Acton, a seventh grader who wanted to play football, refused to consent to random tests and the school barred him from participating. His parents challenged the policy and asked the Court to decide that drug-testing without individualized suspicion violated the Fourth Amendment. The Vernonia majority used T.L.O.'s Fourth Amendment reasonableness balancing to weigh the nature of the intrusion on individual privacy against the state's interests in a drug-free student body. The Court found the testing program valid even without individualized suspicion. The Court emphasized that children in school have lesser liberty and privacy interests than adults do generally and that schools exercise extensive supervisory control over them. Schools' "custodial and tutelary responsibility" includes physical exams and student athletes have minimal expectations of privacy in the locker room. By participating in extra-curricular activities, they effectively volunteer for an even greater level of regulation because they dress and shower together and consent to medical examinations. The Court noted the minimal nature of the intrusion—testers collected urine samples in a minimally intrusive way and no differently from normal communal toilet activities. It emphasized the magnitude of the governmental interests—deterring drug use, protecting children who are especially vulnerable to drug use, and protecting athletes from physical injuries as a result of drug use. The Court declined to require reasonable suspicion as a prerequisite to drug testing. The Court identified several practical difficulties of implementing such a standard: parents who might allow random tests might not consent to accusatory drug tests, teachers might impose drug tests arbitrarily, and it might foster excessive litigation about the reasonableness of reasonable suspicion. Of course, if school officials have reasonable suspicion of drug use, then parents have no basis to object to testing a suspected youth. And, reasonable suspicion provides a check on teachers imposing drug tests arbitrarily.

The Vernonia dissent objected to the majority's rejection of individualized suspicion in favor of random enforcement. Suspicionless testing denied a person the opportunity to avoid being searched simply by engaging in law-abiding behavior. The dissent noted that non-criminal regulatory searches only dispensed with individualized suspicion when the search was not personally intrusive—e.g. searches of businesses and closely regulated industries—or occurred in unique contexts, such as prisons or the military. The dissent regarded searches of the person, especially for bodily by-products, as sufficiently intrusive to require particularized suspicion. It noted that the Court dispensed with individualized suspicion only when the state could not obtain particularized evidence and where undetected wrongdoing posed a substantial threat to others. By contrast, suspicion-based testing was consistent with school disciplinary functions and adequately could control most of the incidents that prompted the school's drug-testing policy.

The Vernonia Court purported to limit its holding to students engaged in interscholastic athletics, but random testing quickly became more pervasive. In Board of Education v. Earls, 536 U.S. 822 (2002), the Court, by a 5–4 margin, extended Vernonia and allowed random, suspicionless testing of every student participating in any extra-curricular activities. The Court emphasized schools' "special needs" and the limited expectation of privacy that children possess there. The Court approved suspicionless drug testing even without a showing of a pervasive drug problem. The majority concluded that "testing students who participate in extracurricular activities is a reasonably effective means of addressing the School District's legitimate concerns in preventing, deterring, and detecting drug use." The dissent objected that Earls represented an unreasonable extension of Vernonia. Apart from the fact that both cases involved students who voluntarily participated in extra-curricular activities, the nature of the drug problem presented in Earls and the type of activities in which students engaged provided no reasonable basis for suspicionless testing. Despite Earls' expansion of random, suspicionless searches, school districts' efforts randomly to search all students have failed. In Doe v. Little Rock School District,

380 F.3d 349 (8th Cir. 2004), the school regularly conducted random searches of all students— ordering them to leave the room after removing everything from their pockets and placing all of their belongings, including their backpacks and purses, on their desks. While the students waited outside their classroom, school personnel searched the items they left behind. A provision in the student handbook purported to authorize searches of all items brought to school. However, the court held that students retained a legitimate expectation of privacy in their personal effects and unlike those who "volunteered" for extra-curricular activities, "the search regime at issue here is imposed upon the entire student body, so the LRSD cannot reasonably claim that those subject to search have made a voluntary tradeoff of some of their privacy interests in exchange for a benefit or privilege."

In York v. Wahkiakum School District No. 200, 163 Wash.2d 297, 178 P.3d 995, 230 Ed. Law Rep. 425 (WA 2008), the Washington Supreme Court interpreted the state constitution—"No person shall be disturbed in his private affairs, or his home invaded, without authority of law." Wash. Const. art. I, § 7—to give student athletes greater protection than that which the Court in Acton and Earls granted under the Fourth Amendment The York Court's analysis considered whether the state's action to require a urine sample disturbed his privacy and whether the law justified the intrusion. Notwithstanding student athletes' greater regulation and reduced privacy in the locker room, York viewed collecting urine samples to be a

significant intrusion on students' privacy. York
rejected the state's legal justification that school
conditions posed unique circumstances and declined
to adopt Vernonia's "special needs" exception in its
interpretation of the state constitution. The Court
feared that the "special needs" exception would
provide no basis on which "to draw a principled line
permitting drug testing only student athletes. If we
were to allow random drug testing here, what
prevents school districts from either later drug
testing students participating in any extracurricular
activities, as federal courts now allow, or testing the
entire student population?"

C. PRE–TRIAL INTERROGATION
OF JUVENILES

Interrogating juveniles implicates both the
punitive or rehabilitative roles of juvenile courts
and the developmental competencies of children as
compared with adults. The Progressive reformers
envisioned non-adversarial juvenile courts in which
judges presided as "benevolent fathers" and in
which an errant child bared his soul. By contrast,
the privilege against self-incrimination is the
bulwark of the adversary system and a procedural
device to formalize equality between the individual
and the state. Courts have struggled with how to
reconcile issues of reduced competence and
procedural justice when police question juveniles.

The Supreme Court has used three different
constitutional strategies to regulate police
interrogation of criminal suspects in the states—

Fourteenth Amendment Due Process voluntariness; Sixth Amendment right to counsel; and Fifth Amendment privilege against self-incrimination. E.g. Brown v. Mississippi, 297 U.S. 278 (S.Ct.1936); Escobedo v. Illinois, 378 U.S. 478 (S.Ct.1964); Miranda v. Arizona, 384 U.S. 436 (S.Ct.1966); LaFave, *Criminal Procedure*. The Fourteenth Amendment due process strategy provided the primary constitutional theory until the early 1960s. The Court recognized that youths' age and inexperience may affect their competence, the validity of waivers of constitutional rights, and the voluntariness of confessions. Long before Gault, the Court instructed trial judges to be particularly sensitive to the dangers of unreliability and unfairness when police interrogate juveniles. In Haley v. Ohio, 332 U.S. 596, 599–601 (S.Ct.1948), police interrogated a fifteen-year-old "lad" in relays beginning shortly after midnight, denied him access to counsel, and confronted him with confessions of co-defendants before he finally confessed at five o'clock a.m. The Supreme Court reversed his conviction and ruled that a confession obtained under these circumstances was involuntary:

> [W]hen, as here, a mere child—an easy victim of the law—is before us, special care in scrutinizing the record must be used. Age 15 is a tender and difficult age for a boy of any race. He cannot be judged by the more exacting standards of maturity. That which would leave a man cold and unimpressed can overawe and overwhelm a lad in his early teens. This is the period of great instability which the crisis of

adolescence produces. . . . [W]e cannot believe that a lad of tender years is a match for the police in such a contest. He needs counsel and support if he is not to become the victim first of fear, then of panic. . . . The age of petitioner, the hours when he was grilled, the duration of his quizzing, the fact that he had no friend or counsel to advise him, the callous attitude of the police toward his rights combine to convince us that this was a confession wrung from a child by means which the law should not sanction.

In Gallegos v. Colorado, 370 U.S. 49, 54 (S.Ct.1962), police extracted a confession from "a child of 14." The Court reiterated that the youth of the accused constituted a special circumstance that may affect the voluntariness of a confession and re-emphasized the vulnerability of youth:

But a 14–year–old boy, no matter how sophisticated, is unlikely to have any conception of what will confront him when he is made accessible only to the police. . . . [W]e deal with a person who is not equal to the police in knowledge and understanding of the consequences of the questions and answers being recorded and who is unable to know how to protect his own interests or how to get the benefits of his constitutional rights. . . . A lawyer or an adult relative or friend could have given the petitioner the protection which his own immaturity could not. Adult advice would have put him on a less unequal footing with his interrogators. Without some adult protection against this inequality, a 14–year–old boy would not be able to know, let alone assert, such constitutional rights as he had.

In Gallegos and Haley, the Supreme Court considered the admissibility of confessions made by younger juveniles, applied the voluntariness test, and concluded that youthfulness constituted a special circumstance that required close judicial scrutiny. The Court focused on the vulnerability of children, the unreliability of juveniles' confessions, the accuracy of the fact-finding process, and juveniles' dependence on adults and need for assistance of parents or counsel.

In In re Gault, 387 U.S. 1 (S.Ct.1967), the Court repeated that "admissions and confessions of juveniles require special caution," and suggested that "[e]ven greater protection might be required where juveniles are involved, since their immaturity and greater vulnerability place them at a greater disadvantage in their dealings with police." Thus, the Court long has recognized that youths are not the equals of adults in the interrogation room and that they require greater procedural safeguards than adults, such as the presence of parents or counsel, to compensate for their vulnerability and susceptibility to coercive influences.

Although Gault recognized that the Fifth Amendment contributed to accurate fact finding and reliable confessions, the Court emphasized that it bolstered the adversary process, functioned to reduce governmental oppression, and maintained a proper balance between the individual and the state:

> The privilege against self-incrimination is, of course, related to the question of the safeguards necessary to assure that admissions or confessions are reasonably trustworthy, that they are not mere fruits of fear or coercion, but are reliable expressions of the truth. The roots of the privilege are, however, far deeper. They tap the basic stream of religious and political principle because the privilege reflects the limits of the individual's attornment to the state and—in a philosophical sense—insists upon the equality of the individual and the state. In other words, the privilege has a broader and deeper thrust than the rule which prevents the use of confessions which are the product of coercion because coercion is thought to carry with it the danger of unreliability. One of its purposes is to prevent the state, whether by force or by psychological domination, from overcoming the mind and will of the person under investigation and depriving him of the freedom to decide whether to assist the state in securing his conviction.

The Gault Court cited Miranda v. Arizona, 384 U.S. 436 (S.Ct.1966), as authority for the assertion that persons, even juveniles, cannot be compelled to testify against themselves. Miranda rights attach whenever an accused is in custody and questioned, and the inherent coercion of custodial interrogation threatens the suspect's ability to exercise the privilege against self-incrimination. The Supreme Court required police to administer the now-familiar Miranda warning as a prelude to "custodial interrogation" because "such an interrogation environment is created for no purpose other than to subjugate the individual to the will of his examiner. This atmosphere carries its own badge of intimidation. To be sure, this is not physical intimidation, but it is equally destructive of human dignity. The current practice of incommunicado interrogation is at odds with one of our Nation's most cherished principles—that the individual may not be compelled to incriminate himself. Unless adequate protective devices are employed to dispel the compulsion inherent in custodial surroundings, no statements obtained from the defendant can truly be the product of his free choice."

Although the Gault decision concerned only delinquents' rights at the adjudicatory hearing, granting delinquents the privilege against self-incrimination effectively extended Miranda rights to juveniles. The Supreme Court has never explicitly held that Miranda applies to juvenile proceedings, but the Court in Fare v. Michael C., 442 U.S. 707 (S.Ct.1979), "assume[d] without deciding that the Miranda principles were fully applicable to the present [juvenile] proceedings." Following Gault, states adopted statutes or juvenile court rules of procedure to provide delinquents with the Miranda safeguards when police subjected them to custodial interrogation during criminal investigations. E.g. Cal. Welf. & Inst. Code §§ 625, 627.5 (West 1984); Conn. Gen. Stat. Ann. § 46b–137(a)(West 1986).

The Supreme Court in Haley, Gallegos, and Gault recognized the special vulnerability of children but it did not explore fully the legal policies that states might adopt to accommodate how youthfulness and immaturity affects juveniles' ability to exercise rights during police interrogation. States employ three alternative policy strategies to protect juveniles during interrogation: 1) judicial review of a juvenile's "knowing, intelligent, and voluntary" waiver of Miranda rights under the "totality of the circumstances," 2) a parental presence *per se* requirement, or 3) consultation with and presence of counsel. The three alternative policies differ in their assessments of the competence of children versus adults, the role of treatment versus punishment, the value of discretion versus rules, and the balance of protecting juveniles versus protecting society. If children are not the functional equals of adults, then how should the law accommodate their vulnerability, immaturity, and limited decision-making capabilities?

1. "TOTALITY OF THE CIRCUMSTANCES"

Should the law treat juveniles' waivers of Miranda rights and confessions differently than adults' because juveniles are less competent than adults to make legal decisions, "confession is good for the soul," the sentences delinquents receive generally are less severe than those of adults, or a rule that encourages children to deny responsibility might teach them a bad moral lesson? If juveniles may waive their Miranda rights, then how should courts evaluate the validity of those waivers and the voluntariness of any ensuing confessions?

The Supreme Court in Fare v. Michael C., 442 U.S. 707 (S.Ct.1979), a 5—4 decision, considered the validity of a Miranda waiver by a 16½–year–old who had several prior arrests, previous experience with police, and "served time" in a youth camp. Fare presented the issue whether the juvenile's request to consult with his probation officer during custodial interrogation constituted an invocation of the right to counsel or the privilege against self-incrimination under Miranda. The Supreme Court distinguished between the unique role attorneys play in the adversarial process to safeguard the privilege against self-incrimination and the role of probation officers. Fare emphasized that a probation officer is not law-trained, cannot represent a juvenile, does not enjoy privileged communications with a probationer, and actually may file the delinquency petition to prosecute a juvenile. The Court held that Michael C.'s request to speak with a probation officer did not invoke either the Fifth Amendment right to silence or the Miranda right to counsel.

The Fare Court then used the "adult" standard— whether the suspect made a "knowing, intelligent, and voluntary waiver under the 'totality of the circumstances' "—to evaluate the validity of the juvenile's waiver of Miranda rights.

> [T]he determination whether statements obtained during custodial interrogation are admissible against the accused is to be made upon an inquiry into the totality of the

circumstances surrounding the interrogation, to ascertain whether the accused in fact knowingly and voluntarily decided to forgo his rights to remain silent and to have the assistance of counsel.

This totality-of-the-circumstances approach is adequate to determine whether there has been a waiver even where interrogation of juveniles is involved. We discern no persuasive reasons why any other approach is required where the question is whether a juvenile has waived his rights, as opposed to whether an adult has done so. The totality approach permits—indeed, it mandates—inquiry into all the circumstances surrounding the interrogation. This includes evaluation of the juvenile's age, experience, education, background, and intelligence, and into whether he has the capacity to understand the warnings given him, the nature of his Fifth Amendment rights, and the consequences of waiving those rights.

Fare did not discuss why juveniles, whom the law deems incompetent to make other important legal decisions, possess the competence to waive constitutional rights unaided. Fare declined to provide children with greater procedural protections than those afforded adults during interrogation. The Court rejected the view that developmental or psychological differences between juveniles and adults required a different rule or special procedural protections. Instead, the Court required children to assert their legal rights clearly and unambiguously, just like adults, and rebuffed the argument that trial courts cannot adequately measure young peoples' exercise or waiver of Miranda rights with the adult standard. Because Michael C. had not affirmatively invoked his right to counsel or his privilege against self-incrimination with technical precision, the Court concluded that he had knowingly and voluntarily waived these rights under the "totality of the circumstances." The Fare majority accepted police interrogation as a legitimate law enforcement tool, posited coerciveness as a fact question in each case, declined to unduly restrict law enforcement with bright-lines, and provided police with considerable latitude to exploit youths' vulnerability.

The Fare dissenters reiterated the Court's historical concern about the special vulnerability of youthful during coercive interrogation. They argued that Miranda should provide greater protection for juveniles and that trial courts should treat "any intimation of a desire" to speak with an adult as "an attempt to obtain advice and a general invocation of the right to silence." They criticized the majority's rule as withdrawing the safeguards of Miranda from those who most need its protections.

a. Custodial Interrogation

Because Fare adopted the Miranda framework, some special issues may arise in the context of juveniles. Miranda requires police to warn suspects of their rights when they are in custody and interrogated in order to offset the "inherent coercion of custodial interrogation." LaFave, *Criminal Procedure*. This raises the questions of when a youth is in custody, what constitutes interrogation, and what warnings police must give a youth before she validly may waive her Miranda rights. Because of the social context of youth, answers to these questions sometimes may be different from those for adults.

The Miranda safeguards come into play when a person has been "taken into custody or otherwise deprived of his freedom of action in any significant way." Berkemer v. McCarty, 468 U.S. 420 (S.Ct.1984). The circumstances must convey restraints functionally equivalent to those of formal arrest to a reasonable person in the defendant's position. LaFave, *Criminal Procedure*. However, courts frequently observe that youths always are in some form of custody—of their parents, in school, or in the presence of police. When a youth's mother brings him to the police station for an interview, at what point does his status become "custody" for purposes of requiring a Miranda warning? For example, in In re Dino, 359 So.2d 586 (La.1978), the juvenile's mother brought him to the police station where he was taken to an office and neither told he could leave nor required to remain during questioning. In concluding that he was in custody, the court considered how the juvenile arrived at the place of questioning, whether the police told him he was free to leave, and whether police questioned the youth as a witness or as a suspect. E.g. LaFave, *Criminal Procedure*.

In J. D. B. v. North Carolina, 131 S. Ct. 2394 (2011), the Supreme Court considered whether youthfulness affected when a juvenile whom police questioned was "in custody" and entitled to a Miranda warning. Police stopped and questioned J. D. B., a 13–year–old, seventh-grade student, near the site of two home break-ins. Five days later, investigator DiCostanzo went to the school and had a uniformed police officer (SRO) remove J. D. B. from his classroom and escort him to a closed-door conference room. Two police officers and two school officials questioned him for about 30—45 minutes without giving him *Miranda* warnings or telling him he was free to leave the room. DiCostanzo only told J.D.B. that he could refuse to answer questions and was free to leave after he made some incriminating admissions. J.D.B. eventually confessed, gave a written statement at DiCostanzo's request, and provided the location of stolen items. The state charged J. D. B. with burglary and theft. His public defender moved to suppress his statements and evidence on the grounds that J.D.B. was in custody when authorities interrogated him without giving a *Miranda* warning. The trial court denied the motion and the North Carolina Supreme Court affirmed, "declin[ing] to extend the test for custody to include consideration of the age . . . of an individual subjected to questioning by police."

Justice Sotomayor, for the majority, framed the issue as "whether the age of a child subjected to police questioning is relevant to the custody analysis of Miranda v. Arizona. It is beyond dispute that children will often feel bound to submit to police questioning when an adult in the same circumstances would feel free to leave. Seeing no reason for police officers or courts to blind themselves to that commonsense reality, we hold that a child's age properly informs the *Miranda* custody analysis." Because police must give a *Miranda* warning when a person is in custody and interrogated, the Court's "custody" focus centers on "the circumstances surrounding the interrogation: and whether given those circumstances, "a reasonable person have felt he or she was at liberty to terminate the interrogation and leave." The J.D.B. majority concluded that

> a child's age "would have affected how a reasonable person" in the suspect's position "would perceive his or her freedom to leave." That is, a reasonable child subjected to police questioning will sometimes feel pressured to submit when a reasonable adult would feel free to go. We think it clear that courts can account for that reality without doing any damage to the objective nature of the custody analysis.

The Court emphasized that children are "less mature and responsible than adults;" that they "often lack the experience, perspective, and judgment to recognize and avoid choices that could be detrimental to them;" and that they "are more vulnerable or susceptible to . . . outside pressures" than adults. It noted that these characteristics led to a host of legal disabilities imposed on children as a class—e.g. the right to alienate property, enter a binding contract, or marry without parental consent—and the use of a "reasonable child" standard in negligence actions. The Court concluded that

> so long as the child's age was known to the officer at the time of police questioning, or would have been objectively apparent to a reasonable officer, its inclusion in the custody analysis is consistent with the objective nature of that test. This is not to say that a child's age will be a determinative, or even a significant, factor in every case. It is, however, a reality that courts cannot simply ignore. . . . [O]fficers and judges need no imaginative powers, knowledge of developmental psychology, training in cognitive science, or expertise in social and cultural anthropology to account for a child's age. They simply need the common sense to know that a 7–year–old is not a 13–year–old and neither is an adult.

The Court remanded the case to the trial court to determine whether J.D.B. was in custody when police interrogated him, taking account of all of the circumstances of the interrogation including his age at the time.

The four dissenting Justices in J.D.B. objected that including consideration of a child's age in the Miranda custody evaluation detracted from the objective nature of the inquiry. "Today's decision shifts the *Miranda* custody determination from a one-size-fits-all reasonable-person test into an inquiry that must account for at least one individualized characteristic—age—that is thought to correlate with susceptibility to coercive pressures." They argued that most juveniles whom police interrogate are near the age of majority and for whom "the one-size-fits-all *Miranda* custody rule may not be a bad fit." In addition, the *Miranda* custody rule takes account of the setting in which questioning and can accommodate the unique circumstances present when the police interrogate youths at school. Finally, they argued that "where the suspect is especially young, courts applying the constitutional voluntariness standard can take special care to ensure that incriminating statements were not obtained through coercion."

The Court in T.L.O. and Vernonia emphasized that students always are in some form of custody. As a result, if a school official questions a student, then does that constitute "custodial interrogation" which the official must precede with a Miranda warning? Courts distinguish between interrogations in school conducted by a police officer about crimes and interrogation by school officials about school-related misconduct. In general, courts reject students' efforts to suppress incriminating statements made to school officials. They emphasize that a school setting is not the inherently coercive environment of the station-house and children spend most of their daily lives there. E.g. State v. V.C. and R.S., 600 So.2d 1280 (Fla.App.1992) (not in custody when questioned because liberty restrictions stemmed from status as students). Moreover, school officials, unlike police officers, are only marginally more coercive than adults in general and requiring a Miranda warning would adversely affect student—school relations. Most courts conclude that interrogation is non-custodial when it is "conducted by school officials in furtherance of their disciplinary duties." Boynton v. Casey, 543 F.Supp. 995 (D.Me.1982); Commonwealth v. Snyder, 413 Mass. 521, 597 N.E.2d 1363 (Mass. 1992).

Where police are present and participate or where school officials act as agents of law enforcement, courts may reach a different result. For example, in In re R.J.E., 630 N.W.2d 457 (Mn.Ct.App.2001), two uniformed security guards removed the 15–year–old juvenile from class, escorted him to a security office and subjected him to a closed door, tape-recorded interrogation by a uniformed school-liaison police officer in the presence of the security guards and a school social worker. The officer never told R.J.E. that he was free to leave or that he could decline to answer any questions. The court held that under such circumstances, the youth was in custody and entitled to a Miranda warning. E.g. In re G.S.P., 610 N.W.2d 651 (Minn.App.2000) (youth removed from class and interrogated by school liaison police officer in presence of school official who told him that he had to answer the questions was entitled to Miranda warning); State v. D.R., 930 P.2d 350 (Wash.Ct.App.1997) (juvenile questioned by police officer in principal's office entitled to Miranda warning because he was in custody and not free to leave).

b. Additional Warnings

If a juvenile confesses while under the jurisdiction of the juvenile court and the state subsequently transfers the youth to criminal court for prosecution as an adult, then may the prosecutor introduce the juvenile's confession in the criminal proceeding? Some courts fear that the informal, non-adversarial nature of the juvenile justice system could lull a youth into a false sense of security and produce a confession that ultimately leads to punishment rather than treatment. Courts differ on whether the police should warn a youth about possible uses of statements in criminal prosecutions rather than in delinquency proceedings. Compare e.g., Harling v. United States, 295 F.2d 161 (D.C.Cir.1961) (any statement made while in police custody is inadmissible in a criminal prosecution following a transfer hearing); State v. Maloney, 102 Ariz. 495, 433 P.2d 625 (1967) (statement inadmissible unless juvenile and parents advised that criminal proceedings are a possibility); with State v. Gullings, 244 Or. 173, 416 P.2d 311 (1966) (statement is admissible as long as elicited in an adversarial atmosphere); Mitchell v. State, 464 S.W.2d 307 (Tenn.Crim.App.1971) (any statement obtained in compliance with Miranda is admissible in criminal prosecution); State v. Kim Thul Ouk, 516 N.W.2d 180 (Minn.1994) (interrogating officers should advise juveniles that adult criminal prosecution could result, but failure to do so does not necessarily invalidate an otherwise valid waiver of rights); State v. Benoit, 126 N.H. 6, 490 A.2d 295

(N.H.1985) (requiring juveniles to be advised of possibility of being tried as adult).

State statutes often provide that interrogation must cease if a juvenile indicates that she wishes to speak with a parent or guardian. E.g. Ark. Code Ann. § 9–27–371(g)(2)(A) (Michie 1998). Some court decisions also treat a juvenile's request to speak with a parent as the functional equivalent of invoking the right to silence. E.g. People v. Burton, 6 Cal.3d 375, 99 Cal.Rptr. 1, 491 P.2d 793 (Cal.1971). Although juveniles in some states may have a statutory right to talk with their parents if they affirmatively request to do, courts do not interpret those statutes to require police to advise juveniles of their right to consult with a parent. E.g. Miller v. State, 338 Ark. 445, 994 S.W.2d 476 (Ark.1999). And, while parents have a right to be notified that their child is in custody, they do not have a constitutional right to be notified prior to their child's interrogation in the absence of a statute or decision that gives them a right to be present. See Chapter 3 B.4.; 3 C.2.; Stone v. Farley, 86 F.3d 712 (7th Cir.1996). Moreover, police officers' statutory duty to notify a juvenile's parents that they have taken the minor into custody does not give the parents a right to speak with their child prior to interrogation or to be present when police question the child. People v. McNeal, 298 Ill.App.3d 379, 232 Ill.Dec. 561, 698 N.E.2d 652 (Ill.App.1998).

c. Application of "Totality of Circumstances" to Juveniles

In subsequent interpretations of Miranda, the Supreme Court in Moran v. Burbine, 475 U.S. 412 (S.Ct.1986), held that a valid waiver required both voluntariness and a "knowing and intelligent" awareness of the right relinquished. LaFave, *Criminal Procedure.* According to Moran, a waiver of rights has two distinct elements—voluntariness and understanding. A voluntary waiver is one free of intimidation, coercion or deception. Comprehension means an understanding of the nature of the rights being relinquished. However, comprehension means only an understanding and awareness of the contents of the Miranda-warning rights themselves, rather than an appreciation of the legal consequences of a waiver. E.g. People v. Cheatham, 453 Mich. 1, 551 N.W.2d 355 (Mich.1996). A youth's awareness that police could not compel him to talk, but would use his statements against him would constitute an adequate understanding of the right to remain silent. E.g., People v. Bernasco, 138 Ill.2d 349, 562 N.E.2d 958 (Ill.1990) (for Miranda purposes, intelligent "means the ability to understand the very words used in the warnings. It need not mean the ability to understand far-reaching legal and strategic effects of waiving one's rights, or to appreciate how widely or deeply an interrogation may probe, or to withstand the influence of stress or fancy"). In Colorado v. Connelly, 479 U.S. 157 (S.Ct.1986), the Court held that absent police coercion, a defendant's mental state alone would not render a confession involuntary. Connelly emphasized that a voluntariness inquiry properly focuses on police conduct, rather than the subjective susceptibility of the defendant. Thus, courts' assessments of Miranda waivers narrowly address a suspect's awareness of and ability to comprehend the warnings and on coercive police conduct that deprives her of the freedom to exercise or to waive those rights.

Despite Fare's suggestion that a juvenile only needs to indicate in "any manner" her desire to invoke Miranda protections, the Court has held that police must cease interrogation only after a defendant has "clearly and unambiguously invoked" her Miranda rights. Davis v. United States, 512 U.S. 452 (S.Ct.1994) (police have no obligation to stop interrogation until defendant makes an unambiguous or unequivocal request for counsel and police have no obligation to clarify an ambiguous reference to counsel). In *Berghuis v. Thompkins*, 103 S. Ct. 2250 (2010), the Court upheld an "implied waiver" and concluded that "The *Miranda* rule and its requirements are met if a suspect receives adequate *Miranda* warnings, understands them, and has an opportunity to invoke the rights before giving any answer or admissions." Thus, *Fare*, *Davis*, and *Berghuis* put the burden on a youth affirmatively to invoke *Miranda* rights clearly, unequivocally, and with adult-like technical precision before the Court will require police to honor her assertion of rights.

Fare remitted evaluations of juveniles' Miranda waivers to trial judges who exercise broad discretion and readily admit statements made by manifestly incompetent youths. Moreover, once a trial judge finds a youth made a valid waiver and gave a voluntary statement, appellate courts reverse only if they find that the trial court's decision was clearly erroneous or an abuse of discretion, a very high threshold. Trial judges consider a youth's age, experience, education, intelligence and comprehension, parental presence, and immaturity among the totality of factors. In addition to characteristics of the youth, courts also examine circumstances of the interrogation itself—whether the youth consulted with family members or an attorney, the methods used, the length of the interrogation, and any other surrounding circumstances. Even for very young juveniles, age is not necessarily a determinative factor that invalidates a waiver or confession.

The vast majority of states use Fare's adult "totality of the circumstances" test to evaluate juveniles' waivers of rights and allow them to waive Miranda rights without adult assistance. E.g. Quick v. State, 599 P.2d 712 (Alaska 1979); Dutil v. State, 606 P.2d 269 (Wash.1980); People v. Lara, 67 Cal.2d 365, 377, 432 P.2d 202, 215 (Cal.1967), cert. denied, 392 U.S. 945 (1968). Judges typically focus on characteristics of the juvenile—e.g., age, education, and I.Q.—and circumstances surrounding the interrogation—e.g., methods used and length of the questioning—to evaluate the validity of waivers and the admissibility of any statement. E.g. West v.

United States, 399 F.2d 467 (5th Cir.1968); People
v. Lara, 67 Cal.2d 365, 432 P.2d 202 (Cal.1967).
Several leading cases provide extensive lists of
"totality" factors for trial judges to consider when
they assess juveniles' waiver of rights—age,
education, physical condition, presence of or
opportunity to consult with parent or other adult,
length of interrogation, method of interrogation,
knowledge of the charges, subsequent repudiation of
the statement, understanding of the warnings
given, warning of possible transfer to criminal court,
and the like. E.g., Fare v. Michael C. (S.Ct.1979);
State v. Williams, 535 N.W.2d 277 (Minn.1995)
("totality factors" include juvenile's age, maturity,
intelligence, education, prior criminal experience,
any physical deprivations during interrogation,
presence or absence of parents, length and legality
of detention, lack of or adequacy of warnings, and
the nature of the interrogation).

While appellate courts identify many factors, they
do not assign controlling weight to any particular
one and instead remit the weighing of factors to the
trial judge's discretion. Most courts apply the
"totality" standard conservatively. Courts routinely
find valid Miranda waivers when police testify that
they advised a juvenile of her rights and she
answered "yes" when asked if she understood them.
Trial judges find and appellate courts uphold
Miranda waivers as voluntary even when police
employ overtly coercive interrogation techniques
and obtain waivers from very young children or
those with mental deficiencies. See e.g. W.M. v.
State, 585 So.2d 979 (Fla.4th Dist.Ct.App.1991)

(valid waiver by a 10–year old boy with an I.Q. of 70, placed in a learning disability program, described by teachers as having difficulty understanding directions, with no prior record, questioned by police for nearly 6 hours, knowingly and voluntarily confessed to nearly every unsolved burglary on the police blotter.) Courts readily admit confessions of illiterate, mentally retarded juveniles with IQs in the 60s, whom psychologists testify are incapable of abstract reasoning. E.g., People v. Cheatham, 453 Mich. 1, 551 N.W.2d 355 (Mich.1996) (valid waiver by an illiterate juvenile with an IQ of 62 because "[l]ow mental ability in and of itself is insufficient to establish that a defendant did not understand his rights"); State v. Cleary, 161 Vt. 403, 641 A.2d 102 (Vt.1994) (valid waiver by juvenile with only a limited ability to read or write and an IQ of 65). When judges apply the "totality" test, they exclude only the most egregiously obtained confessions and then only on a haphazard basis. E.g. In re W.C., 657 N.E.2d 908 (Ill.1995) (valid waiver by thirteen-year old who was "illiterate and moderately retarded with an IQ of 48 . . . the equivalent developmentally of a six- to seven-year old"). Because appellate courts do not substitute their own evaluations of facts for those of a trial judge, they only reverse a trial judge's ruling if it is clearly erroneous, an abuse of discretion, or without substantial support in the record. As a result, courts often uphold trial judges' decisions based on extreme facts.

Appellate courts regard a juvenile's request to talk with her parent or police preventing a parent from conferring with her child as significant factors that may undermine the voluntariness of a waiver or statement. In State v. Presha, 163 N.J. 304, 748 A.2d 1108 (N.J. 2000), the court noted that "it is difficult for us to envision prosecutors successfully carrying their burdens ... [when] there has been some deliberate exclusion of a juvenile's parent or legal guardian from the interrogation." In Moran v. Burbine, the Court held that police need not inform an adult defendant who had not invoked his right to counsel that an attorney was available and wanted to consult with him. By contrast, courts are more likely to suppress a confession as involuntary where police deliberately deceive a parent about her child's whereabouts during interrogation, refuse to inform a child of her parent's presence and request to see her, or deny a juvenile's requests to see his parent. E.g. In re Lashun H., 284 Ill.App.3d 545, 219 Ill.Dec. 823, 672 N.E.2d 331 (Ill.App.1996); State v. Johnson, 221 Mont. 503, 719 P.2d 1248 (Mont.1986) (request to call parent is assertion of Fifth Amendment privilege). A juvenile's repeated requests to talk with a parent both before and after police administer a Miranda warning may undermine the validity of a waiver or the voluntariness of a confession. State v. Burrel, 697 N.W.2d 579 (Minn. 2005).

d. Juveniles' Competence to Exercise Miranda Rights

Can a typical juvenile make a "knowing, intelligent, and voluntary" waiver decision? Do youth possess the cognitive ability, developmental capacity, or maturity of judgment to understand and exercise constitutional rights? Developmental psychologists' evaluations of juveniles' understanding of Miranda report that most juveniles who receive the warnings do not understand the language, much less the legal concepts, well enough to waive their rights in a "knowing and intelligent" manner. Social scientists assessed whether juveniles could paraphrase the words in the Miranda warning, whether they could define six critical words such as "attorney," "consult," and "appoint," and whether they could give correct true-false answers to twelve re-wordings of the warnings. Thomas Grisso, *Juveniles' Capacities to Waive Miranda Rights: An Empirical Analysis*, 68 Cal. L. Rev. 1134 (1980); Thomas Grisso, *Juveniles' Waivers of Rights: Legal and Psychological Competence* (1981). Most juveniles who received the warnings performed at a level below that of an adult comparison group and did not understand them well enough to waive their rights "knowingly and intelligently." Younger juveniles exhibited even greater difficulties understanding their rights and youth who lacked comprehension waived their rights more readily. Jodi L. Viljoen and Ronald Roesch, "Competence to Waive Interrogation Rights and Adjudicative Competence in Adolescent Defendants: Cognitive Development, Attorney Contact, and Psychological Symptoms," 29 *Law & Hum. Behav.* 723 (2005).

Typically, delinquents come from lower income households and they may lack the verbal skills or capacity to understand legal abstractions or exercise legal rights effectively. Immaturity, inexperience, and lower verbal competence than adults render youths especially vulnerable to coercive police interrogation tactics. Children's greater dependence on adults and societal expectations of youthful obedience to authority also make youths more vulnerable. Inexperienced youths may waive their rights and talk in the short-sighted and unrealistic belief that their interrogation will end more quickly and secure their release. People with lower social status than their interrogators typically respond more passively, talk more readily, acquiesce to police suggestions more easily, and speak less assertively. Thus, Fare's requirement that youths invoke their Miranda rights clearly, unambiguously, and with adult-like technical precision runs contrary to developmental psychological research findings about adolescent competence and to the normal social reactions and verbal styles of most delinquents whom police interrogate.

Empirical studies of police interrogation of sixteen- and seventeen-year-old juveniles charged with a felony compared their responses with those of adults. Barry C. Feld, *Kids, Cops, and Confessions: Inside the Interrogation Room* (2013); Barry C. Feld, "Real Interrogation: What Actually Happens When Cops Question Kids," 47 Law & Society Rev. 1 (2013). These older delinquents waived their Miranda rights (93%) at a somewhat higher rate than research reports for adults interrogated (around 80% or more). Juveniles, like adults, with prior felony arrests were significantly more likely to invoke Miranda. Juveniles' higher waiver rates may reflect their lack of understanding or inability to invoke Miranda rights or less prior justice system involvement than adults. After they waived their Miranda rights, police interrogated them in much the same way as they did adults. Police used similar maximization and minimization interrogation techniques, seemed to work from the same standard script, and used the same tactics. Juvenile and adult suspects exhibited comparable ability to cooperate or to resist the tactics employed and provided incriminating evidence at about the same rates. In short, the law treats juveniles just like adults and police question them just as they do older suspects. While developmental psychological research suggests that sixteen- and seventeen-year-old juveniles function more or less on a par with adults, it also reports that younger juveniles do not understand their Miranda rights, lack adjudicative competence, and remain at greater risk to give false confessions.

Young people and suspects with mental retardation are especially vulnerable to coercive questioning and are more likely to give false confessions. Juveniles are greatly overrepresented among those who give false confessions, and younger adolescents are at greater risk than older ones. Steven A. Drizin and Richard A. Leo, "The Problem of False Confessions in the Post–DNA World," 82 *N. Car. L. Rev.* 891 (2004) studied 125 cases DNA-exonerations, many of which included proven false confessions, and which involved a disproportionate number of juveniles and reported that juveniles comprise approximately one-third

(33%) of false confessors and police elicited more than half of those false confessions from youths ages fifteen and under. Samuel Gross, et. al., "Exonerations in the United States: 1989 through 2003," 95 *J. Crim. L. and Criminology* 523 (2005) studied 340 exonerations and reported that false confessions occurred in 15% of cases, that juveniles accounted for 42% of all false confessors, and that among the youngest juveniles—those aged twelve to fifteen—more than two-thirds (69%) confessed to crimes they did not commit. Significantly, exonerated juveniles who confess falsely involve only the small population of youths whom states prosecuted as adults. Another study by Joshua A. Tepfer, et al., "Arresting Development: Convictions of Innocent Youth," 62 *Rutgers L. Rev.* 887 (2010), focused on factors associated with wrongful convictions of 103 youths—defined as those under the age of twenty at the time of their offense. One-third (31.1%) of juvenile exonerees gave false confessions, a rate of false confessions almost double that of young-adult DNA exonerees (17.8%). Moreover, youths who confessed falsely tended to be younger than those who did not. These two findings—a higher rate of false confessions by juveniles and an age skew toward younger offenders—highlight the special vulnerability of young suspects. Developmental psychologists and legal analysts attribute juveniles' overrepresentation among false confessors to developmental immaturity, diminished competence relative to adults, and increased susceptibility to interrogation techniques. Juveniles have fewer life experiences or psychological resources on which to draw and with which to resist the pressures of interrogation. Their impulsive decision-making, limited ability to consider long-term consequences and greater desire to obey and please authority figures heightens their risk. Their nascent judgment makes them less likely to appreciate the gravity of talking. Juveniles' immaturity, inexperience, and propensity to comply with authority increases the likelihood that they will waive *Miranda* without understanding the warning or appreciating the consequences. Juveniles' lower social status relative to adult interrogators and societal expectations of youthful obedience to authority create additional pressures to waive. The isolation, stress, and anxiety associated with interrogation intensify their desire to extricate themselves by the short-term expedient of confessing. Juveniles have limited language skill, understanding, and attention compared with adults, and these differences affect their performance during interrogation. Their reduced appreciation of legal rights or consequences increases their vulnerability to manipulative tactics. They think less strategically and more readily assume responsibility for or confess falsely to protect a peer than do adults. Limited ability to appreciate consequences renders them more susceptible than adults to police tactics and even alters their perceptions of events. Juveniles are more likely than are adults to comply with authority figures, to tell police what they think they want to hear, and to respond more submissively to negative feedback.

2.   PARENTAL PRESENCE

Because most younger juveniles lack the cognitive competence or legal ability of adults to understand the process and to exercise or waive their rights, some states have experimented with alternative strategies to compensate for youths' special vulnerabilities. By statute or court decisions, these jurisdictions use concrete guidelines or per se rules to assure the validity of a juvenile's waiver of rights or confession. They typically require the presence of an "interested adult," such as a parent, or consultation with an attorney. E.g., Lewis v. State, 259 Ind. 431, 288 N.E.2d 138 (Ind.1972); People v. Saiz, 620 P.2d 15 (Colo.1980); Commonwealth v. A Juvenile, 449 N.E.2d 654 (Mass.1983). For example, in In re E.T.C., 141 Vt. 375, 378, 449 A.2d 937 (Vt.1982), the Vermont Supreme Court held that the state constitution imposed three criteria to establish a valid waiver by a juvenile: the youth "must be given the opportunity to consult with an adult . . .; that adult must be one who is not only generally interested in the welfare of the juvenile but completely independent from and disassociated with the prosecution, e.g. a parent, legal guardian, or attorney representing the juvenile; and . . . the independent interested adult must be informed and be aware of the rights guaranteed to the juvenile." About ten states provide juveniles with the right to the presence of a parent or interested adult by statute. E.g,. Ind. Code § 31–32–5–1; Iowa Code Ann. § 232.11; N.H.Stat. Ann. § 169–B:121; W.Va. Code § 49–5–8(d). The Colorado Children's Code § 19–2–511 (2000) provides that

No statements or admissions of a juvenile made as a result of the custodial interrogation of such juvenile by a law enforcement official concerning delinquent acts ... shall be admissible in evidence against such juvenile unless a parent, [or] guardian ... was present at such interrogation and the juvenile and his parent, [or] guardian ... were advised of the juvenile's right to remain silent and that any statements made may be used against him in a court of law, of his right to have counsel appointed if he so requests at the time of the interrogation; except that, if a public defender or counsel representing the juvenile is present at such interrogation, such statements or admissions may be admissible even though the juvenile's parent, or guardian ... was not present.

Courts regularly suppress statements obtained during custodial interrogation if police fail to adhere to the required procedural safeguards. People v. J.D., 989 P.2d 762 (Colo.1999); State v. Walker, 352 N.W.2d 239 (Iowa 1984). Colorado courts apply this provision strictly and require parental presence at interrogation even if a juvenile misleads police and falsely informs them that he is an adult. Nicholas v. People, 973 P.2d 1213 (Colo.1999). Other jurisdictions with a parental presence rule only require police to make a good faith and diligent effort to comply with the parental presence requirement, but admit confessions where the suspect misrepresents his age. Stone v. State, 268 Ind. 672, 377 N.E.2d 1372 (Ind. 1978).

States advance several reasons to require parental presence at interrogation. Parental presence will mitigate the dangers of untrustworthy statements and reduce coercive influences. In re the Interest of Jerrell C.J., 283 Wis.2d 145, 699 N.W.2d 110 (WI 2005). Their presence will enhance the accuracy of any statements obtained, involve them at the initial stages, ensure that police fully advise and juveniles actually understand those advisories, and relieve police of the burden of making judgments about a youth's competency. Their presence reduces the likelihood of police coercion and enables them to testify about any unfair tactics employed. Lewis v. State, 259 Ind. 431, 288 N.E.2d 138 (Ind. 1972). These states recognize that most juveniles lack the maturity to understand their rights or the competence to waive them and believe that a parent may reduce a juvenile's fear and isolation and provide them with access to legal advice. If most juveniles lack maturity of judgment or legal competence, then special safeguards will protect them from their own limitations.

States use several variations to provide juveniles with greater protections at interrogation than those afforded by Miranda and Fare. Some require police to give a Miranda warning to the juvenile and the interested adult, to provide them with an opportunity to consult, and obtain consent to any subsequent waiver from both of them. E.g., Lewis v. State, 259 Ind. 431, 288 N.E.2d 138 (Ind.1972); Commonwealth v. A Juvenile, 389 Mass. 128, 449 N.E.2d 654 (Mass.1983). Some states require a parent to be present at interrogation and bar statements obtained after police warned both the juvenile and parent and provided an opportunity to consult, but then excluded the parent. Conn. Gen. Stat. § 46b–137(a) (West Supp. 1986) (bars statements "unless made by such child in the presence of his parent" and after both were advised of rights); In re Robert M., 22 Conn.App. 53, 576 A.2d 549 (Conn.App.1990) ("parental presence" requirement prohibits statements obtained when police separated juvenile from her parent after warnings). However, an otherwise valid confession obtained in violation of these state prophylactic provisions still may be admissible in federal delinquency prosecutions. E.g. United States v. Wilderness, 160 F.3d 1173 (7th Cir.1998) (federal law, rather than state law, determines admissibility in federal prosecution).

Some states use a "two-tier" approach and treat younger juveniles differently than older youths. Several require parental presence for juveniles under the age of fourteen year, but allow older youths to waive that requirement. E.g. In re B.M.B., 955 P.2d 1302 (Kan.1998) ("We cannot ignore the immaturity and inexperience of a child under 14 years of age and the obvious disadvantage such a child has in confronting custodial police interrogation."); State v. Presha, 748 A.2d 1108 (N.J.2000) ("adult's absence will render the young offender's statement inadmissible as a matter of law, unless the parent or legal guardian is truly unavailable."). Other states actually require a juvenile below the age of fourteen years to consult with an interested adult, but provide older juveniles only with the opportunity to consult with an interested adult as a prerequisite to a valid waiver. E.g., Commonwealth v. A. Juvenile, 389 Mass. 128, 449 N.E.2d 654 (Mass.1983); Commonwealth v. Berry, 410 Mass. 31, 570 N.E.2d 1004 (Mass.1991). Several states' statutes incorporate variations of these interested adult requirements. Conn. Gen. Stat. § 46b–137 (1981); Ind. Code Ann. § 31–32–5–1 (West 1998) (waiver only with counsel or after "meaningful consultation" with and in the presence of parent or guardian who "has no interest adverse to the child"); N.M. Stat. Ann. § 32A–2–14(E), (F) (1987) (confessions by child under thirteen years of age inadmissible, rebuttable presumption of inadmissibility by any child thirteen or fourteen); W.Va. Code § 49–5–2(l) (Supp. 1996) (statements by juvenile under fourteen years of age inadmissible unless made in parents' presence).

In order for parents to fulfill their intended roles, states require that the juvenile have an opportunity for "meaningful consultation." "The meaningful consultation requirement . . . is an added protection afforded only to juveniles. This additional safeguard applicable to juvenile waivers may be satisfied by actual consultation of a meaningful nature or by the express opportunity for such consultation, which [may then be] forsaken in the presence of the proper authority by the juvenile, so long as the juvenile knowingly and voluntarily waives his constitutional rights." Hickman v. State, 654 N.E.2d 278, 281 (Ind.Ct.App.1995). Typically, parental presence and an opportunity for parent and child to confer in private satisfy the requirement. E.g. Patton v. State, 588 N.E.2d 494 (Ind.1992).

Courts that require parental presence assume that parent and child share an identity of interests, that the parent adequately can understand the legal situation, and that they can function as an effective advisor. However, a parent's presence during interrogation may not provide the envisioned benefit for the child and may increase, rather than decrease, the coercive pressures youths experience. Research indicates that most parents do not directly advise their children about the waiver decision and that those who did almost always urged their child to waive his or her rights. Research on adults' ability to understand and exercise their Miranda rights casts doubt on the competence of even well-intentioned parents to assist their children. Parents seldom have legal training and may not understand or appreciate their child's legal problems. Parents' potential conflict of interest with the child, their emotional reactions to their child's arrest, or their own intellectual or social limitations may prevent them from playing the supportive role envisioned. Cases abound of instances in which parents coerce their children to confess. E.g. Anglin v. State, 259 So.2d 752 (Fla.Dist.Ct.App.1972); In the Matter of C.P., 411 A.2d 643 (D.C.Ct.App.1980); Commonwealth v. Philip S., 611 N.E.2d 226 (Mass.Sup.Jud.Ct.1993). The only empirical study of parents' role during questioning reports that if parents attend a juvenile's interrogation, then police try either to enlist them as allies or to neutralize their presence. Feld, *Kids, Cops, and Confessions.*

Police assure parents that no one blames them for their child's misconduct. Officers emphasize to parents that the role of the police is to learn the truth and try to enlist parents as collaborators. Prior to an interview, officers advise parents that they share a common goal—to learn the truth—but caution them that their presence could inhibit their child's ability to be honest. If a parent attends an interrogation, then the officer seats the parent behind the child and admonishes him or her not to participate in questioning—to render the parent passive and unobtrusive. Passivity reduces parents' psychological role as an ally and increases police's ability to get a statement. The investigator then conducts the interrogation as though he were alone with the suspect.

3.   ASSISTANCE OF COUNSEL

Rather than relying on judges' discretionary review of the "totality of the circumstances" or parents' presence, a few states require the presence of an attorney or consultation with counsel prior to a juvenile's waiver of Miranda rights. Waivers of Miranda involve tactical and strategic considerations as well as an abstract awareness of the meaning of the rights themselves. A per se requirement of consultation with counsel prior to any waiver recognizes youths' immaturity, lack of experience with law enforcement, and provides the only effective means to protect their interests. Several professional groups have endorsed the appointment of and consultation with counsel as a prerequisite to any juvenile's waiver of rights. The

National Advisory Committee Task Force on Juvenile Justice recommended that during police interrogation, states prohibit juveniles from "waiv[ing] the right against self-incrimination without the advice of counsel." National Advisory Committee on Criminal Justice Standards and Goals, *Report of the Task Force on Juvenile Justice and Delinquency Prevention* (1976). The American Bar Association's Juvenile Justice Standards recommend that "[t]he right to counsel should attach as soon as the juvenile is taken into custody, . . . when a petition is filed, . . . or when the juvenile appears personally at an intake conference, whichever occurs first." American Bar Association—Institute of Judicial Administration, *Juvenile Justice Standards Relating to Pretrial Court Proceedings* (1980); American Bar Association, *A Call For Justice* (1995).

A few states require an attorney to represent juveniles at interrogation and bar youths from waiving the right to counsel without the written consent of a parent. Iowa Code Ann. § 232.11(1)(a) (West 1998) provides that "A child shall have the right to be represented by counsel . . . [f]rom the time the child is taken into custody for any alleged delinquent act that constitutes a serious or aggravated misdemeanor or felony . . . and during any questioning thereafter by a peace officer or probation officer." A juvenile below the age of sixteen years may not waive the right without written consent of her parent and an older juvenile only may waive if there has been a "good faith" effort to notify the youth's parent or guardian that the child has been taken into custody and of their right to visit and confer with the child. E.g. In re J.A.N., 346 N.W.2d 495 (Iowa 1984) (excluded the confession obtained from a 14 year old youth obtained in the absence of counsel or without parental consent); State v. Walker, 352 N.W.2d 239 (Iowa 1984) ("For children less than sixteen, the statute provides that no waiver of counsel is valid unless accompanied by the written consent of the parent. For the child who is at least sixteen years of age, the statute replaces written parental consent with the requirement that good faith efforts be made to notify the parent. . . .") Similarly, the court in In the Interest of J.D.Z., 431 N.W.2d 272 (N.D.1988), construed a statute that required "representation by legal counsel at all stages of any proceedings" to include the mandatory assistance of counsel during police interrogation. Requiring youths to consult with counsel prior to any waiver protects them against their immaturity and lack of experience and recognizes that only attorneys, rather than parents, possess the necessary skills to assist a child in the adversarial process.

Mandatory, non-waivable appointment of counsel protects juveniles' rights, helps courts efficiently to handle cases, and assures that any waiver decisions truly are "knowing" and "intelligent." Clearly, a rule requiring lawyers to represent juveniles at interrogation, as well as throughout the process, could substantially affect juvenile justice administration. The ability of police to obtain waivers from and interrogate youths likely would decrease. Indeed, some judges decry the adverse effects that such procedural safeguards have on police interrogation, share the "societal outrage against crime," and rue the consequences of per se rules on the efficient repression of crime. In re Thompson, 241 N.W.2d 2, 5 (Iowa 1976) ("It is apparent most courts, required to deal pragmatically with an ever-mounting crime wave in which minors play a disproportionate role, have considered society's self-preservation interest in rejecting a blanket exclusion for juvenile confessions.") At one point, Texas prohibited juveniles from waiving rights without the assistance and concurrence of counsel. Tex. Fam. Code Ann. § 51.09 (Vernon 1973); In re R.E.J., 511 S.W.2d 347 (Tex.Civ.App.1974). However, Texas amended the statute and allowed juveniles to waive their rights after they have received a Miranda warning from a magistrate. Tex. Fam. Code Ann. § 51.095 (West 2000). The Pennsylvania Supreme Court adopted an "interested adult" rule, but then abandoned it in favor of a "totality" approach because the "protection of juveniles against the innate disadvantages associated with the immaturity of most youth may . . . be achieved in a manner that affords more adequate weight to the interests of society and of justice." Commonwealth v. Christmas, 502 Pa. 218, 465 A.2d 989 (Pa.1983). Thus, most states reject the one procedural safeguard that most effectively would protect youths from their own vulnerability during interrogation and instead adopt a discretionary "totality" policy that places youths at a practical disadvantage compared with adults.

4.   MANDATORY RECORDING OF JUVENILE INTERROGATION

For the past decade, virtually every legal analyst and policy group has advocated audio or videotape recordings of interrogations to reduce coercion, to minimize the dangers of false confessions to which juveniles are particularly prone, and to make the process more visible and transparent. The Wisconsin Supreme Court in In the Interest of Jerrell C.J., 283 Wis. 2d 145, 699 N.W.2d 110 (WI 2005), invoked its supervisory power to control the admissibility of evidence in courts and required police electronically to record all custodial interrogation of juveniles that occurs at a place of detention. The Court offered a number of reasons to require recording. Electronic recording provides courts with the best evidence from which to determine, under the totality of the circumstances, whether a juvenile's waiver and confession is voluntary. It provides courts with a "more accurate and reliable record of a juvenile's interrogation" and "eliminates conflicts in evidence." It will "reduce the number of disputes over Miranda and voluntariness issues." It creates an objective record and an independent basis to resolve disputes between police and defendants about *Miranda* warnings, waivers, or statements. It will protect police officers whom suspects wrongfully accuse of improper tactics. It will enhance interrogations by enabling police to focus on the suspect's responses rather than taking notes and reduce the need for a second person to witness a statement which may chill a suspect's willingness to talk. It will protect the rights of the accused by providing an independent record with which courts can resolve credibility contests between police and juveniles which police invariably win. A complete record enables fact-finders to decide whether a statement contains facts known to a guilty perpetrator or police supplied them to an innocent suspect during questioning. It enables police to focus on suspects' responses, to review details of an interview not captured in written notes, and to test them against subsequently discovered facts.

D. CONFIDENTIALITY AND PRE–TRIAL IDENTIFICATION PROCEDURES

The Supreme Court in Gault noted that

it is frequently said that juveniles are protected by the process from disclosure of their deviational behavior. . . . that it is the law's policy to 'hide youthful errors from the full gaze of the public and bury them in the graveyard of the forgotten past.' This claim of secrecy, however, is more rhetoric than reality. Disclosure of [juvenile] court records is discretionary with the judge in most jurisdictions. Statutory restrictions almost invariably apply only to the court records, and even as to those the evidence is that many courts routinely furnish information to the FBI and the military, and on request to government agencies and even to private employers. Of more importance are police records. In most States the police keep a complete file of juvenile 'police contacts' and have complete discretion as to the disclosure of juvenile records.

The Court in United States v. Hall, 452 F.Supp. 1008 (S.D.N.Y.1977), noted that the Federal Youth Corrections Act which, like the juvenile court, had as its goal "the rehabilitation of the young persons in this country who have made their first mistake, so to speak. . . . The evils of a criminal record are well known. The convicted are forever branded as untrustworthy members of society. Their job prospects are permanently compromised; they are often the subject of suspicion and mistrust. . . . [Sealing or expunging ensures] that the defendant no longer has a criminal 'record' and he can resume his life anew without the stigma of a conviction." However, the Court in United States v. Johnson, 28 F.3d 151 (D.C.Cir.1994) cautioned that "[w]hen yesterday's juvenile delinquent becomes today's adult criminal the reasons behind society's earlier forbearance disappear." Thus, confidentiality issues involve gathering, using, storing, disseminating, and disposing of identification evidence and police and court records.

Identification procedures collect "non-testimonial" evidence including "fingerprints, palm prints, footprints, measurements, blood specimens, urine specimens, saliva samples, hair samples, or other reasonable physical examination, handwriting exemplars, voice samples, photographs, and lineups or similar identification procedures requiring the presence of a juvenile." N.C. Gen. Stat. § 7A–596 (Michie 1997). Because these involve physical rather than testimonial evidence, the Fifth Amendment does not prevent police from collecting these data. LaFave, *Criminal Procedure*. After police gather the evidence, they also create physical records which may persist long after their immediate use in legal proceedings. Identification procedures and evidence, records of juvenile arrests and convictions, and pre-trial publicity raise important issues for juvenile justice administration. To what extent, if any, should states modify the criminal procedures used for adults when they gather identification evidence of juveniles? How should state policies balance protecting public safety against the consequences of subjecting delinquents to routine criminal booking procedures? How should state policies balance the legitimate interests of law enforcement in creating records against the dangers that such dossiers may permanently label, stigmatize, and adversely affect youths' employment prospects and adult life trajectory?

The policy dilemma of identification procedures includes creation, subsequent use, and storage of records and subjecting delinquents to routine, adult criminal booking procedures. Progressive reformers created a separate juvenile court to eliminate the trappings of the criminal process and the creation of lasting criminal records. Increasingly, many routine features of the adult criminal justice system comprise components of the juvenile process as well. States obviously require identification evidence for effective law enforcement and confidentiality restrictions should not bar police from obtaining it. But provisions authorizing its routine collection erode many distinctions between the juvenile and adult systems.

1. LINEUP, PHOTOGRAPH, AND FINGERPRINT IDENTIFICATION PROCEDURES

Initially, the Fourth Amendment is the threshold to obtain identification evidence from a suspect. LaFave, *Criminal Procedure*. Police need either search probable cause to believe that fingerprints or other identification evidence will provide evidence of a crime, arrest probable cause to conduct a search incident to arrest, or a valid consent. E.g. Lanes v. State, 767 S.W.2d 789 (Tex.Crim.App.1989) (probable cause required to fingerprint juvenile); Davis v. Mississippi, 394 U.S. 721 (S.Ct.1969) (exclusion of fingerprints seized in violation of Fourth Amendment). If police have valid search authority, then most states will fingerprint and photograph juveniles according to routine adult criminal booking procedures. Patricia Torbet, et al, *State Responses to Serious and Violent Juvenile Crime* (1996).

The Supreme Court in United States v. Wade, 388 U.S. 218 (S.Ct.1967), held that an adult criminal defendant has a Sixth Amendment right to counsel when placed in a post-indictment lineup. The Court reasoned that such a confrontation between the accused and the victim or witness constitutes a "critical stage" in the proceedings that requires the presence of counsel in order meaningfully to cross-examine witnesses. The Wade Court reasoned that the assistance of counsel at pre-trial line-ups would lessen the dangers of unreliable eyewitness identification and suggestibility, reduce the possibility of mistaken identification and erroneous convictions, and ensure a fair trial.

In Kirby v. Illinois, 406 U.S. 682 (S.Ct.1972), a plurality of the Court declined to extend the right to counsel to identification procedures conducted before the state indicted or formally charged a defendant. Kirby reasoned that the Sixth Amendment right to counsel attaches only at or after the "formal initiation" of adversarial proceedings. The dissent in Kirby contended that the dangers of misidentification and the need for assistance of counsel occurred regardless of formal initiation of criminal proceedings. Most victims and witnesses identify defendants before the state formally charges them because that identification provides the essential link between a crime and the accused necessary to support charges. Kirby's refusal to extend the right to counsel to these earlier confrontations leaves uncharged defendants with only the less adequate safeguards afforded by due process. Manson v. Brathwaite, 432 U.S. 98 (S.Ct.1977); Neil v. Biggers, 409 U.S. 188 (S.Ct.1972); LaFave, *Criminal Procedure.*

A few state supreme courts rejected the Kirby ruling on state constitutional grounds and extended the right to counsel to pre-indictment identification procedures. E.g. Blue v. State, 558 P.2d 636 (Alaska 1977); People v. Bustamante, 30 Cal.3d 88, 634 P.2d 927, 177 Cal.Rptr. 576 (Cal.1981). These decisions balanced protection of a suspect from prejudice with the State's interest in prompt and purposeful investigation and concluded that an in-custody suspect who is in custody should have the assistance of counsel at any lineup unless exigent circumstances exist and delay to provide counsel would unduly interfere with a prompt investigation. These state courts reason that once the investigation proceeds beyond an immediate on-the scene show-up, and especially once police have the defendant in custody at the station house, no further compelling law enforcement exigency exists that offsets the dangers of prejudice to the suspect.

State courts routinely apply adult criminal procedural rules to identification cases in juvenile courts. E.g. Davis, *Rights of Juveniles*; Jackson v. State, 17 Md.App. 167, 300 A.2d 430 (Md.App.1973) (following Wade—Kirby distinction on right to counsel at identification only after formal initiation of proceedings); In re Daniel T., 446 A.2d 1042 (R.I.1982). For juveniles, as for adults, the "formal initiation" of the adversarial process triggers the right to counsel. Because states do not use indictments or complaints in delinquency proceedings, filing a delinquency petition typically marks "formal initiation" of the process. E.g. In re M.A., 310 N.W.2d 699 (Minn.1981).

States also apply adult criminal procedure rules to juvenile photo identifications. In United States v. Ash, 413 U.S. 300 (S.Ct.1973), the Supreme Court held that a suspect did not have a constitutional right to have counsel present when a witness viewed an out-of-court photographic display. In In re M.B., 513 P.2d 230 (Colo.Ct.App.1973), the court approved a juvenile photo identification without the presence of counsel. E.g., In re Love, 646 A.2d 1233 (Pa.Super.1994) (no right to counsel during photo identification prior to arrest).

States allow police to photograph and fingerprint juveniles whom they have arrested. Torbet, *State Responses*. State laws vary considerably with regard to the offenses for which they may fingerprint and photograph juveniles and the subsequent use and storage of identification evidence. Some states allow police to fingerprint and photograph juveniles arrested for any offense. E.g. Conn. Gen. Stat. § 46b–133 (West 2000), Idaho Code § 20–516 ("juvenile taken into custody may be fingerprinted and photographed"); Tex. Fam. Code § 58.002 (Vernon 2000) (may photograph or fingerprint child taken into custody for felony or misdemeanor punishable by confinement). Some states require police to take fingerprints and photographs of juveniles fourteen years or older and arrested for a felony, for certain serious offenses, or for youths placed in detention. E.g. Va. Code Ann. § 16.1–299 (West 2000); N.Y. Fam. Ct. Act § 306.1 (McKinney 1999); Idaho Code § 20–516 (2000).

State laws vary with regard to subsequent use and storage of identification evidence. Some states require local police agencies to retain identification evidence in separate and confidential law enforcement files, rather than to transmit it to a central repository. E.g. N.Y. Fam. Ct. Act § 306.1

(McKinney 1999); Or. Stat. § 419A.250 (2000). Others require police agencies to file those records with a central state criminal justice record depository. E.g. Okla Stat. Tit. 10 § 7307–1.6 (West 1998); Idaho Code § 20–516 (2000). Some states authorize police to transfer fingerprint information to a state repository only if the court adjudicated the juvenile delinquent for a felony, whereas others call for destruction of those records once the reasons for taking fingerprints and photographs have been fulfilled. E.g. Neb. Rev. Stat. § 43–252 (1998); N.J. Stat. § 2A:4A–61 (West 1999). The American Bar Association, *Juvenile Justice Standards Relating to Records and Information* (1980), recognized that law enforcement agencies need identification evidence whether an offender is a juvenile or adult. If the police or juvenile court concludes that the youth did not commit the offense for which they collected the evidence, then the ABA recommended that law enforcement agencies destroy the fingerprints and photographs. Retaining identification records after the state has satisfied legitimate law enforcement needs creates a continuing danger of subsequent disclosure and stigmatization.

State laws also vary with respect to the confidentiality of juvenile court records and sharing them with other law enforcement agencies, schools, and welfare agencies. For example, many states require juvenile courts to notify a youth's school if a juvenile is arrested for a violent crime or one in which she used a deadly weapon. Torbet, *State Responses*. Chapter 6 examines the use of records of delinquency conviction to enhance subsequent criminal sentences. Chapter 7 examines the shift from closed, confidential hearings to open, public trials.

2.   PRETRIAL PUBLICITY

Chapter 7 explores juveniles' right to a "public trial," the right of the press to attend or publish information obtained in closed delinquency proceedings, and legislative efforts to balance protecting juveniles with enhancing visibility and accountability of the juvenile justice system. In Smith v. Daily Mail Publishing Co., 443 U.S. 97 (S.Ct.1979), the Supreme Court addressed the validity of a state statute that prohibited newspapers from publishing, without written approval of the juvenile court, the name of any youth charged as an offender. During the initial criminal investigation, newspapers learned the identity of the juvenile from witnesses independently of the juvenile court and subsequently published his name. The Court rejected the state's claim that protecting the anonymity of juvenile offenders and preserving the confidentiality of delinquency proceedings constituted a compelling state interest that justified the restrictions on information dissemination. Despite the state's desire to avoid stigmatizing and labeling a young offender, the Court held that the First Amendment protects newspapers' right lawfully to publish truthful information about matters of public significance even if the disclosure adversely affects the confidentiality of delinquency proceedings.

CHAPTER 4

PRELIMINARY PROCEDURES: INTAKE AND DIVERSION

A. INTRODUCTION

Several officials make decisions that affect the processing of youths in the juvenile justice system. Police officers may adjust a case informally on the street or at the station-house, route it to a diversion program, or refer it to court intake for formal processing. K.S.A. § 38–2330(d)(1) (2007) ("A juvenile taken into custody by a law enforcement officer shall be brought without unnecessary delay to an intake and assessment worker . . ."). Police also make the initial decision whether to take a youth to a pretrial detention facility pending further review by a prosecutor, probation officer, or juvenile court judge. See Chapter 5. Probation officers in a juvenile court intake-unit may refer a youth to the juvenile court for formal adjudication or may dispose of the case through informal supervision or diversion to a program run by the juvenile court or some other social services agency. Juvenile court intake workers and juvenile court judges also review the cases of any youth held in pretrial detention. Even after formal adjudication, a juvenile court judge may choose from a wide array of dispositional alternatives ranging from continuing a case without a finding of delinquency, informal or formal probation, out-of-home placement, or commitment to a state training school. See Chapter 8.

Juvenile justice decision-making is a cumulative process; decisions made by initial participants, for example, police or juvenile court intake officers, affect the decisions subsequent actors make, for example, prosecutors, juvenile court judges, probation officers and correctional personnel. Thus, juvenile court sentencing practices reflect decisions made by other actors at other stages of the process who screen and winnow the youths who appear on the formal docket. If police refer a case to juvenile court, typically an intake probation officer will screen it to decide whether to process the case formally or informally. Probation officers close or informally adjust around half of the cases referred to juvenile court intake. Over the past three decades, the percentage of delinquency referrals resulting in prosecutors filing formal delinquency petitions has ranged between about 41 and 58 percent. In 2002, court officials filed formal petitions in 58 percent of juvenile court referrals, the highest rate in decades and ten percent higher than a decade earlier. Snyder and Sickmund, *National Report.* A child's family background, attitude and demeanor, and race, as well as the referral offenses and prior record influence intake decision-making.

After a youth is referred to juvenile court, either the local prosecuting authority or the juvenile court's probation intake department decides whether to process a case formally or informally. E.g. 3 V.S.A. § 163(a) (2008) ("The attorney general shall develop and administer a juvenile court diversion project . . ."). These administrative gatekeepers handle many referrals to intake with informal dispositions: dismissal, counseling, warning, diversion, referral to another agency, community service, or informal probation. Snyder and Sickmund, *National Report*. Typically, cases remain open pending successful completion of the informal, voluntary disposition at which time court services personnel dismiss them. In the majority of cases processed formally, the prosecuting authority or a probation officer files a petition—a charging document—to initiate the juvenile court process. A petition compares legally with a prosecutor filing a complaint or information or a grand jury indictment in the adult criminal process. The relationship between the screening functions of juvenile court intake staff and the charging functions of prosecutors offices vary from state to state and county to county within a state.

Once the prosecutor or probation officer files a formal delinquency petition, the juvenile court arraigns the juvenile on the petition. The right to counsel attaches in juvenile court only after the state files a petition. Judges appoint counsel to represent juveniles at the arraignment and at subsequent hearings. However, rates of representation vary widely from state to state and from county to county within a state. Barry C. Feld, *Justice for Children: The Right to Counsel and Juvenile Courts* (1993). Even though delinquents are formally entitled to legal representation, many youths appear in juvenile court without assistance of counsel. See Chapter 7. For youths held in pretrial detention, the juvenile court also conducts a detention hearing to determine the youth's custody status pending further court processing and may appoint counsel for this hearing as well. See Chapter 5. At the arraignment, a juvenile admits or denies the allegations in the petition. For youths held in detention, the judge also decides their pretrial custody status. The detention hearing represents one of the most significant decisions that juvenile court judges make because the initial decision to detain a juvenile also may affect subsequent dispositions. In many cases, juveniles admit the allegations of the petition at the arraignment and the court quickly disposes of their cases, often without appointment of a defense attorney. In other cases, the judge appoints a public defender or court-appointed lawyer who confers briefly with the juvenile before the youth admits or denies the allegations in the petition. The vast majority of youths plead guilty and juvenile courts decide only a small faction of delinquency cases in formal contested trials, often called adjudicatory hearings.

The President's Commission on Law Enforcement and Administration of Justice, *The Challenge of Crime in a Free Society* (1967), provided impetus for the Supreme Court due process decisions that significantly reformed juvenile court procedures. The Crime Commission critically examined many aspects of juvenile justice administration, acknowledged that the great hopes Progressives held for juvenile courts often remain unfulfilled, and made several policy recommendations that the Gault decision incorporated and state legislatures later enacted. The Crime Commission suggested that the juvenile court ultimately might evolve into a two-track system with separate criminal social control for serious offenders and social welfare functions for most youths. In such a two-track system, public officials would divert and handle informally most minor delinquents and status offenders. Most juveniles commit trivial offenses, out-grow their delinquencies normally, and do not require formal intervention. By the 1970s, the Crime Commission recommendations led to changes in judicial and legislative policies to divert less serious offenders from juvenile court.

The Gault decision increased the procedural formality and administrative costs of processing offenders in juvenile courts and provided additional impetus to handle minor juvenile cases informally. Diversion programs constitute one reform strategy to minimize formal intervention and to provide supervision or services informally. Just as the original juvenile court diverted youths from adult criminal courts, theoretically diversion programs shift away from juvenile court youths who otherwise would enter that system. Proponents of diversion contend that it provides an efficient gate-keeping mechanism, constitutes the first-line of case-sorting and routing, and avoids stigmatizing or labeling minor offenders. Diversion conserves scarce judicial resources and provides an informal means to respond to misbehavior that the more formal system might otherwise ignore. It provides faster, more efficient and flexible access to re-integrative community resources and rehabilitative services than via a formal process. Although Gault subjected juvenile courts to greater procedural formality and judges' decisions to appellate oversight, police and intake gate-keepers continue to make low-visibility discretionary decisions on an informal basis on the periphery of the system.

B. INTAKE

States rely on intake screening to avoid inappropriate and unnecessary detention of juveniles and to ensure consistent and objective decisions by "juvenile intake services . . . administered by probation officers acting as juvenile probation intake officers . . ." Neb. Rev. Stat. § 29–2260.01. Courts have described the unique function of Probation Intake—"to attempt 'adjustment' of incidents before a petition is filed and the matter sent through the court process of adjudication. Where it is apparent that an ultimate adjudication of delinquency will serve no useful purpose and/or that the informal adjustment procedure will accomplish the same result to the satisfaction of all actual or prospective parties, the matter is adjusted and never reaches adjudication." In re Luis R., 399 N.Y.S.2d 847, 92 Misc.2d 55 (N.Y.Fam.Ct.1977). The Supreme Court in *Schall v. Martin*, 457 U.S. 253, n. 9 (1984), summarized the intake process in conjunction with the decision to hold a youth in pre-trial detention:

> Every accused juvenile is interviewed by a member of the staff of the probation department. This process is known as "probation intake." In the course of the

interview, which lasts an average of 45
minutes, the probation officer will gather what
information he can about the nature of the
case, the attitudes of the parties involved, and
the child's past history and current family
circumstances. His sources of information are
the child, his parent or guardian, the arresting
officer and any records of past contacts between
the child and the Family Court. On the basis of
this interview, the probation officer may
attempt to "adjust," or informally resolve, the
case. Adjustment is a purely voluntary process
in which the complaining witness agrees not to
press the case further, while the juvenile is
given a warning or agrees to counseling
sessions or, referral to a community agency. In
cases involving designated felonies or other
serious crimes, adjustment is not permitted
without written approval of the Family Court.
If a case is not informally adjusted, it is
referred to the "presentment agency."

State laws structure the screening and gate-
keeping functions of juvenile courts in various ways.
In some jurisdictions, prosecutors decide whether to
file a formal petition or to divert or adjust a
juvenile's case informally. "The county attorney,
within its sole discretion, may designate for
diversion or divert the prosecution of a juvenile
accused of an incorrigible or a delinquent act to a
community based alternative program or to a
diversion program administered by the juvenile
court." Arizona Juv. Ct. R. Proc 2(C). In other states,
juvenile court probation officers conduct an intake

screening at which they decide to divert, supervise informally, or refer juveniles to the prosecuting authority for the filing of a formal petition. Courts regard an intake conference as an indispensable element of the juvenile justice process and may dismiss delinquency petitions filed without conducting such a mandated preliminary inquiry. E.g., In re Kevin Eugene C., 599 A.2d 1233, 90 Md.App. 85 (Md.Ct.Spec.App.1992).

State statutes or juvenile court rules specify in varying detail the types of cases to handle informally or formally and the criteria probation staff or prosecutors should use to make these decisions. Typically, screening decisions focus on whether sufficient evidence exists to establish juvenile court jurisdiction and whether formal proceedings are in the best interest of the child or the public. E.g. Tex. Fam. Code Ann. § 53.01 (Vernon 2000). Most states vest preliminary screening authority in the juvenile court intake probation staff to make these determinations. E.g., Haw. Rev. Stat. § 571–31.2 (1998); Iowa Code Ann. § 232.28 (West 1998) (intake officer shall consult with law enforcement, interview complainant, victim or witnesses, confer with child and parent, and, after consultation with county attorney when necessary, decide whether to file a petition). If the intake officer declines to file a delinquency petition, some jurisdictions require the prosecuting authority to review the case at the request of the complainant and vest final charging authority in the prosecutor. E.g., D.C. Code Ann. § 16–2305(c) (1998 Repl.).

Statutes and juvenile court rules describe with varying precision both with whom intake staff should consult, what type of inquiry or investigation they should conduct, and what criteria they should consider in deciding whether to adjust a referral informally or proceed formally. For example, California court rules mandate the presiding juvenile court judge, in cooperation with probation, welfare, prosecuting attorney, law enforcement, and other agencies, to establish an intake program to evaluate referrals and to pursue appropriate action. Cal. R. Ct. 1404(a) (1999). The intake unit evaluates cases to determine whether the juvenile court has jurisdiction, whether sufficient evidence exists to support a petition, whether non-judicial agencies or programs in the community can better deal with the case, and whether the welfare of the child or protection of the public allow informal supervision or require formal proceedings. To make these determinations, the probation officer or social worker conducts an investigation and determines whether to request the prosecutor to file a petition or to settle the matter at intake by taking no action, by counseling the child, or by referring the child to other agencies or community programs. The rules limit a program of informal supervision to six months.

Court rules also specify the criteria that probation officers should consider when they decide to handle a case informally or formally. The criteria include: the sufficiency of the evidence to establish jurisdiction; for less serious offenses, whether the child previously has presented any significant problems in the home, school, or community; whether the matter reflects a temporary family crisis which has been or can be resolved; whether other community resource better suited to serve the needs of the child exist; the attitudes of the child and the parent or guardian; the age, maturity, and abilities of the child; the child's prior dependency or delinquency history; any recommendations by the referring party; the attitudes of the victims; and any other factors that indicate that settling the case at intake would serve the welfare of the child and protect the public. Cal. R. Ct. 1405 (1999)

Filing a delinquency petition represents the formal initiation of the process and the point at which a juvenile's right to counsel attaches. In re M.A., 310 N.W.2d 699 (Minn.1981) ("right to counsel attaches at the time the formal petition is filed. At this point, there is a definite commencement of the adversary proceedings."). Gault shifted the theoretical focus of juvenile courts from those of a social welfare agency to a more formal, legal and adversarial entity. In the past, states allocated the screening and charging functions between prosecutors—executive branch—and court intake staff—judicial branch—in various ways. Either juvenile court intake screened cases and referred to the prosecutor to review those cases recommended for formal petitions or prosecutors screened referrals initially and then delegated to intake the authority to handle informally those cases which did not require a formal petition.

The Washington State statute represents one of the earliest and most comprehensive efforts to structure diversion and an example of the increasing prosecutorial dominance of the intake screening process. Wash. Rev. Code §§ 13.40.070; 13.40.080 (1998). It uses offense criteria to frame referral and routing decision, authorizes prosecutors to refer to court intake the less serious cases, and gives prosecutors greater authority to structure diversion programs and to file formal charges. Other states authorize court intake officers to conduct a preliminary investigation, but require court personnel to forward to the prosecutor cases involving felonies or violent misdemeanors. E.g. Tex. Fam. Code Ann. § 53.01 (Vernon 2000). Traditionally court intake personnel decided whether to proceed formally, but as a result of recent legislative changes, prosecutors increasingly control the decision whether or not to file a petition. E.g. In the Matter of Appeal in Maricopa County, 122 Ariz. 252, 594 P.2d 506 (Ariz.1979); In re Baron C., 77 Md.App. 448, 550 A.2d 740 (Md.Ct.Spec.App.1988) (prosecutor makes ultimate decision to file petition and intake may not adjust informally).

1.   PROCEDURAL RIGHTS AT INTAKE

Probation officers typically summon non-detained youth to an intake conference with a ticket, citation, or official letter. Intake staff informs the juvenile and her parents that the outcome of the conference may result in the filing of a delinquency petition, the likely allegations in the petition, and the possible consequences. They may advise the youth of the right to remain silent, that the juvenile court would not adversely consider a juvenile's silence, and other procedural rights available at trial, such as the right to counsel, to confront and cross-examine witnesses. W.S.A. § 978.234 (2008). Intake staff also may advise a youth and parent that information they divulge can be used in civil damages actions by people who suffered personal injury or property damage caused by the juvenile's offense.

Courts occasionally consider what procedural rights youth enjoy when they meet with a probation officer at intake, such as the right to counsel or privilege against self-incrimination. Juvenile courts design the intake conference to be informal—people sitting in a conference room or in an office around a desk. Intake officers attempt to elicit full disclosure about the referral incident, including information about the nature of the offense, any accomplices, the location of missing property, and the like. Under many informal diversion procedures, youth make admissions which have evidentiary value because "the juvenile . . . must take responsibility for the actions which led to the current accusation." Fla. Stat. § 983.303(4)(a) (1998). Should a probation officer administer a Miranda warning to a juvenile at intake screening or prior to participating in a diversion program? Should intake appoint counsel for a juvenile? If a juvenile admits involvement in an offense at intake, can the probation officer testify about those statements if she eventually decides to file a formal delinquency petition rather than to handle the matter informally? Because the intake conference occurs prior to filing formal charges, unless privately retained, attorneys rarely accompany juveniles at this stage of the proceedings.

The court in In the Matter of Frank H., 337 N.Y.S.2d 118 (N.Y.Fam.Ct.1972), considered whether an intake conference constituted a critical stage for which a juvenile court should appoint a lawyer. The Supreme Court's critical stage analyses focuses on whether a defendant requires counsel to protect other rights, such as the privilege against self-incrimination, the ability to confront and cross examine witnesses, or to preserve procedural rights that must be invoked during pre-trial procedures. LaFave, *Criminal Procedure*. The court in Frank H. concluded that an intake conference did not constitute a critical stage that required appointment of counsel because no adverse legal consequences could follow if a child appeared without a lawyer. A New York statute granted statutory use immunity and barred use of any statements that a child made at intake in any subsequent delinquency or criminal proceedings. N.Y. Fam. Ct. Act § 735 (McKinney 2000) ("no statement made during a preliminary conference may be admitted into evidence at a fact-finding hearing . . ."). The statutory immunity encouraged youths' candor, cooperation, and full-disclosure at the conference. Because nothing a juvenile said could incriminate her, the court held that the juvenile did not require either a Miranda warning or appointment of counsel. The court observed that the decision whether or not to file a petition is a social-work decision as much as a legal one and an attorney could play only a limited role at intake. Because the authority of the probation officer created an implied compulsion, the statute barred the admission not only of primary evidence but also other evidence derived from statements made at the intake conference. E.g. In re Luis R., 399 N.Y.S.2d 847, 92 Misc.2d 55 (N.Y.Fam.Ct.1977). Even without a statutory immunity, some courts have found that the policy of encouraging a juvenile's candid and frank discussion precluded the subsequent use of statements made by a juvenile to a probation officer during an intake conference. E.g., In re Wayne H., 24 Cal.3d 595, 156 Cal.Rptr. 344, 596 P.2d 1 (Cal.1979).

Although Frank H. found that the statutory immunity obviated the need for counsel, even without such an immunity provision, juveniles do not enjoy a constitutional right to a Miranda warning at intake. In Minnesota v. Murphy, 465 U.S. 420 (S.Ct.1984), the Supreme Court held that an adult probationer was not in custody when his probation officer interviewed him in her office. Even though conditions of probation required him to meet with and respond truthfully to his probation officer's questions, the Court found that probation officers did not exert the type of inherently coercive pressures associated with police custodial interrogation. An informal intake conference is even less coercive because a parent typically accompanies a youth. Moreover, regardless of whether an intake conference constitutes custodial interrogation, a probation officer simply could administer a Miranda warning at the start of the meeting, obtain a "knowing, intelligent, and voluntary" waiver, and then testify as to any statements obtained in subsequent delinquency or criminal proceedings. E.g. Tenn. R.Juv. Ct. Proc. 12 (West 1998) (probation officer at intake conference shall immediately give child a Miranda warning); W.S.A. § 938.243 (2008) (intake worker shall advise juvenile of "right to remain silent").

In some instances, police may attempt to piggy-back on a summons to appear at an intake conference. For example, Deshawn E. v. Safir, 156 F.3d 340 (2d Cir.1998), involved a police practice of intercepting youths summoned to appear at the Probation Department for an intake conference and interrogating them. The immunity statute in Frank H. only applied at intake conferences, so police who questioned a youth with proper Miranda warnings could obtain admissible statements. Moreover, because youths who accompanied police to an interrogation room were not in custody, failure to administer Miranda warnings would not necessarily bar the admissibility of statements.

C. DIVERSION

Despite the theoretical rationale for handling youths informally and outside the juvenile justice system, a question remains whether states effectively have implemented diversion reforms or instead converted them into an additional tool of social control that extends further into the normal adolescent population. Although voluntary participation and non-justice system implementation provided the original premises of diversion reforms, if program personnel can induce a youth to participate in a program by the threat of filing a petition, then do youths truly participate voluntarily? Do diversion programs restrict themselves to youths who otherwise would have entered the juvenile system or do they have a "net-widening" effect and encompass youths whom police previously would have counseled, reprimanded, or released in the absence of such program options?

In some jurisdictions, diversion decisions remain in the hands of police officers. For example, the Texas "first offender program" authorizes police officers to refer youths whom they take into custody for non-violent misdemeanors to a juvenile board. Tex. Fam. Code Ann. § 52.031 (Vernon 1998). If the child and her parents consent to program participation, the board may impose dispositions which include restitution, community service, counseling or other rehabilitative services, and periodic reporting to the police or other agencies. If a child refuses or fails to participate, the board refers the case to juvenile court.

The State of Washington has a comprehensive statute to structure and formalize the diversion process. E.g. Wash. Rev. Code §§ 13.40.070; 13.40.080 (1998). Because Washington adopted its diversion statute in 1976, appellate courts have answered several common legal and policy questions about administration of diversion. The statute centralizes diversion decisions and authorizes prosecutors and court intake personnel, rather than police officers, to make them. The prosecutor exercises primary screening authority to charge or to divert although she may delegate that screening authority for non-felony cases to juvenile probation officers. The statute uses offense criteria to define eligibility for diversion, to formalize the diversion agreement, to impose limitations on the length and nature of diversion dispositions, and to assure some degree of procedural regularity in the making and revoking of diversion contracts. Wash. Rev. Code § 13.40.070 (1998). Prosecutors must divert first-time misdemeanants and may divert any youth whom they do not charge with a felony, who does not have a prior record which includes felonies, who has not previously been committed to an institution or diverted, or who does not request formal prosecution. The statute formalizes diversion by allowing a juvenile to enter an agreement in lieu of prosecution. Wash. Rev. Code § 13.40.080 (1998). It specifies the types of dispositions that a diversion contract may impose, for example, community service of up to 150 hours, restitution, counseling, and the like. It limits the length of diversion dispositions to six months for a misdemeanor and one year for a felony.

The diversion process also provides basic procedural rights. A juvenile receives the assistance of counsel at intake and during the diversion conference to obtain advice about the terms of the diversion contract. Wash. Rev. Code § 13.40.080(8) (1998). The statute specifies the procedural rights available to a youth if the diversion unit subsequently revokes the diversion agreement. These rights include: termination only for violating terms of the agreement, notice prior to a termination hearing, the right to confront and cross-examine witnesses, and the assistance of counsel. Essentially, the Washington diversion statute creates a non-judicial guilty plea and authorizes non-custodial dispositions. Because the informal guilty plea authorizes dispositions equivalent to a probation status, the statute provides procedural safeguards similar to those used to revoke probation. The statute also includes diverted offenses in a juvenile's delinquency record if she subsequently re-offends.

Because the Washington statute formalized diversion, appellate courts have reviewed several aspects of diversion administration. A youth has a right to be considered for diversion in lieu of prosecution, but does not enjoy an absolute right to be accepted into a diversion program. E.g. State v. Chatham, 28 Wash. App. 580, 624 P.2d 1180 (Wash.Ct.App.1981). As long as the diversion unit provides a full and fair determination of eligibility, it properly may reject a youth. A determination of eligibility for diversion requires individualized consideration and a prosecutor may not adopt a policy of processing formally certain categories of offenses otherwise eligible for diversion. E.g. State v. W. S., 40 Wash. App. 835, 700 P.2d 1192 (Wash.Ct.App.1985). If a juvenile declines to enter a diversion program, a prosecutor may charge the delinquent with a more serious offense than originally contemplated absent a showing of "actual vindictiveness." E.g. State v. McDowell, 102 Wash.2d 341, 685 P.2d 595 (Wash.1984). As a result, prosecutors may threaten to file more serious charges as a way to induce juveniles to accept a diversionary disposition. Finally, as long as intake properly obtains a juvenile's waiver of counsel, the state may include diverted offenses in a juvenile's delinquency history to enhance subsequent juvenile sentences. State v. Quiroz, 107 Wash.2d 791, 733 P.2d 963 (Wash.1987).

States increasingly adopt procedures to govern diversion agreements. These typically require a juvenile to admit his involvement in the delinquent act and to voluntarily and intelligently enter into a diversion contract which may include supervision for six months or more. E.g. Ark.C.A. § 9–27–323 (2008). Youths enter into diversion agreements— written in "simple, ordinary, and understandable language"—and agree to non-judicial probation supervision, participation in court-approved education, counseling, or treatment programs, or in teen courts or juvenile drug courts. E.g. Ark.C.A. § 9–27–323(e)(1–4) (2008). Other states establish diversion programs to accomplish a number of goals: to provide alternatives to formal adjudication, to reduce the caseloads of juvenile courts, to reduce recidivism, and to collect restitution. E.g. Minn. Stat. Ann. § 388.24 (West 2000). Components of diversion programs include: developing court intake and prosecutorial screening criteria; providing counseling; performing chemical dependency assessments and making referrals to treatment agencies where appropriate; connecting diverted offenders with community resources; and monitoring juveniles' performance and compliance.

Some states' diversion programs emphasize restorative justice which attempts to balance competency development, accountability, and community protection. Competency development focuses on a youth's needs and attempts to enhance his ability to function as a productive, responsible citizen. Community protection emphasizes monitoring, social control, and public safety. Accountability emphasizes restitution, community service and victim-offender mediation to increase offenders' appreciation of the consequences of misbehavior. E.g., Minn. Stat. Ann. § 611A.775 (West 1998); Fla. Stat. Ann. § 985.303 (West 1998). Typically, a restorative justice board meets with a non-violent, first-offender who must accept responsibility for her behavior and waive her right to a speedy trial and to counsel. The juvenile, her parents, victims, and other community members meet with the panel which may impose sanctions including: restitution, work for the victim or community service, and participation in counseling, education or treatment services. A written contract formalizes the agreement between the juvenile and the panel. If a youth successfully completes the sanctions imposed, the prosecutor may not file a petition. E.g. Fla. Stat. Ann. § 985.303 (West 1998). If the juvenile rejects the recommended sanctions or fails to complete them successfully, then the prosecutor may file a delinquency petition.

CHAPTER 5
PRETRIAL DETENTION

A. INTRODUCTION

Police take most juveniles into custody without a warrant and then must decide whether to release them immediately to their parents, to hold them for further investigation, to question them at the police station, or to detain them in a non-secure or secure facility. Typical custody statutes require police immediately to notify a parent when they take a child into custody. Custody and detention statutes include a presumption that police should release a child to her parents unless she meets detention criteria. See Chapter 3.A.3. If police do not release her, then several justice system actors participate in decisions about a youth's interim status pending further investigation—intake screening, prosecutorial charging, and court hearing.

Initially, a police officer decides whether or not to take a youth into custody. If the officer brings a juvenile to a detention facility, then an intake probation officer or detention worker attempts to contact a parent and decides whether to release or detain the youth. If the detention facility staff decides to hold the juvenile in custody, then the prosecutor must promptly file a delinquency petition. Finally, at a detention hearing, a juvenile court judge must decide whether or not to release the juvenile pending adjudication and disposition. Under statutory time limits, these different justice system actors make their respective decisions within 48 to 72 hours after police take a youth into custody. If a judge detains a youth, the juvenile may spend a month or more in confinement pending a plea or adjudication and disposition. Snyder and Sickmund, *National Report.*

Jurisdictions distinguish between placing a youth in a shelter care, or a detention or secure detention facility. A shelter care facility is any public or private structure or group home, other than a detention facility, used to provide either temporary placement for children prior to a dispositional order or for longer term care following disposition. E.g. Kan. Stat. Ann. § 38–1502 (1997); Minn. Stat. Ann. § 260B.015 Subd. 17 (West 2000) (physically unrestricting facility); N.Y. Fam. Ct. Act § 301.2(5) (McKinney 2000). A detention facility is a secure public or private building used to hold accused or adjudicated offenders. E.g. Kan. Stat. Ann. § 38–1502 (1997); Minn. Stat. Ann. § 260B.015 Subd. 16 (West 2000) (physically restricting facility); N.Y. Fam. Ct. Act § 301.2(4) (McKinney 2000). Most detention facilities are secure structures. Staff control all entrances and exits or rely on locked rooms and buildings, fences and physical restraint to control residents. E.g. Kan. Stat. Ann. § 38–1502 (1997). A shelter care facility is not a secure lock-up, whereas a detention facility is the functional equivalent of an adult jail. The differences between shelter and secure facilities are important because federal and state laws prohibit placing status offenders in secure detention facilities with delinquents. E.g. In re Ronald S., 69 Cal.App.3d

866, 138 Cal.Rptr. 387 (Cal.App.1977); 42 U.S.C. 5633(a)(12)(A) (2000) (courts may not place status offenders in juvenile detention or correctional facilities).

Juvenile courts' jurisdictional and statutory authority to take juveniles into custody also defines the power of police officers, probation intake workers, and juvenile court judges to detain youths. Recall, statutes authorize police to take juveniles into custody for criminal law violations, for non-criminal status offenses, and when they find children in circumstances that endanger their health, safety, and welfare. Although states give police broad authority initially to intervene, it does not necessarily follow that justice system officials need to detain all youths taken into custody pending further proceedings. States' detention statutes define with differing degrees of specificity the criteria for holding juveniles. Although statutory language varies greatly, detention criteria focus on three general elements: the danger a youth poses to him or herself; the danger he or she poses to others; or his or her likelihood of flight. E.g. Va. Code Ann. § 16.1–248.1 (Michie 1998) (release of the juvenile poses an unreasonable danger to the person or property of others, a substantial threat of serious harm to the juvenile, or the juvenile has threatened to abscond or has a record of willful failure to appear in court); Minn. Stat. Ann. § 260B.171 (West 2000) (release to parents unless there is reason to believe that the child would endanger self or others or not return for a court hearing); Ga. Code Ann. § 15–11–18.1 (1998). Pretrial detention represents a significantly different process in the ways states process juvenile and adult criminal defendants because of juvenile courts' broader jurisdiction and states' protective policies toward children.

B. RIGHT TO BAIL

The Eight Amendment to the Constitution provides, *inter alia*, that "Excessive bail shall not be required." The Supreme Court in Stack v. Boyle, 342 U.S. 1 (S.Ct.1951), held that

> federal law has unequivocally provided that a person arrested for a non-capital offense *shall* be admitted to bail. This traditional right to freedom before conviction permits the unhampered preparation of a defense, and serves to prevent the infliction of punishment prior to conviction. . . . Unless this right to bail before trial is preserved, the presumption of innocence . . . would lose its meaning. The right to release before trial is conditioned upon the accused's giving adequate assurance that he will stand trial and submit to sentence if found guilty.

For adults, "giving adequate assurance" may take the form of posting monetary bail or pledging other assets as collateral, paying a premium to a bail-bondsman who posts the bail, release on personal recognizance, supervised released, or release to a third-party. LaFave, *Criminal Procedure*. Theoretically, bail functions to assure a defendant's presence at trial. Pretrial release enables the defendant to aid in the preparation of a defense, to secure witnesses, and to avoid punishment before trial. Judges set bail based on a defendant's flight risk and examine indicators of stability and reliability to keep court appearances to make this decision. Relevant factors bearing on flight risk include the seriousness of the offense charged and possible penalty if convicted, aggravating circumstances indicating dangerousness, character and reputation, financial assets, family status, roots in the community, prior failure to appear in court, and employment status.

States' juvenile codes take three different positions on juveniles' right to post bail to secure pretrial release: some allow bail as a discretionary matter similar to adults; some deny youths any right to bail; and most are silent on the issue. A few states explicitly grant juveniles a statutory right to bail. E.g. Ga. Code Ann. § 15–11–19 (1998) (judge shall apply bail provisions to juveniles in the same manner as applied to adult criminal defendants); State in Interest of Banks, 402 So.2d 690 (La.1981). Some allow bail as a matter of the trial judge's discretion. E.g. Neb. Rev. Stat. § 43–253 (Michie 1994). Although bail functions to assure an adult defendant's court appearances, most states and courts conclude that a child's freedom should not depend on her ability to pay for it. Juveniles have neither money nor property of their own to post as collateral with a bail bondsman. A monetary bail system for juveniles therefore conditions juveniles' freedom on their families' financial resources. Because many delinquents' families are poor, a money bail system would detain many juveniles because of poverty rather than public policy. In addition, minors can not enter into binding contracts, so bail bondsmen would be reluctant to issue a policy for their release without a solvent adult co-signer. Finally, money bail could be inappropriate if the court detains a child because release could endanger her welfare.

Most states' detention statutes either prohibit or do not authorize judges conditionally to release juveniles on the posting of monetary bail or a security bond. E.g. Or. Rev. Stat. § 419C.179 (1995). State courts that have considered delinquents' constitutional challenges to denial of bail consistently have concluded that a "properly administered" juvenile detention statute provides an "adequate alternative" to an adult's right to bail. E.g. In re William M., 3 Cal.3d 16, 473 P.2d 737, 89 Cal.Rptr. 33 (Cal.1970); Doe v. State, 487 P.2d 47 (Alaska 1971); Morris v. D'Amario, 416 A.2d 137 (R.I.1980). In the leading case of L.O.W. v. District Court, 623 P.2d 1253 (Colo.1981), the court rejected a juvenile's constitutional challenge to denial of bail and concluded that the detention law's presumption for release and statutory criteria—"welfare of the child or community"—provided a suitable alternative to a money bail system. The court reasoned that bail functioned solely to ensure adult defendants' presence at trial, but juvenile detention statutes also protect the child and the community. The court emphasized that a money bail system would be inappropriate because most juveniles lacked financial resources. Moreover, a bail system adversely could affect a youth who suffered abuse at home or whose parents declined to receive him.

When a state files a motion to transfer a juvenile to criminal court for prosecution as an adult, some courts are more receptive to a constitutional claim for pre-trial release on bail. They reason that when the state seeks to deny a juvenile the protection of the juvenile court, the youth is entitled to commensurately greater constitutional protection. E.g. In re K.G., 89 Ohio Misc.2d 16, 693 N.E.2d 1186 (Ohio Com.Pl.1997). Other courts, by contrast, continue to deny juveniles a right to bail until after the court decides to transfer them to criminal court. E.g. State v. M.L.C., 933 P.2d 380 (Utah 1997). They reason that the protective and rehabilitative policies of the juvenile court prevail until such time as the judge determines the youth's adult criminal status.

C. PRETRIAL DETENTION

A recurring tension in juvenile justice policy is when and how to recognize adolescents' unique developmental characteristics—immaturity, vulnerability, and dependency. Sometimes, the Supreme Court or state lawmakers encounter opportunities to recognize youths' developmental limitations and to provide them with greater procedural safeguards than those afforded adult criminal defendants. Despite developmental differences, the Court in Fare v. Michael C. used the same legal standard to evaluate juveniles' and adults' waivers of Miranda rights and effectively put vulnerable youths at a practical disadvantage. On the other hand, sometimes the Supreme Court and law makers have the option to use procedures that treat delinquents at least as well as adult defendants and instead employ less effective safeguards in juvenile courts, for example, denial of the right to a jury trial. Pretrial detention procedures for juveniles and adults represent another instance in which states pursue different policies and use different procedures.

In United States v. Salerno, 481 U.S. 739 (S.Ct.1987), the Supreme Court upheld the constitutionality of the Federal Bail Reform Act of 1984, 18 U.S.C. § 3141 et seq. (2000), which allowed the federal government preventively to detain an adult pending trial if the government demonstrates by clear and convincing evidence in an adversary hearing that no release conditions "will reasonably assure . . . the safety of any other person and the community." The Salerno majority concluded that "crime prevention" served a legitimate regulatory purpose and did not constitute pre-trial punishment. The Bail Reform Act provided for an adversary hearing, a standard of proof of "clear and convincing" evidence, and specified a narrow range of extremely serious offenses as the predicates for preventive detention. 18 U.S.C. § 3142(f) (1988).

By contrast, in Schall v. Martin, 467 U.S. 253 (S.Ct.1984), the Court considered the constitutionality of a much less precise juvenile statute that authorized preventive detention if the juvenile court judge found that "there is a serious risk that he may before the return date commit an act which if committed by an adult would constitute a crime." N.Y. Fam. Ct. Act § 320.5 (McKinney 2000). In a 6–3 decision Justice Rhenquist reversed lower courts that struck down the statute and held that the law satisfied Fourteenth Amendment due process requirements of fundamental fairness.

The Schall majority considered whether the pretrial detention statute served legitimate state objectives and whether it provided adequate procedural safeguards. The Court found that the state had a compelling interest to prevent crime and juveniles committed a significant amount of crime. The Court asserted that preventive detention protected youths from their own folly, noted the prevalence of similar detention statutes among the states, and minimized juveniles' liberty interests. "[J]uveniles, unlike adults, are always in some form of custody." The Court found that detention did not punish juveniles and characterized conditions of confinement as the consequences of legitimate regulatory practices, akin to parental controls. "Children, by definition, are not assumed to have the capacity to take care of themselves. They are assumed to be subject to the control of their parents, and if parental control falters, the State must play its part as parens patriae."

After concluding that preventive detention served legitimate policy goals, the Court considered the adequacy of the statute's procedures. The Schall majority did not use the Court's ordinary due process analyses—the nature of the private interests at stake, the risk of erroneous fact-finding, and the burden of additional procedural safeguards to avoid those risks—to assess juveniles' challenges to detention procedures. Mathews v. Eldridge, 424 U.S. 319 (S.Ct.1976). Instead, it asserted that the statute provided for notice and an expedited hearing at which juveniles received assistance of counsel. It found that a judge's finding of probable cause satisfied the Fourth Amendment requirements of Gerstein v. Pugh, 420 U.S. 103 (S.Ct.1975).

The Court rejected the juveniles' contention that the statutory criterion—"serious risk" of a future crime—was unconstitutionally vague. It asserted that "from a legal point of view there is nothing inherently unattainable about a prediction of future criminal conduct." Despite the majority's confidence that judges accurately could predict youths' future dangerousness, the Court declined to specify what criteria judges should use, what evidence would satisfy those criteria, or the state's burden of proof. The majority insisted that its role only was to assure that the law comported with constitutional minimum standards rather than to draft a model statute.

Justice Marshall, writing for three dissenting justices, objected that the statute failed to achieve a legitimate state objective or to provide adequate procedural safeguards. Marshall noted that the statutory criterion—"serious risk" of future crime— failed to specify either the type or seriousness of the anticipated crime or the probability of its occurrence. More fundamentally, the dissent objected that judges lacked the ability reliably to predict future dangerousness and thus could not prevent future crimes.

Predictive judgments pervade the juvenile and criminal justice systems—juvenile detention, sentencing, and transfer decisions and adult bail release, sentencing, probation and parole, and even death penalty decisions. Social scientists have conducted extensive research to assess the validity, accuracy, and reliability of predictions of future crime. Empirical research on judges' and clinicians' ability to predict dangerousness consistently report that they lack the technical capacity accurately to predict future behavior and they invariably over-predict and erroneously confine as potential offenders many more people than subsequently would commit additional offenses if released. E.g. Feld, *Bad Kids*. In addition to the inherent fallibility of predicting dangerousness, juvenile court judges make their decisions within a relatively short time frame and based on incomplete information about a youth's background.

Justice Marshall objected that the state could not achieve its crime prevention goals because most detained juveniles are not dangerous or violent offenders. States detain larger proportions of violent offenders than they property offenders, but property offenders comprise a much larger number of youths on juvenile courts' dockets. As a result, prosecutors charge most detained juveniles with property or drug crimes rather than violent offenses. Snyder and Sickmund, *National Report*. The dissent also criticized the Court for denigrating juveniles' liberty interests and characterizing confinement in a detention facility as similar to parental custody.

Justice Marshall also criticized the majority's analysis of the detention procedures. He noted that the statute lacked any substantive criteria or objective guidelines. It failed to describe either the type or weight of evidence a judge should consider or to specify the burden of proof the state must satisfy to establish the probability of a future serious crime. As a result, the statute gave judges broad discretion which the dissent feared they could apply in an arbitrary, capricious, or discriminatory manner.

Empirical research confirms the adverse impact of discretionary detention decisions on racial minority and female offenders. Without objective criteria, validated indicators or "risk assessment" instruments, detention statutes remit speculative predictions about future behavior to each judge's discretion and lend themselves to discriminatory decisions. Empirical studies of juvenile court decision-making report that after controlling for the seriousness of the offense, prior record, and other legally relevant variables, judges detain a disproportionately larger number of minority offenders than they do similarly situated white juveniles. Joan McCord, Cathy Spatz Widom, and Nancy A. Crowell, *Juvenile Crime, Juvenile Justice* (2001) [hereinafter McCord, *Juvenile Crime*]; Snyder and Sickmund, *National Report*. The prevalence of Disproportionate Minority Confinement (DMC) provided the impetus for amendments to the Federal Juvenile Justice and

Delinquency Prevention Act to reduce racial disparities in pretrial detention and institutions. 42 U.S.C. § 5601 (1994). Female juveniles also experience higher rates of pretrial detention than do male juveniles whom prosecutors charge with minor and status offenses. Meda Chesney–Lind and Randall G. Shelden, *Girls, Delinquency, and Juvenile Justice* (1998). The disproportionate detention of females provided one impetus to divert and de-institutionalize status offenders.

D. DETENTION PROCEDURES

Schall held that the procedures used to detain juveniles provided adequate "protection against erroneous and unnecessary deprivations of liberty." The Court compared them with the Fourth Amendment probable cause procedures for arrested adults established in Gerstein v. Pugh, 420 U.S. 103 (S.Ct.1975). Gerstein held that any post-arrest liberty restraints required a prompt judicial probable cause determination because prolonged detention entailed a Fourth Amendment seizure of the person. Gerstein noted that the exigent circumstances that justified warrantless arrests without a prior judicial determination of probable cause disappeared once police took a defendant into custody. The Court did not require states to provide arrested defendants with an adversarial probable cause determination. It reasoned that a judge found probable cause in an ex parte proceeding when she issued a warrant before an arrest and held that the Fourth Amendment did not require a more formal, adversarial proceeding if a judge found probable cause after an offender's arrest.

The Schall majority concluded that the juvenile preventive detention procedures satisfied Gerstein because the juvenile received notice of the charges at an informal initial appearance, the court made a record of the appearance, a parent accompanied the juvenile, and the judge advised the juvenile of the right to remain silent and the right to counsel. The Schall majority suggested that a juvenile court judge made a probable cause determination at the initial appearance and asserted that in any event, the state filed a petition and conducted a formal probable cause hearing within three days of the initial appearance.

After Gerstein granted criminal defendants the right to a prompt judicial determination of probable cause, the Court in County of Riverside v. McLaughlin, 500 U.S. 44 (S.Ct.1991), defined a prompt hearing as one that occurred within 48–hours of arrest. After the McLaughlin decision, the California Supreme Court in Alfredo A. v. Superior Court of Los Angeles County, 6 Cal.4th 1212, 865 P.2d 56, 26 Cal.Rptr.2d 623 (Cal.1994), considered the time period within which a juvenile court must conduct a prompt probable cause and detention hearing. Under California law, a prosecutor must file a delinquency petition within 48–hours after police take a youth into custody. However, the juvenile court in Alfredo A. adopted a policy to hold a detention and probable cause hearing within 72–hours after police arrested a youth without a warrant, rather than within 48–hours as would be the case for adults under McLaughlin. The California Supreme Court concluded that the Supreme Court did not intend automatically to apply McLaughlin's 48–hour rule to juvenile detention hearings. Alfredo A. distinguished McLaughlin's 48–hour promptness rule because adult defendants received only a probable cause determination whereas juveniles required a judicial determination of probable cause and a finding that the juvenile satisfied statutory detention criteria. Alfredo A. also noted that the Supreme Court decided Schall based on Fourteenth Amendment due process considerations such as informality and flexibility rather than by strict application of the Fourth Amendment.

The Alfredo A. dissent objected to the majority's failure to apply McLaughlin's 48–hour promptness requirement to detained juveniles. It noted that court and statutes uniformly require juveniles to receive a probable cause determination prior to continued detention. E.g. Moss v. Weaver, 525 F.2d 1258 (5th Cir.1976) (Gerstein's probable cause requirement applicable to juveniles); R.W.T. v. Dalton, 712 F.2d 1225 (8th Cir.1983) (status offenders entitled to probable cause determination). It argued that nothing in McLaughlin's promptness analysis limited its holding to adult defendants. Other states' statutes and rules of juvenile court procedure differ on whether juvenile court judges must conduct a prompt probable cause hearing within 48–hours as required for adults or within 72–hours in conjunction with a detention hearing, as approved in Alfredo A. E.g. Minn. Stat. Ann. § 260B.172 (West 2000); Mn. Rule Juv. Proc. 5.04 (probable cause finding within 48–hours); Fla. Stat. Ann. § 985.215 (West 2000); Fla. Stat. Ann. § 985.215 (West 2000) (probable cause determination within 24 hours of being taken into custody); Tex. Fam. Code § 54.01 (Vernon 2000) (non-adversarial probable cause finding within 48–hours).

Gerstein and most states' juvenile codes do not require a formal, adversarial probable cause determination. However, state laws and rules of procedure grant juveniles the right to counsel at a detention hearing because the juvenile court judge considers other factors when it decides a youth's pretrial custody status. E.g. Minn. Rule Juv. Proc. 5.07 (West 2000); Tex. Fam. Code § 54.01 (Vernon 2000) (if a child was not represented initially at a detention hearing, when court appoints counsel, juvenile entitled to a de novo hearing within two days after attorney files a formal request); A.R.S. § 8–221 (Supp. 2001); Haas v. Colosi, 40 P.3d 1249 (Ariz.App.2002) (right to counsel in all proceedings that may result in detention). At the beginning of a detention hearing, the judge advises the juvenile and parents of the child's right to be represented by counsel and, unless waived, appoints counsel for an indigent youth.

In addition to finding probable cause, a juvenile court judge decides whether or not the youth meets the statutory detention criteria. Detention provisions contain a presumption that juveniles should be released, rather than detained, after police take them into custody or indicate a preference for the "least restrictive alternative." If police or intake staff does not release a juvenile immediately, then prosecutors must file a petition and the court must conduct a detention hearing within the specified time—48– to 72–hours. The specificity of detention criteria vary with state statutes and court rules. However, all focus primarily on a juvenile's danger to him or herself or to others in the community or risk of non-appearance for court hearings. E.g. Cal. Welf. & Inst. Code § 628 (West 2000). Some states require decision-makers to use risk assessment instruments to refine detention decisions and to narrow the population of youths eligible for detention. Risk assessment instruments focus on juveniles' prior history of failure to appear, prior offenses, crimes committed pending adjudication, and probation or parole status at the time she was taken into custody. E.g. Fla. Stat. Ann. § 985.213 (2000). Other courts have adopted criteria, such as those proposed by the American Bar Association, *Juvenile Justice Standards Relating to Interim Status* (1980), to regularize judges' detention decisions. E.g. Facilities Review Panel v. Coe, 187 W.Va. 541, 420 S.E.2d 532 (W.Va.1992).

Juvenile courts must make individualized decisions about a youth's eligibility for detention and may not adopt a uniform policy automatically to detain all juveniles charged with certain offenses. E.g. In re William M., 3 Cal.3d 16, 473 P.2d 737, 89 Cal.Rptr. 33 (1970). However, some states have enacted laws that create a rebuttable presumption that a youth who commits a felony while using a handgun constitutes a danger to him or herself or the community. E.g. Colo. Rev. Stat. § 19–2–204(3) (1994). Courts have upheld such laws because they provide an evidentiary presumption that the youth fits the detention criteria, but which the juvenile may rebut with other evidence that overcomes the presumption. E.g. People v. Juvenile Court, City and County of Denver, 893 P.2d 81 (Colo.1995).

E. CONDITIONS OF CONFINEMENT AND ADULT JAILS

The Schall Court denigrated juveniles' liberty interests and trivialized the institutional conditions under which most states detain juveniles. States confine the majority of juveniles' in pretrial detention centers prior to trial rather than in post-adjudication commitments to training schools or other correctional facilities. E.g. Feld, *Bad Kids.* Unfortunately, custodial jail-like conditions prevail in many juvenile detention facilities around the nation. States detain more than half of all youths in overcrowded facilities operated above their designed capacity. Snyder and Sickmund, *National Report.*

Juvenile detention centers function similar to and closely resemble conditions in adult jails. The Supreme Court in Florence v. Board of Chosen Freeholders of Burlington, N.J., 132 S.Ct. 1510 (2012), allowed jailors to conduct strip searches without individualized suspicion of adults arrested for minor offenses prior to entry into the general in jail population to safeguard the security and health of the jail population. Even prior to Florence, lower courts had authorized the routine strip-search of juveniles on their first admission to a detention center without individualized suspicion. E.g. N.G. v. Connecticut, 382 F.2d 225 (2nd Cir. 2004); Smook v. Minnehaha County Juvenile Detention Center, 457 F.2d 806 (8th Cir. 2006). In N.G., the court used the T.L.O. and Earls reasonableness balancing framework to weigh state and individual interests and concluded that suspicionless strip searches were reasonable even for youths admitted for violating a court order based on a status offense. The court emphasized the state's responsibility to act *in loco parentis* for juveniles in custody and found that detention facilities' "special needs" made searches without a individualized suspicion reasonable. The state's primary, non-law enforcement purposes in searching were "to protect the children from harm inflicted by themselves or other inmates, and to protect the safety of the institution." A strong dissent in N.G. objected that suspicionless strip-searches were severely intrusive and equated the level of Fourth Amendment protection afforded to young status offenders with that of prison inmates convicted of felonies. Moreover, the students subjected to suspicionless drug-testing in Vernonia and Earls had voluntarily engaged in the activity that required suspicion-less drug-testing, unlike the N.G. detainees.

In addition to institutional conditions inherent in confinement, pre-trial imprisonment significantly affects detained juveniles and their families.

Detention adversely affects youths' current employment and future job prospects, disrupts educational continuity, and separates them from their families. Negative self-labeling and the prisonization experience impair juveniles' ability to prepare a legal defense. Although most judges do not base initial decision systematically on offense criteria or other legally relevant factors, juveniles held in detention experience an increased likelihood of conviction and institutional confinement compared with non-detained youths. Feld, *Bad Kids*. After controlling for offense and prior records, juvenile courts processed more detained youths further into the system, adjudicated them delinquent more frequently, and sentenced them more severely than youths who remained at liberty.

Many policy analysts and professional organizations recommend that states use offense criteria, risk assessment instruments, or other administrative guidelines to reduce excessive pre-trial detention, to reserve detention for high risk youths, and to develop less restrictive alternatives for youths who pose minimal threat to public safety. The Annie E. Casey Foundation has sponsored efforts to reduce the use of pre-trial detention and to improve conditions of confinement through its Juvenile Detention and Alternatives Initiative (JDAI) (http://www.aecf.org). Some recommend that judges detain only those youths whom prosecutor charge with a serious violent crime which, if proven, would likely result in commitment to a secure facility, who escaped from an institution, or who had a demonstrated history of prior failures to appear.

ABA, *Juvenile Justice Standards Relating to Interim Status.*

In non-urban areas, police and juvenile courts often lack access to juvenile detention facilities and detain youths in adult jails under conditions even worse than those experienced by adult inmates. E.g. D.B. v. Tewksbury, 545 F. Supp. 896 (D.Or.1982) (condemning conditions of confinement for juveniles held in adult jails). Among its other purposes, the Federal Juvenile Justice and Delinquency Prevention Act (JJDP Act), 42 U.S.C. § 5602(a)(9) (2000), attempted "to assist State and local governments in removing juveniles from jails and lockups for adults." The JJDP Act requires states to submit a plan to carry out its purposes and to describe their implementation and compliance with jail-removal mandate. Among the other statutory requirements, the state plans require jailors not to detain juveniles in institutions in which they have contact with adults who are awaiting trial or who have been convicted of a crime—"sight and sound separation." 42 U.S.C. § 5633(13) (1998). However, institutional segregation frequently amounts to juveniles' solitary confinement in small cells which causes anxiety, exacerbates mental disorders, and increases risk of suicide. If properly segregated, states may detain delinquents in an adult jail for 24–hours if they are taken into custody outside a metropolitan area, if no acceptable alternative placement is available, and if distance or travel safety precludes transporting a youth to a juvenile detention facility. Despite the JJDP Act jail-removal mandate, states confine many youths in adult lockups despite the inability of jailors to assure youths' safety, to meet adolescents' unique nutritional needs or to provide educational and physical programs necessary for healthy development. Campaign for Youth Justice, *Jailing Juveniles: The Dangers of Incarcerating Youth in Adult Jails in America* (2007). States hold most youths transferred to criminal court for adult prosecution in jails rather than juvenile detention facilities, even though many juveniles are not convicted and only about one-quarter of those convicted receive a prison sentence.

CHAPTER 6

WAIVER OF JUVENILE COURT JURISDICTION

Between the mid–1980s and the early–1990s, many politicians advocated a get-tough response to increases in violent crimes, homicide, and offenses committed with guns by youths, especially by urban black males. Feld, *Bad Kids*. Public opinion and political leaders questioned juvenile courts' ability either to rehabilitate serious young offenders or to protect public safety. Legislative strategies to crack down and prosecute larger numbers of youths as adults included lowering the minimum age for transfer, increasing the number of offenses excluded from juvenile court jurisdiction, and shifting discretion from the judicial branch—judges in a waiver hearing—to the executive branch—prosecutors making charging decisions. Patricia Torbet, et al., *State Responses to Serious and Violent Juvenile Crime: Research Report* (1996). Although fourteen is the minimum age for transfer in most jurisdictions, some states permit waiver of youths as young as ten years or specify no minimum age and others states require adult prosecution of children as young as thirteen. Snyder and Sickmund, *National Report*. These strategies de-emphasized rehabilitation and individualized consideration of the offender, stressed personal and justice system accountability and punishment, based transfer decisions on a serious offense or prior record, and exposed waived youths to substantial sentences as adults. This chapter examines the boundary of children's "adult" criminal responsibility, the processes states use to decide whether to prosecute youths in juvenile or criminal courts, and the penal consequences of prosecuting youths as adults.

A. INTRODUCTION

Every state uses one or more statutory devices to prosecute some youths below the maximum age of juvenile court jurisdiction as adults. Although states' transfer laws vary considerably, all rely on variations of three general strategies—judicial waiver, legislative offense exclusion, and prosecutorial direct file—to prosecute children in criminal court. Barry C. Feld and Donna M. Bishop, "Transfer of Juveniles to Criminal Court," *Oxford Handbook of Juvenile Crime and Juvenile Justice* (2012). Each of these waiver strategies allocates to a different branch of government—judicial, legislative, or executive—the decision whether to try a youth in juvenile or criminal court. Judicial waiver allows juvenile court judges to transfer jurisdiction after conducting a hearing to determine whether a youth is amenable to treatment or poses a danger to the public. By contrast, legislatures may define juvenile courts' jurisdiction simply to exclude from their jurisdiction youths charged with serious offenses without any hearing. Finally, in about a dozen states, juvenile and criminal courts share concurrent jurisdiction and prosecutors can direct file or charge youths with serious crimes in either system without any judicial review of their charging or forum-selection decision. All waiver strategies attempt to reconcile the cultural conceptions of children as immature and innocent with the frightening reality that some youths commit heinous crimes. Waiver policies choose between conflicting constructions of young people as dependent and vulnerable and as autonomous and responsible, define the boundaries of criminal adulthood, and retrospectively ascribe criminal responsibility to some youths.

The jurisprudential disjunctions between the deterministic, rehabilitative premises of the juvenile justice system and the free will, punishment assumption of the criminal justice system emerge starkly in transfer laws. Although juvenile courts theoretically attempt to rehabilitate all young offenders, a small but significant number of youths may confound their efforts. These may be older delinquents nearing the maximum age of juvenile court jurisdiction, chronic recidivists who have not responded to prior intervention and for whom additional treatment may not succeed during the time remaining, or youths charged with serious crimes like rape, robbery, or murder who deserve longer sentences than those available in juvenile courts. Chronic juvenile offenders commit a disproportionate amount of serious and violent crime. Highly visible or serious offenses evoke community outrage or fear and legislators adopt harsh sanctions to punish them and to secure political advantage. Politicians and the public may view these youths as mature, sophisticated criminals rather than as children.

Waiver laws provide an important jurisdictional safety valve—they permit the expiatory sacrifice of some youths to quell political and public clamor, allow judges to demonstrate that they can protect the public, enable legislators to deflect pressures to lower the maximum age of juvenile court jurisdiction, and allow prosecutors and politicians to demonstrate that they are "tough on crime." Transfer laws implicate sentencing policy debates such as the tensions between rehabilitation, incapacitation, or retribution, between focusing on needs of the offender or the seriousness of the offense, between discretion and rules, and between indeterminacy and determinacy. Waiver laws attempt to reconcile contradictory impulses engendered when a child is a criminal and a criminal is a child.

The technical and administrative details of states' transfer laws vary considerably, but judicial waiver, legislative offense exclusion, and prosecutorial direct file represent the three general methods employed. E.g. Feld and Bishop, "Transfer of Juveniles to Criminal Court"; Snyder and Sickmund, *National Report*. Judicial waiver laws allow a juvenile court judge to waive jurisdiction on a discretionary basis after conducting a hearing to determine whether a youth is amenable to treatment, poses a danger to public safety, or simply if retaining jurisdiction "would be contrary to the best interests of the juvenile or of the public." These individualized assessments reflect the sentencing discretion juvenile courts routinely exercise and rely upon clinical evidence and social information about the youth as well as circumstances of the offense.

Legislative offense exclusion provisions frequently supplements judicial waiver provisions. This approach emphasizes the seriousness of the offense committed and reflects the retributive values of the criminal law. Legislatures create juvenile courts and possess considerable latitude to define their jurisdiction and to exclude youths from juvenile court based on their age and offense. A number of states, for example, exclude youths sixteen or older and charged with murder or a capital offense from juvenile court jurisdiction. E.g. Minn. Stat. Ann. § 260B.015 Subd. 5 (West 2000). Other states exclude even longer lists of offenses, such as criminal sexual conduct, arson, kidnapping, aggravated robbery, or the like. E.g. Alaska Stat. § 47.12.030 (Michie 2000); D.C. Code Ann. § 16–2301 (2000); Feld and Bishop, "Transfer of Juveniles to Criminal Court."

About a dozen states use a third method—prosecutorial waiver or direct file. In these states, juvenile and criminal courts share concurrent jurisdiction over certain ages and offenses—e.g., older youths charged with serious crimes—and prosecutors may select either a juvenile or criminal court in which to prosecute them. Snyder and Sickmund, *National Report*; Feld and Bishop, "Transfer of Juveniles to Criminal Court." Because of the constitutional doctrine of separation of powers, courts ordinarily do not review discretionary executive decisions and judicial opinions characterize prosecutorial transfer as an ordinary charging decision. E.g. Manduley v. Superior Court of San Diego County, 27 Cal.4th 537, 117 Cal.Rptr.2d 168, 41 P.3d 3 (Cal. 2002).

Each waiver strategy has supporters and critics. Proponents of judicial waiver endorse juvenile courts' rehabilitative philosophy, argue that individualized transfer decisions provide an appropriate balance of flexibility and severity, and allow for broader consideration of the child in the context of the offense. Critics object that judges lack valid or reliable clinical tools with which to accurately assess youths' amenability to treatment or to predict dangerousness and that their exercise of standardless discretion results in inconsistent and discriminatory decisions. Proponents of offense exclusion favor just deserts sentencing policies, advocate sanctions based on more objective factors such as offense seriousness and criminal history and value consistency, uniformity, and equality. Critics question whether legislators can remove judicial discretion without making the process excessively rigid and over-inclusive or simply shifting discretion to prosecutors in their charging decisions. Proponents of direct file claim that prosecutors can act as more neutral and objective gatekeepers than either "soft" judges or "get tough" legislators. Critics observe that prosecutors succumb to political pressures and symbolically posture on crime issues, exercise their discretion just as subjectively and idiosyncratically as do judges, and foster geographic variability in justice administration. Feld and Bishop, "Transfer of Juveniles to Criminal Court."

Selecting a waiver strategy from among these competing and contradictory claims implicates fundamental sentencing policy issues. For example, should waiver policy reflect juvenile or criminal court jurisprudence and focus primarily on individualized treatment of the offender or on punishment for serious offenses? If policy makers endorse criminal law's retributive values, then transfer decisions lend themselves to relatively mechanical rules based on present offense or prior record, excluded offenses, or presumptive waiver guidelines. If waiver policies reflect a commitment to offenders' rehabilitation, then judges require a more indeterminate and discretionary process to make individualized, clinical assessments of youths' amenability to treatment or dangerousness.

B. JUDICIAL WAIVER

Juvenile courts in most states exercise original and exclusive jurisdictions over youths below the age of eighteen years who violate the criminal law. From juvenile courts' inception, judges could deny some young offenders its protections and transfer them to criminal court. Judicial waiver hearings reflect juvenile courts' individualized, offender-oriented approach to deciding whether to treat a youth as a juvenile or to punish him as an adult. In Kent v. United States, 383 U.S. 541 (S.Ct.1966), the Court formalized the waiver process and required juvenile courts to provide some procedural due process protections. The Court did not require a formal hearing simply because juvenile courts conferred special benefits on delinquents, but because the decision whether or not to waive jurisdiction involved a factual dispute about the offender whose resolution required an adversarial hearing. The statute in Kent required the judge to conduct a "full investigation" although it gave the court "a substantial degree of discretion as to the factual considerations to be evaluated, the weight to be given them, and the conclusions to be reached." Kent concluded that the loss of juvenile court protections through a waiver decision was a "critically important" action that required a hearing, assistance of counsel, access to social investigations and other records, and written findings and conclusions capable of review by a higher court. "[T]here is no place in our system of law for reaching a result of such tremendous consequences without ceremony—without hearing, without effective assistance of counsel, without a statement of reasons." Although the Court decided Kent in the context of a federal statute adopted by Congress for the District of Columbia, its language suggested an underlying constitutional basis for requiring procedural due process in any judicial waiver decision. Kent's procedural requirements anticipated many of the safeguards that the Court later required for delinquency adjudications in In re Gault, 387 U.S. 1 (1967).

Subsequently, in Breed v. Jones, 421 U.S. 519 (S.Ct.1975), the Court applied the double jeopardy clause of the Fifth Amendment to delinquency convictions. The ruling required states to decide whether to try and sentence a youth as a juvenile or as an adult before proceeding to trial on the merits of the charge.

Kent and Breed provided the formal procedural framework within which judges conduct waiver hearings. However, the substantive bases on which judges decide to waive jurisdiction pose the principal difficulty. Until recently, waiver statutes allowed judges to transfer jurisdiction based on their assessment of subjective factors such as a youth's amenability to treatment or threat to public safety. The Court in Kent, for example, appended to its opinion a list of substantive criteria that juvenile court judges could consider when they conducted a "full investigation":

> An offense falling within the statutory limitations ... will be waived if it has prosecutive merit and if it is heinous or of an aggravated character, or—even though less serious—if it represents a pattern of repeated offenses which indicate that the juvenile may be beyond rehabilitation under Juvenile Court procedures, or if the public needs the protection afforded by such action.
>
> The determinative factors which will be considered by the Judge in deciding whether the Juvenile Court's jurisdiction over such offenses will be waived are the following:
>
> 1.   The seriousness of the alleged offense to the community and whether the protection of the community requires waiver.

2. Whether the alleged offense was committed in an aggressive, violent, premeditated or willful manner.

3. Whether the alleged offense was against persons or against property, greater weight being given to offenses against persons especially if personal injury resulted.

4. The prosecutive merit of the complaint, i.e., whether there is evidence upon which a Grand Jury may be expected to return an indictment. . . .

5. The desirability of trial and disposition of the entire offense in one court when the juvenile's associates in the alleged offense are adults. . . .

6. The sophistication and maturity of the juvenile as determined by consideration of his home, environmental situation, emotional attitude and pattern of living.

7. The record and previous history of the juvenile, including previous contacts with the Youth Aid Division, other law enforcement agencies, juvenile courts and other jurisdictions, prior periods of probation to this Court, or prior commitments to juvenile institutions.

8. The prospects for adequate protection of the public and the likelihood of reasonable rehabilitation of the juvenile (if he is found to have committed the alleged offense) by the use

of procedures, services and facilities currently available to the Juvenile Court.

States' judicial decisions and waiver statutes specify amenability criteria in various ways and frequently incorporate the general and contradictory list of Kent factors. However, waiver decisions are highly discretionary and judges need not assign equal weight to each of the waiver criteria. E.g. United States v. Nelson, 90 F.3d 636 (2d Cir.1996).

Some states limit jurisdictional waiver to felony offenses and establish a minimum age for criminal prosecutions, typically sixteen, fifteen, or fourteen. Snyder and Sickmund, *National Report*. Of the states that specify a minimum age for transfer, fourteen years of age is the most common and corresponds with the common law age of criminal responsibility. Other states impose neither offense limitations nor minimum age restrictions and remit the adulthood determination to each judge's discretion. Some states permit waiver at different ages for different offenses, for example, a sixteen-year-old charged with any felony, but a fourteen-year-old charged with murder or other serious crimes. Snyder and Sickmund, *National Report*.

1. WAIVER PROCEDURES

Prosecutors initiate a judicial waiver hearing by filing a transfer motion along with a delinquency petition. To avoid double-jeopardy under Breed v. Jones, the judge may not allow the juvenile to plead to the offenses alleged in the petition until the court determines whether it will try the youth in juvenile or criminal court. In a few states, a juvenile may request transfer or initiate a waiver proceeding. For example, a juvenile who wants a jury trial or who has an extensive prior record but whom the prosecutor charged with a relatively minor offense might prefer a trial in criminal rather than in juvenile court. However, absent statutory authority, courts do not allow youths to waive themselves to criminal court. In re K.A.A., 410 N.W.2d 836 (Minn.1987) (juvenile may not waive jurisdiction for some short-term benefit that ignores her own best interests); In re Anna Marie S., 99 Cal.App.3d 869, 160 Cal.Rptr. 495 (Cal.App.1979) (state interest in treating amenable juveniles under juvenile court law precludes youth from selecting forum for trial).

a. Probable Cause and Substantive Criteria

A judicial waiver hearing considers two separate issues: probable cause and whether the youth meets the substantive waiver criteria. State procedures often separate these distinct inquiries into two phases. E.g. N. C. Gen. Stat. §§ 7A–609; 7A–610 (1999). In Michigan, for example, court rules explicitly provide that a waiver hearing consists of two phases:

(1) First Phase. The first-phase hearing is to determine whether there is probable cause that an offense has been committed which if committed by an adult would be a felony, and that there is probable cause that the juvenile who is 14 years of age or older committed the offense . . .

(2) Second Phase. If the court finds the requisite probable cause at the first-phase hearing . . . the second-phase hearing shall be held to determine whether the interests of the juvenile and the public would best be served by granting the motion. Mich. R. Court–Probate Court 5.950 (West 1999)

The first inquiry addresses whether probable cause exists to believe that the child committed an offense and meets the age criteria. If the waiver statute restricts transfer eligibility to felonies or serious felonies committed after a specified age, then the judge must find probable cause that the youth meets those criteria. In many states, allegations of serious offenses create a presumption for waiver or shift the burden of proof to the juvenile to show why the juvenile court should retain jurisdiction. Judges must make specific probable cause findings to properly allocate burdens of proof in the waiver hearing. For example, in Minnesota, if the court finds probable cause to believe that a juvenile is sixteen- or seventeen-years of age and committed an offense for which the adult sentencing guidelines presume commitment to prison, then the waiver statute presumes that juvenile court will waive jurisdiction and the youth bears the burden of proof to show that it should retain jurisdiction. Minn. Stat. § 260B.125 Subd. 2a (West 2000). Courts routinely approve the use of offense criteria to create a rebuttable presumption for waiver and to shift the burden of proof to the juvenile. E.g. In re L.J.S., 539 N.W.2d 408 (Minn.Ct.App.1995); State in the Interest of A.L. 271 N.J.Super. 192, 638 A.2d

814 (N.J.Super.App.Div.1994). Some states only allow the prosecutor to use evidence that would be admissible at the adjudicatory hearing or trial to establish probable cause. E.g. N.C. Gen. Stat. § 7A–609(c) (2000); R.J.D. v. State, 799 P.2d 1122 (Okl.Cr.App.1990); People v. Hana, 443 Mich. 202, 504 N.W.2d 166 (Mich.1993) (only "legally admissible evidence" may be used to establish probable cause).

If the judge finds probable cause, then she must decide whether the youth meets the substantive criteria to waive jurisdiction. Some states focus on a child's amenability to treatment and instruct the judge to consider criminal sophistication, potential for rehabilitation, prior interventions, delinquent history and offense seriousness. Others states legislatively or judicially adopted the criteria appended to the Kent decision. Still other states focus on "the best interests of the juvenile and the public" and mandate judicial assessment of the seriousness of the offense, the juvenile's culpability in committing the offense, prior record, programming history, and the adequacy of punishment or treatment programs available in the juvenile system. Mich. Comp. Laws § 712A.4 (West 2000); Minn. Stat. § 260B.125 (West 2000). Juveniles have mounted due process and "void for vagueness" challenges to waiver statutes that allow judges to transfer a child found "not amenable to treatment" or "not a fit and proper subject." However, the vast majority of courts have rejected these constitutional challenges and upheld the statutes as sufficiently precise. E.g. Donald L. v.

Superior Court, 7 Cal.3d 592, 102 Cal.Rptr. 850, 498 P.2d 1098 (Cal.1972); State v. Smagula, 117 N.H. 663, 377 A.2d 608 (N.H.1977).

Although judges conduct waiver hearings informally and more like sentencing hearings than criminal trials, they are adversarial proceedings for which courts appoint counsel to assist juveniles. E.g. Kent v. U.S.; Mich. Comp. Laws § 712A.4 (West 2000) (right to counsel and appointment of counsel); N.C. Stat. § 7A–609 (counsel shall represent juvenile). Both the state and the juvenile may submit evidence relevant to the waiver criteria and may cross-examine the testimony and submissions of the other party. For example, a juvenile may cross-examine the probation officer who prepares a social report about the bases for her recommendations. E.g. In the Matter of Appeal in Maricopa County Juvenile Action No. JV127231, 183 Ariz. 263 902 P.2d 1367 (Ariz.Ct.App.1995). Counsel's role includes gathering favorable evidence, scrutinizing reports and recommendations of court personnel, and developing alternative placements to treat the youth within the juvenile process. Haziel v. United States, 404 F.2d 1275 (D.C.Cir.1968).

State laws differ on the burden of proof and who bears it in waiver proceedings. Because juvenile courts exercise original and exclusive jurisdiction and the state files a motion to commence transfer proceedings, the prosecution bears the initial burden of proof. Some states allow the judge to waive a youth based on a preponderance of the

evidence. E.g. Md. Cts. & Jud. Proc. Code Ann. § 3–
817(c); In re F.S., 586 P.2d 607 (Alaska 1978).
Others require the prosecutor to persuade the judge
to waive jurisdiction by clear and convincing
evidence. E.g. Minn. Stat. § 260B.125 (West 2000).
The state's burden of proof beyond a reasonable
doubt only applies to delinquency trials and not
waiver hearings. In re Winship, 397 U.S. 358
(S.Ct.1970); Chap. 7.A.2. In some states, once the
prosecutor establishes probable cause to believe that
a youth committed certain offenses, then the statute
shifts the burden to the juvenile to prove why she
should remain in juvenile court. E.g. Minn. Stat.
§ 260B.125 (West 2000). Courts regularly approve
presumptions that shift the burden to demonstrate
fitness to the juvenile. E.g. Sheila O. v. Superior
Court, 125 Cal.App.3d 812, 178 Cal.Rptr. 418
(1981); People v. Jones, 958 P.2d 393, 18 Cal.4th
667, 76 Cal.Rptr.2d 641 (Cal.1998).

Many states' laws include a provision of "once
waived, always waived." Once a juvenile court
waives jurisdiction over a child, prosecutors may file
any subsequent charges against a chronological
juvenile in criminal court. E.g. Ala. Code §§ 12–15–
1(8), 12–15–34(h) (2000); Miss. Code Ann. § 43–21–
157(8) (2000); Snyder and Sickmund, *National
Report.*

b. Evidence in Waiver Hearings

Courts characterize waiver hearings as
dispositional or sentencing proceedings and do not
apply rules of evidence as strictly as in criminal

trials. E.g. People v. Hana, 443 Mich. 202, 504 N.W.2d 166 (Mich.1993). Although a waiver hearing is an adversarial proceeding, a judge may base her findings on "informal but reliable evidence" including hearsay testimony. E.g. Three Minors, 684 P.2d 1121 (Nev.1984); Smith v. State, 475 So.2d 633 (Ala.Crim.App.1985); State v. Wright, 456 N.W.2d 661 (Iowa 1990). Courts normally admit police arrest and offense records, probation reports and social histories despite their hearsay content. E.g. In re T.D.S., 289 N.W.2d 137 (Minn.1980); People v. Taylor, 76 Ill.2d 289, 29 Ill.Dec. 103, 391 N.E.2d 366 (Ill.1979).

The Michigan Supreme Court in People v. Hana, 443 Mich. 202, 504 N.W.2d 166 (Mich.1993), considered whether Fifth and Sixth Amendment evidentiary limitations applied during the second or dispositional phase of the waiver hearing. At the waiver hearing, the state introduced statements obtained from the defendant. The Hana court held that Fifth and Sixth Amendment interrogation restrictions did not affect the admissibility of the statements in the waiver hearing because waiver was dispositional only and preceded any determination of guilt or innocence. Although the majority emphasized the flexibility and simplicity of the process, the dissent analogized between waiver and sentencing hearings and the Fifth Amendment limitations imposed by Estelle v. Smith, 451 U.S. 454 (S.Ct.1981). The dissent argued that because waiver increased the severity of the defendant's sentence, Estelle limited the authority of the state to compel or to use the defendant's statements.

Waiver hearings often focus on a juvenile's amenability to treatment and judges require expert testimony from psychologists or psychiatrists about her diagnosis and prognosis. Statutes and court rules authorize judges to obtain clinical evaluations to assess a child's amenability to treatment. If the state requires psychological or psychiatric evidence either to prove that a youth is not amenable to treatment or to rebut clinical evidence of fitness offered by a juvenile, then obtaining access to a child for a forensic assessment poses potential Fifth Amendment self-incrimination issues. In Estelle v. Smith, 451 U.S. 454 (S.Ct.1981), the Court held that the privilege against self-incrimination applied to court-ordered psychiatric examinations conducted for adult post-conviction sentencing hearings and restricted clinicians' permissible access and testimonial disclosures. Since Estelle, some state courts have held that any court-ordered psychological evaluation to determine amenability violates a youth's Fifth Amendment rights. E.g., R.H. v. State, 777 P.2d 204 (Alaska Ct.App.1989); In the Interest of A.D.G., 895 P.2d 1067 (Colo.Ct.App.1994) (juvenile has a privilege against self-incrimination and cannot be compelled to submit to interview over his objection). Other states require a youth's attorney to accompany her at a clinical interview. E.g. Christopher P. v. State, 816 P.2d 485, 489 (N.M.1991).

Courts and legislatures attempt to balance the need for psychiatric evidence in waiver hearings with the strictures against compelled self-incrimination. Some states resolve the dilemma by requiring a juvenile to submit to a psychiatric or psychological examination in order to obtain a clinical evaluation and then provide use immunity and limit any references to clinical evidence in subsequent delinquency or criminal trials. E.g. In re S.R.J., 293 N.W.2d 32 (Minn.1980); United States v. A.R., 38 F.3d 699 (3d Cir.1994) (no statements made by juvenile in psychiatric interview could be used in subsequent criminal proceeding). Other jurisdictions bar a juvenile from introducing expert testimony on the youth's amenability to treatment if she does not submit to an examination by an expert for the state. E.g., Commonwealth v. Wayne W., 606 N.E.2d 1323, 1330 (Mass.1993) (juvenile who testifies waives his privilege and may be compelled to respond to questions posed by the State). If a youth's attorney obtains a clinical evaluation to aid the defense in a waiver hearing, some states allow the prosecution to call the psychiatrist as a witness in its subsequent criminal trial. The court in State v. Rhomberg, 516 N.W.2d 803 (Iowa 1994), held that the doctor-patient privilege did not apply because the juvenile consulted the psychiatrist for litigation rather than to aid in treatment.

If a juvenile testifies about the alleged offense at a certification hearing, then may the prosecutor introduce that testimony in a subsequent delinquency or criminal trial? E.g., Simmons v. United States, 390 U.S. 377, 394 (S.Ct.1968) (defendant's testimony in support of a motion to suppress evidence on Fourth Amendment grounds can not be used against him at trial). In Ramona R. v. Superior Court, 693 P.2d 789 (Cal.1985), the

California Supreme Court granted juveniles use-immunity for any statements made during a certification hearing and barred their use in any subsequent delinquency or criminal trial. The court in Ramona R. analogized to the dangers of self-incrimination posed for probationers in revocation hearings and reasoned that without use-immunity, a juvenile could not contest a certification motion. In other jurisdictions, statutes grant juveniles immunity to testify at a waiver hearing. E.g. N.J. Stat. Ann. § 2A:4A–29 (West 2000) (no testimony at a waiver hearing will be admissible in any hearing to determine delinquency or guilt of a crime); State v. Ferguson, 255 N.J.Super. 530, 605 A.2d 765 (N.J.Super.Ct.App.1992); Commonwealth v. Ransom, 446 Pa. 457, 288 A.2d 762 (Pa.1972) (evidence given at a waiver hearing inadmissible in any other proceedings).

In practice, judges focus on three sets of factors to assess youths' amenability to treatment and dangerousness. First, a youth's age and the time remaining within juvenile court jurisdiction limit the court's sentencing options and provide impetus to waive older juveniles, particularly those accused of a serious offense. Judges waive older youths more readily than younger offenders. Second, judges focus on a youth's treatment prognosis as reflected in clinical evaluations and prior treatment interventions. Once youth exhaust available correctional resources, transfer becomes more likely. Finally, judges assess a youth's dangerousness based on the seriousness of the offense, the prior record, and whether the youth used a firearm.

Waiver criteria framed in terms of amenability to treatment or dangerousness give judges wide discretion. Lists of contradictory substantive factors, such as those appended in Kent, do not provide adequate guidance and instead allow judges selectively to emphasize one variable or another to justify any decision. The subjective nature of waiver decisions, the absence of guidelines to shape outcomes, and the lack of valid or reliable clinical instruments with which to classify youths allows judges to make unequal and disparate decisions without effective procedural or appellate checks. Empirical evaluations indicate that judges may apply waiver statutes in an idiosyncratic, unfair, and biased manner. Feld, *Bad Kids*; Feld and Bishop, "Transfer of Juveniles to Criminal Court." Different states' rates of judicial waiver for similar types of offenders vary considerably. Within a single jurisdiction, judges interpret and apply waiver statutes inconsistently from county to county and from court to court. In some states, rural judges waive jurisdiction over similarly-charged youths more readily than do urban judges. Even within a single urban county, several judges in the same court decided cases of similarly-situated offenders differently. Youths' race consistently affects waiver decisions and judges transfer minority juveniles at higher rates than they do comparable white offenders. Snyder and Sickmund, *National Report*; Feld and Bishop, "Transfer of Juveniles to Criminal Court."

c. Appellate Review of Waiver Decisions

Kent required trial judges to make specific findings of fact and conclusions of law to permit meaningful appellate review. If a judge's transfer order does not include a sufficient statement of reasons, then appellate courts reverse for specific findings. E.g. People v. Dunbar, 423 Mich. 380, 377 N.W.2d 262 (Mich.1985); C.L.A. v. State, 137 Ga.App. 511, 224 S.E.2d 491 (Ga.App.1976). They also reverse trial judges if they fail to adhere to statutory procedures or to make required findings. E.g., Harden v. Commonwealth, 885 S.W.2d 323, 325 (Ky.App.1994) (reasons for transfer "must be specific enough to permit meaningful review for the purpose of determining whether there has been compliance with the statute"); State v. Collins, 694 So.2d 624 (La.App.1997) (trial court must specifically address the transfer criteria); State v. Sonja B., 395 S.E.2d 803, 807 (W.Va.1990) (juvenile judge failed to review psychological evaluations or comply with statutory requirement to make a detailed analysis of child's mental condition, maturity, emotional attitude, and other personal factors). Appellate courts occasionally fault a judge for failing to consider a juvenile's amenability to treatment and focusing solely on the seriousness of the alleged offense. E.g. In the Matter of J.D.W., 881 P.2d 1324 (Mont.1994); In the Matter of J.K.C., 891 P.2d 1169 (Mont.1995).

Transferred juveniles frequently appeal judges' adverse waiver decisions while unsuccessful prosecutors appeal in cases in which the juvenile court denied the transfer motion. Most states do not allow juveniles to appeal a transfer order until there is a final judgment, i.e. a criminal conviction. E.g., In re Clay, 246 N.W.2d 263 (Iowa 1976); State ex rel. Snellgrove v. Porter Circuit and Juvenile Courts, 386 N.E.2d 680 (Ind. 1979) (holding that "there is not right to an immediate appeal, but rather . . . must await final determination of criminal prosecution authorized by waiver." For example, Florida law does not treat waiver transfers as final orders and requires conviction in criminal court before the defendant may appeal. In the Interest of R.J.B. v. State, 408 So.2d 1048 (Fla. 1982). Other states allow a juvenile to appeal a waiver decision because it terminates juvenile court jurisdiction and constitutes a final order. In re I.Q.S., 309 Minn. 78, 244 N.W.2d 30 (Minn.1976); State ex rel. Atcheson, 575 P.2d 181 (Utah 1978); State v. Harwood, 572 P.2d 1228 (Idaho 1977) ("order waiving juvenile jurisdiction constitutes final order . . . and further proceedings shall be held in abeyance pending determination of that question."). States allow prosecutors to bring an immediate appeal if a judge denies a waiver motion because Breed v. Jones would preclude criminal reprosecution if the state first tried the youth in juvenile court. E.g. People v. Martin, 67 Ill.2d 462, 367 N.E.2d 1329 (Ill.1977).

Appellate courts seldom reverse waiver decisions on substantive grounds and defer to trial judges' discretion either to retain or to waive jurisdiction. In part, the vague and contradictory statutory criteria, such as those appended in Kent, limit appellate courts' ability to rigorously review trial judges' discretionary decisions. Ordinary standards of review—"substantial evidence," "clearly erroneous," or "abuse of discretion"—and appellate courts' deference to trial courts' fact-finding lead them to affirm juvenile judges' substantive decisions, most often to waive jurisdiction. E.g. Jeremiah B. v. State, 823 P.2d 883 (Nev.1991). On the other hand, appellate courts appear more inclined to substitute their judgment of the facts and reverse trial judges' decisions to retain jurisdiction over the juvenile. E.g. People v. Jones, 958 P.2d 393, 18 Cal.4th 667, 76 Cal.Rptr.2d 641 (Cal.1998); In re D.F.B., 433 N.W.2d 79 (Minn.1988). Not surprisingly, cases in which appellate courts order a juvenile transferred to criminal court typically involve youths charged with serious offenses. E.g. People v. Fultz, 554 N.W.2d 725 (Mich.1996); People in the Interest of Y.C., 581 N.W.2d 483 (S.D.1998).

C. LEGISLATIVE OFFENSE EXCLUSION

Legislative exclusion statutes remove from juvenile court jurisdiction youths of a certain age and charged with certain offenses. Legislatures enact juvenile court statutes and define their jurisdiction, powers, and purposes in many different ways. For example, states currently set juvenile courts' maximum age jurisdiction at seventeen, sixteen, or fifteen-years-old as a matter of state policy and without constitutional infirmity. See Chapter 2. Because juvenile courts exist only as creatures of the legislature, what lawmakers create, they also may take away. "[T]he legislature could

. . . withhold the protection of the doctrine of *parens patriae* from all juveniles exceeding fifteen years of age. What the legislature may do absolutely, it may do conditionally. . . ." State v. Green, 218 Kan. 438, 544 P.2d 356 (Kan.1975); People v. Jiles, 43 Ill.2d 145, 148, 251 N.E.2d 529, 531 (Ill.1969) (nothing in the federal or state constitutions requires a state to maintain a juvenile court). If a legislature defines juvenile court jurisdiction to include only youths below a jurisdictional age and whom prosecutors charge with a non-excluded offense, then, by statutory definition other chronological juveniles are adult criminal defendants.

More than half the states exclude at least some offense from juvenile court jurisdiction, most commonly serious crimes by older juveniles. Snyder and Sickmund, *National Report*; Feld and Bishop, "Transfer of Juveniles to Criminal Court." For example, some states exclude youths sixteen years of age or older and charged with murder, rape, or kidnapping. E.g. Alaska Stat. § 47.12.030 (West 2000). Others exclude youths charged with those offenses at age fifteen, e.g. La. Child. Code Art. 305, at age fourteen, e.g. Va. Code § 16.1–2691 (West 2000), at age thirteen, e.g. Ok. Tit. 10 § 7306–1.1 (West 2000), or with no minimum age restriction, e.g. Nev. Stat. § 62.040 (West 2000). Some states exclude capital offenses by youths aged fourteen or older and longer lists of serious crimes by those aged sixteen or older. E.g. Md. Stat. § 3–804 (West 2000).

Youths excluded from juvenile court have challenged their automatic adulthood and trial in

criminal courts as violations of the Fourteenth
Amendment's due process and equal protection
clauses. Youths argue that prosecution in criminal
court violates due process because they do not
receive procedural safeguards required by Kent and
judges do not review the prosecutors' charging
decisions that led to their removal. Juveniles argue
that the legislative decision to classify youths
charged with certain offenses as adults violates
equal protection because it constitutes an irrational
and arbitrary classification. E.g. Cox v. United
States, 473 F.2d 334 (4th Cir.1973), cert. denied,
414 U.S. 869 (1973), United States v. Bland, 472
F.2d 1329 (D.C.Cir.1972), cert. denied, 412 U.S. 909
(1973); People v. Thorpe, 641 P.2d 935 (Colo.1982).

After the Kent decision, the United States
Congress amended the waiver provision of the
District of Columbia's Juvenile Code at issue in that
case. Following the amendments, juvenile court
jurisdiction continued until age eighteen for most
offenses but Congress excluded from its jurisdiction
youths sixteen-or seventeen-years of age and
charged with violent crimes such as murder and
armed robbery. D.C. Code § 16–2031(3)(A) (Supp.
1970). In United States v. Bland, 472 F.2d 1329
(D.C.Cir.1972), cert. denied, 412 U.S. 909 (1973),
the leading case on legislative offense exclusion
statutes, the prosecutor charged sixteen-year-old
Bland with armed robbery—an excluded offense—
and prosecuted him as an adult in criminal court.
Bland argued that he should receive Kent
procedural safeguards as a prerequisite to waiver
because of the critical differences between juvenile

and criminal prosecution. He asserted that the consequences for the juvenile are the same whether a judge waived jurisdiction or a legislature excluded and a prosecutor charged a youth in criminal court. The Bland majority rejected his argument that the comparable consequences flowing from legislative or prosecutorial waivers necessitate comparable procedural safeguards. It declined to impose any procedural requirements or to review prosecutors' charging decisions. It relied on the well-established separation-of-powers doctrine that judges do not review prosecutors' exercises of discretion unless they intentionally create discriminatory or invidious classifications. In a challenge to a prosecutorial waiver statute, the court in Cox v. United States, 473 F.2d 334 (4th Cir.1973), cert. denied, 414 U.S. 869 (1973), specifically rejected procedural safeguards to limit the exercise of prosecutorial discretion.

Courts do not review prosecutors' charging decisions because constitutional separation of powers denies the judicial branch the power to compel or control discretionary decisions made by members of the executive branch. Unless prosecutors' decisions create invidious classifications based on race, religion, or the like, that violate equal protection, courts do not review decisions about whether and whom to charge with what offenses. E.g., Oyler v. Boles, 368 U.S. 448, 456 (S.Ct.1962); Wayte v. United States, 470 U.S. 598 (S.Ct.1985); United States v. Armstrong, 517 U.S. 456 (S.Ct.1996). Judicial reluctance to encumber prosecutors' discretion stems from a fear of intruding on sensitive legal and policy judgments. If judicial review entailed the power to compel prosecutors to present or dismiss a case, then judges might prevent prosecutors from maximizing enforcement effectiveness through selective prosecution or force them to misallocate resources. Courts decline to review prosecutors' decisions because of the need to maintain secrecy during an investigation. A fitness hearing prior to the filing of charges could divulge confidential sources. Additionally, the factors that influence prosecutors' charging decisions—evaluations of evidence and guilt, resource allocation, and other enforcement policies and priorities—seldom provide a written record for pretrial judicial review.

Courts review claims of selective or discriminatory enforcement by prosecutors only when the defendant presents clear evidence of an intentional equal protection violation, for example, selecting some defendants on the basis of their race and not prosecuting other similarly-situated offenders of a different race. E.g. United States v. Armstrong, 517 U.S. 456 (S.Ct.1996). In order to prevail, the defendant must demonstrate both that the "prosecutorial policy had a discriminatory effect and that it was motivated by a discriminatory purpose." Thus, a defendant must establish that charging decisions have an invidious impact *and* an improper motive. Under Armstrong, a youth prosecuted in criminal court for an excluded offense would have an almost insuperable burden to show that the prosecutor intentionally charged him because of his race and declined to prosecute as adults other youths of different races who committed the same offense.

A strong dissent in Bland decried the offense-exclusion statute as a transparent effort to evade Kent's due process requirements. Unlike a judicial waiver hearing, offense-exclusion allows prosecutors to waive a juvenile based on the probable cause of a charging decision and without a hearing, consideration of amenability to treatment, a statement of reasons, or the appointment of counsel. However, many prosecutorial decisions have great consequences for defendants—the decision not to charge, the decision to charge conduct as a misdemeanor rather than a felony, the decision to invoke any one of several applicable statutes.

Offense-exclusion legislation forecloses any consideration of a youth's amenability to juvenile treatment. The only factual issues involved in a charging decision relate to the nature of the offense, probable cause, and provable legal guilt. A criminal trial provides the most rigorous review of a prosecutor's initial factual determinations—proof beyond a reasonable doubt. Offense exclusion laws focus on the crime charged rather than characteristics of the offender.

Youths have argued that offense-exclusion laws violate equal protection by creating an arbitrary and irrational statutory distinction—criminal or delinquent status—based on serious or minor offenses. Courts reject such claims and note that classification on the basis of offenses involves neither an inherently suspect class nor an invidious discrimination and the loss of juvenile treatment does not infringe upon a fundamental right or preferred liberty that requires strict judicial scrutiny. E.g. United States v. Bland, 472 F.2d 1329 (D.C.Cir.1972). Courts find a rational basis to distinguish between youths charged with serious and minor offenses as a class because legislators reasonably believe that serious offenders are not amenable to treatment, pose a danger to public safety, would cost too much to try to rehabilitate, would be detrimental to the rehabilitation of other more amenable youths in the juvenile system, or simply because they deserve more punishment for their offenses. Rehabilitative juvenile courts assume that offenders differ and that no direct relationship exists between their offenses and their real needs. Legislators conclusively presume that youths who commit serious crimes differ from those who commit minor offenses.

When statutes exclude youths from juvenile court based on allegations of certain offenses and then a criminal court subsequently convicts them of non-excluded, lesser included offenses, jurisdictions differ as to whether the court should sentence the youth as an adult or return the youth to juvenile court for a delinquency disposition. Some courts hold that the excluded offenses also subsume all lesser included offenses and that once the state tries a youth as an adult, he cannot invoke the post-verdict sentencing benefits of the juvenile court. E.g. State v. Morales, 240 Conn. 727, 694 A.2d 758 (Conn.1997); State v. Behl, 564 N.W.2d 560 (Minn.1997). Other jurisdictions provide that a youth convicted of a lesser-included, non-excluded offense should be sentenced as a juvenile unless the state conducts a post-conviction waiver hearing to decide whether to sentence him as an adult. E.g. 705 Ill. Comp. Stat. 405 § 5–130 (West 2000); Or. Rev. Stat. § 419C.361 (West 2000); Ky. Rev. Stat. Ann. § 640.010(3) (Michie 2000). Decisions like Morales and Behl which divest jurisdiction on the basis of the charges filed, rather than the ultimate conviction, invite prosecutors to over-charge youths to exclude them from juvenile court and to obtain longer sentences in criminal court. Conviction of a lesser-included, non-excluded offense repudiates the prosecutor's evaluation of the seriousness of the crime that warranted adult prosecution. Judicial policies that militate against reviewing a prosecutor's charging decision before trial do not preclude re-examining it after the fact. One rationale of Bland was that a criminal jury trial provided the best evaluation of the prosecutor's offense-based evaluation. If a jury convicts a youth of a lesser offense that would not exclude him as an adult under the legislative criteria, then juvenile court jurisdiction over the offender should be revived for purposes of disposition. Basing dispositions on the conviction offense provides an important check on prosecutors' abuse of discretion.

D. CONCURRENT JURISDICTION AND PROSECUTORIAL DIRECT FILE

Some states' create concurrent jurisdiction in juvenile and criminal courts over certain offenses and give prosecutors discretion to direct file or

charge youths of certain ages with the same offense
in either forum. Unlike offense-exclusion where
charges only for certain offenses can result in
criminal prosecution, direct file laws give
prosecutors even greater discretion to choose the
forum. For example, Arkansas' juvenile and
criminal courts share concurrent jurisdiction over
youths sixteen years or older who commit any
felony, and over youths fourteen years of age or
older who commit one of eighteen enumerated
violent crimes or who have three prior felony
convictions. A prosecutor can charge a youth with
the same offense in either justice system. E.g. Ark.
Code Ann. § 9–27–318(b) (Michie 1997). Similarly,
in Florida, the state attorney may direct file a
criminal charge against any youth sixteen or
seventeen years of age who committed any felony as
well as against any youth fourteen or fifteen years
of age who committed one of fifteen enumerated
offenses, including murder, robbery, and sexual
battery, "when in the state attorney's judgment and
discretion the public interest requires that adult
sanctions be considered or imposed." Fla. Stat. Ann.
§ 985.227(1)(a)–(b) (West 1997). In direct file
jurisdictions, the prosecutor makes two types of
decisions: whether probable cause exists to believe
that the youth committed a particular offense and, if
that offense is one for which concurrent jurisdiction
exists, whether to charge the youth in juvenile or
criminal court. Prosecutors' expertise to evaluate
sufficiency of evidence or to select charges does not
provide any unique professional insight for the
juvenile or criminal court forum selection decision.

About a dozen states allow prosecutors to charge youths of certain ages and offenses in either the juvenile or criminal justice systems. Snyder and Sickmund, *National Report*; Feld and Bishop, "Transfer of Juveniles to Criminal Court." Unlike legislative offense-exclusion, in which the offense alleged determines juvenile or criminal jurisdiction, direct file laws allow the prosecutor to select the forum without engaging in any charging subterfuges. In most direct file states, the statute provides no guidelines, standards, or criteria to control the prosecutors' choice of forum. Two states guide prosecutors' jurisdictional discretion with Kent-like statutory criteria. E.g. Neb. Rev. Stat. 43–276 (1997); Wyo. Stat. Ann. § 14–6–273(b)(i)–(vii) (1997). Unlike a judicial waiver hearing, where psychologists and court services personnel can provide a judge with information about a youth's maturity, criminal sophistication, or amenability to treatment based on clinical evaluations, social service reports, and forensic interviews, prosecutors typically lack access to personal information because of juveniles' Fifth Amendment privilege against self-incrimination. The absence of specific criteria or review procedures contributes to idiosyncratic and inconsistent practices and geographic variability in forum selection decisions.

Although youths have challenged direct file laws that delegate discretion to prosecutors to choose a youth's juvenile or criminal status, appellate courts invoke the rationale of Bland and reject their claims. In upholding its direct file law, the Florida Supreme Court noted that "prosecutorial discretion

is itself an incident of the constitutional separation
of powers, and that as a result the courts are not to
interfere with the free exercise of the discretionary
powers of the prosecutor in his control over criminal
prosecutions." State v. Cain, 381 So.2d 1361
(Fla.Sup.Ct.1980); Jahnke v. State, 692 P.2d 911
(Wyo.Sup.Ct.1984) (discretion vested in prosecutor
to proceed against a youth in either the juvenile or
criminal court does not violate the constitution).
Based on Bland's separation of powers rationale,
courts uphold prosecutorial waiver statutes with
virtual unanimity. E.g. Walker v. State, 309 Ark.
23, 827 S.W.2d 637 (Ark.1992); Chapman v. State,
259 Ga. 592, 385 S.E.2d 661 (Ga.1989); Myers v.
District Court, 518 P.2d 836 (Colo.1974).

In Manduley v. Superior Court, 27 Cal.4th 537,
117 Cal.Rptr.2d 168, 41 P.3d 3 (Cal.2002), the
California Supreme Court reviewed juveniles'
challenges to Proposition 21 which abrogated the
judicial waiver statute and granted prosecutors
authority to direct file criminal charges against
youths as young as fourteen years of age for
enumerated serious offenses. Juveniles claimed that
the provisions violated separation of powers by
giving prosecutors, rather than judges, the
authority to determine the sentence imposed.
However, the Court emphasized prosecutors'
traditional charging discretion and noted that many
decisions made before the filing of charges affect
subsequent dispositional options without
unconstitutionally intruding on the judicial
sentencing function. The Court rejected the
juveniles' due process challenge by noting that

unlike the situation in Kent, where the juvenile court had original and exclusive jurisdiction, they do not possess any protected interest in being subject to the jurisdiction of the juvenile court and therefore enjoyed no right to procedural protections. The Court rejected the juveniles' equal protection analysis by emphasizing that many statutes impose different penalties for the same course of conduct and prosecutors enjoy discretion to choose among such alternatives as long as they do not do so on a discriminatory basis.

The singular deviation from appellate approval of prosecutorial waiver occurred in State v. Mohi, 901 P.2d 991 (Utah 1995), where the Utah Supreme Court struck down the state's direct file provision because it denied waived juveniles the "uniform operation" of state laws. The Utah statute, like those in other concurrent jurisdictions, allowed prosecutors to charge some youths with serious offenses in juvenile court while prosecuting other youths charged with identical offenses in criminal court. Mohi argued that the legislation created an unreasonable and arbitrary classification because it did not provide any reasons to permit similarly-situated youths to receive such disparate consequences. The Mohi court construed a provision of the state constitution which required "uniform operation" of laws to require treating similarly-situated offenders similarly, unless the differences in treatment reasonably tended to further the statutory objectives. Because the statute contained no criteria or guidelines to guide prosecutors' forum selection decisions, the court could find no reasons for prosecutors to charge some youths in criminal court and other youths of the same age with the same offenses in juvenile court. Although the court conceded the legislature's broad authority to create classes of youths for adult prosecution—for example, serious offenders, repeat offenders, or those who used guns—the court required lawmakers to specify relevant criteria rather than to create a system which allowed prosecutors' decisions to create the classification.

1.   REVERSE WAIVER, TRANSFER BACK, AND BLENDED SENTENCING

Progressive reformers created separate juvenile courts and correctional institutions to avoid confining vulnerable youths in prisons with adults. Legislative policies to transfer more and younger juveniles to criminal courts expose more youths to adult correctional consequences. Because many excluded offenses carry mandatory minimum sentences, juveniles charged and convicted as adults also face greater prospects of incarceration. Juveniles confined in prisons are more likely to be victims of violent attacks, more likely to experience sexual assaults, and more likely to commit suicide than those confined in juvenile facilities. Feld, *Bad Kids*.

In order to restore some flexibility to a prosecutor-dominated process and to allow for appropriate dispositions of amenable younger offenders, many states allow judges to reverse waive or transfer back to juvenile court cases that originated in criminal court as a result of excluded offenses or prosecutorial direct file charging decisions. E.g., N.Y. Crim. Proc. Law § 725.10 (McKinney 1992); Feld and Bishop, "Transfer of Juveniles to Criminal Court." More than half of direct file and excluded offense jurisdictions allow a criminal court judge either to return a youth to juvenile court for trial or sentencing, or to impose a juvenile or youthful offender sentence in lieu of an adult criminal sentence. E.g. Ark. Code Ann § 9–27–318(d) (Michie 1993 & Supp. 1995); Fla. Stat. § 985.233 (West 1997); Neb. Rev. Stat. § 43–261 (1993); Ga. Code Ann. § 15–11–5(b)(2)(B) (1994); Md. Code Art. 27 § 594A (Michie 1997). In some states, laws that place a youth initially in criminal court create a presumption of unfitness and shift the burden of proof to the juvenile to demonstrate why the judge should return her to juvenile court for trial or disposition. E.g., Walker v. State, 803 S.W.2d 502 (Ark.1991); Wyo. Stat. Ann. § 14–6–237(g)(Supp. 1995). In other excluded offense jurisdictions, the prosecutor may make a "reverse waiver" decision. In Georgia, for example, the criminal court has exclusive jurisdiction over youths thirteen to seventeen years of age and charged with murder, rape, or armed robbery, but the district attorney "may, after investigation and for extraordinary cause," prosecute the youth in juvenile court instead. Ga.Code Ann. § 15–11–5(2)(C) (1997). In most states, however, a criminal court judge makes "reverse waiver" or "transfer back" decisions under provisions that recreate the

Kent-style proceedings that originally impelled states to adopt offense exclusion or direct file laws.

In lieu of transfer-back provisions, some states give criminal court judges the option to sentence a youth as a delinquent. In Florida, for example, except for juveniles convicted of offenses punishable by death or life imprisonment, criminal court judges retain the option to sentence youths convicted as adults "to the department for treatment in an appropriate program for children outside the adult correctional system or be placed in a community control program for juveniles." Fla. Stat. Ann. § 985.233(1)(a) (West 1997). When deciding whether to impose juvenile delinquency or adult criminal sanctions, the statute requires judges to review a pre-sentence investigation report, to conduct a sentencing hearing, and to base the decision on eight enumerated criteria that closely mirror those appended in Kent. E.g. Troutman v. State, 630 So.2d 528 (Fla.1993). A similar procedure exists in Arkansas, where juvenile and criminal courts share concurrent jurisdiction over certain ages and offenses, and the prosecutor elects in which forum to try the case. Ark. Code Ann. § 9–27–318 (Michie 1997). A youth charged in criminal court may request the judge to conduct a transfer hearing at which the court will consider "the seriousness of the offense," whether the juvenile is "beyond rehabilitation under existing rehabilitation programs," and the prior record, "character traits, mental maturity, and any other factor which reflects upon the juvenile's prospects for rehabilitation." Ark. Code Ann. § 9–27–318 (e) (Michie 1997). Using these Kent-like criteria, the court must find that the juvenile should be tried as an adult "by clear and convincing evidence," a higher standard of proof than required in many states' judicial waiver proceedings. Ark. Code Ann. § 9–27–318 (f) (Michie 1997).

Another strategy to sentence serious young offenders is "blended sentencing." Torbet, *State Responses*. These laws attempt to meld the rehabilitative sentencing authority of juvenile courts with the threat of criminal sanctions and provide longer delinquency sentences that would otherwise be available in juvenile courts. Delinquency sentences differ from criminal sentences because juvenile courts lose authority over offenders when they attain the maximum dispositional age or some other statutory termination date. As a result, when juvenile courts sentence older chronic offenders or youths convicted of serious crimes, they may be unable to impose sanctions proportional to the youth's culpability and seriousness of the offense. Statutes that increase juvenile courts' punitive capacity or give criminal courts a juvenile sentencing option represent another type of offense-based sentencing strategy for violent and persistent offenders. Blended sentencing laws meld the authority of juvenile with criminal courts, provide longer sentences than juvenile courts otherwise could impose, or increase the rehabilitative options available to criminal courts. E.g. Feld, *Bad Kids*; Torbet, *State Responses*. Blended sentences provide juvenile courts with the option to punish as well as to treat and criminal courts with a treatment alternative to imprisonment for some youths. Several variants of youthful offender, blended or extended jurisdiction sentences exist depending on whether prosecutors try the youth initially in juvenile or in criminal court.

A youthful offender status preserves therapeutic sentencing options for youths tried as adults in criminal court. It provides an intermediate sentencing option for juveniles tried as adults and for young adult offenders. These laws place youths aged sixteen to twenty-one years at the time of sentencing either in separate facilities or in age-segregated sections within adult facilities, limit the sentence to a shorter period than that authorized for adults, and provide some relief from collateral consequences of conviction following successful completion of the sentence. The California Youth Authority Act enables criminal court judges to sentence young adults and waived youths convicted as adults to the Youth Authority for housing and programs, rather than to prison, and retains jurisdiction until age twenty-five. Cal. Welf. & Inst. Code § 1731.5 (West 2000). Florida prosecutors charge many juveniles in criminal court and the state's Youthful Offender law provides judges with an alternative to sentencing them as adults. Fla. Stat. § 958 (2000). A criminal court judge may sentence a youth either as a youthful offender or to prison following Kent-type statutory criteria. Other states give judges the option to sentence youths convicted as adults to a youthful offender status in lieu of prison. Torbet, *State Responses*.

A second version of blended sentencing allows juvenile court judges to impose enhanced sentences beyond those used for ordinary delinquents for youths tried in juvenile court. Barry C. Feld, *Violent Youth and Public Policy: A Case Study of Juvenile Justice Law Reform*, 79 Minn. L. Rev. 965 (1995); Torbet, *State Responses*. New Mexico, Minnesota, and Texas represent different versions of these enhanced sanctions for youths tried in juvenile court. New Mexico classifies juveniles as a "delinquent offender," "youthful offender," or "serious youthful offender." N.M.Stat.Ann. § 32A–2–3(C), (H), (I) (Michie 2000). The prosecutor charges a youth in one of these categories based on age and offense. A youth sixteen or seventeen years of age and charged with first degree murder constitutes a serious youthful offender whom the court *must sentence* as an adult. Youthful offenders consist of juveniles aged fifteen to eighteen years of age charged with specified aggravated or violent crimes. Delinquents and youthful offenders enjoy a statutory right to a jury trial in juvenile court and the same judge presides whether a case is tried as a juvenile or criminal proceeding. Following conviction as a youthful offender, the judge conducts a quasi-waiver sentencing hearing to decide whether to sentence the juvenile as an adult or as a youthful offender. Based on the judge's assessment of a youth's "amenability to treatment or rehabilitation," she may impose either an adult criminal sentence or a juvenile disposition with jurisdiction extended until age twenty-one. N.M. Stat.Ann. § 32A–2–20 (Michie 2000).

Minnesota proceeds against some serious young offenders in Extended Jurisdiction Juvenile (EJJ) prosecutions. Minn.Stat.Ann. § 260B.130 (2000). Youths eligible for EJJ prosecution include sixteen- and seventeen years olds charged with presumptive commitment to prison offenses, youths whom judges declined to waive to criminal courts, and younger juveniles whom judges determine meet offense-based public safety criteria in an EJJ hearing. Feld, *Violent Youth*; In re L.J.S., 539 N.W.2d 408 (Minn.Ct.App.1995) (upholding authority of prosecutor to designate older juveniles as EJJs). Although tried in juvenile courts, EJJ youths receive adult procedural safeguards including the right to a jury trial. The right to a jury is an essential component of this quasi-adult status, because judges impose both a delinquency disposition and a stayed criminal sentence pending successful completion of the juvenile sentence. Minn. Stat. Ann. § 260B.130 (2000). EJJ status extends juvenile dispositional jurisdiction until age twenty-one rather than age nineteen, as for ordinary delinquents. If an EJJ youth violates conditions of the juvenile sentence, then the court may revoke the juvenile probation and execute the criminal sentence. Trying youths in juvenile courts with criminal procedural safeguards preserves access to juvenile correctional resources, provides longer periods of correctional supervision, and retains the possibility of adult incarceration if youths fail on probation or re-offend. Several other states have emulated this blended sentencing strategy. Torbet, *State Responses*.

Texas adopted a determinate sentencing law for juveniles convicted of certain violent crimes to provide an alternative to sentencing them either as delinquents or adults. Tex. Fam. Code Ann. §§ 53.045, 54.04(d)(3) (Vernon 2000). If a youth is indicted and convicted of one of the enumerated violent crimes, then "the court or jury may sentence the child to commitment to the Texas Youth Commission with a possible transfer to the institutional division or the pardons and paroles division of the Texas Department of Criminal Justice for a term of not more than" forty years for a capital or first degree felony, twenty years for a second degree felony, or ten years for a third degree felony. Tex. Fam. Code Ann. § 54.04(d)(3) (Vernon 2000). Juveniles receive the same procedural rights as do criminal defendants including a jury trial. Juveniles begin their sentences in juvenile facilities and, at age eighteen, a court conducts a sentencing hearing using Kent-like criteria to decide whether to retain them in the juvenile correctional system until age twenty-one or to complete their determinate sentence in the adult correctional system. Other states have enacted laws like Texas' that enable a juvenile court judge to sentence youth convicted of serious crimes for terms beyond juvenile courts' dispositional jurisdiction or to complete their sentence in adult correctional facilities. E.g. Torbet, *State Responses*.

Although states' statutes differ in many details, blended sentencing strategies share common features. Because these laws provide adult criminal procedural safeguards, they can acknowledge the reality of juvenile punishment. Once a state grants the right to a jury trial and other criminal procedural safeguards, it retains the option to punish youths and gains greater flexibility to treat them as well. Trying juveniles with criminal procedural rights preserves the option to extend jurisdiction for a period of several years or more beyond that available for ordinary delinquents. Blended sentencing provisions embody the procedural and substantive convergence between juvenile and criminal courts, provide a conceptual alternative to binary waiver statutes, and recognize that adolescence constitutes a developmental continuum that requires an increasing array of graduated sanctions.

E.   JUVENILES IN CRIMINAL COURT

Recent changes in waiver laws have increased the numbers of chronological juveniles charged, tried, and sentenced as adults. States annually try more than 200,000 chronological juveniles as adults because their juvenile court jurisdiction ends at fifteen or sixteen years of age rather than at seventeen and try an additional 55,000 youths as adults as a result of transfer provisions. Feld and Bishop, "Transfer of Juveniles to Criminal Court." During the 1990s, many states amended waiver laws without analyzing their systemic impacts on various components of the juvenile or criminal justice systems. An influx of young offenders into criminal courts imposes greater demands on prosecutorial and judicial resources without corresponding increases in criminal justice personnel. In many states, waived juveniles' pretrial detention status remains ambiguous and may result in lengthy confinement pending an appeal by the youth or by a prosecutor if a judge denies a waiver motion. As criminal courts impose more severe sentences on younger offenders, prison populations may increase without any corresponding increases in bed-space or age-appropriate programs.

Adult criminal courts sentence waived young offenders primarily on the basis of the seriousness of their present offense. The emphasis on the present offense reflects ordinary criminal sentencing practices as well as the failure to include juvenile delinquency adjudications systematically in young adults' criminal histories. As a result, criminal courts often sentence violent and persistent young offenders significantly differently. The former may receive substantial sentences of imprisonment, including "life without parole" for homicide, Miller v. Alabama, 132 S.Ct. 2455 (2012), and until Roper v. Simmons, 543 U.S. 551 (2005), the death penalty. Moreover, violent youths often receive these disparate consequences simply because judges, legislators, or prosecutors decided to try them as adults rather than as juveniles. By contrast, persistent young property offenders often receive more lenient sentences as adult first offenders than do their delinquent counterparts whom judges retain as juveniles. Feld, *Bad Kids*.

1. USE OF DELINQUENCY CONVICTIONS TO ENHANCE ADULT SENTENCES

Criminal courts traditionally lacked access to offenders' delinquent histories because of the confidentiality of juvenile court records, the functional and physical separation of juvenile and criminal court staff, and the difficulty of maintaining integrated offender criminal histories across both systems. Juvenile courts' practices of sealing or purging records to avoid stigmatizing offenders impeded use of juvenile records to identify career offenders and to enhance subsequent adult sentences. Although extensive juvenile criminality provides the most reliable indicator of the onset of a criminal career, failure to combine criminal histories across both systems may enable serious young offenders to avoid the punishment their chronic offending deserves.

Policies on access to juvenile records pose a conflict between the rehabilitative goals of the juvenile court and the public safety interests in identifying career criminals. Although juvenile courts traditionally restricted access to records to avoid stigmatizing youths for minor offenses or who desisted from further offending, confidentiality of records may be inappropriate for youths who continue offending into adulthood. Despite the traditional confidentiality of and restricted access to juvenile courts records, states increasingly use prior juvenile convictions to enhance adult sentences. About half the states provide for structured consideration of juvenile records when criminal courts sentence young adult defendants by including them in their sentencing guidelines' criminal history score. Torbet, *State Responses.*

A number of states and the federal sentencing guidelines include some juvenile prior convictions in an adult defendant's criminal history score. In United States v. Johnson, 28 F.3d 151, 307 U.S.App.D.C. 284 (D.C.Cir.1994), the trial judge increased the defendant's sentence based on the criminal history points he received for his extensive juvenile record. The majority noted that the state's interest in punishing recidivists over-rode the protective policy of sealing juvenile records and concluded that the guidelines reasonably could equate juvenile with adult convictions and sentences as a rough indicator of relative culpability. The dissent in Johnson criticized the Sentencing Guidelines' equation of juvenile and adult sentences of confinement because juvenile courts sentenced youths for treatment and rehabilitation rather than for punishment. The dissent argued that a juvenile sentence of confinement may reflect inadequacies of a youth's home environment or the absence of community treatment resources, rather than the culpability associated with an adult's sentence of confinement. California's "three-strikes" sentencing law includes juvenile adjudications as prior felony convictions for purposes of sentence enhancements. Cal. Penal Code § 667(d)(3) (West 1994) (a prior juvenile adjudication shall constitute a prior felony conviction for purposes of sentence enhancement if the juvenile was 16 years of age or older and convicted of one of 23 serious offenses enumerated in the California transfer statute); People v. Smith, 110 Cal.App.4th 1072, 1 Cal.Rptr.3d 901 (Cal. Ct. App. 2003) (defendant acquired two prior "strikes" from a delinquency adjudication for multiple crimes arising out of the same incident). Some states include a juvenile record as a discretionary factor to consider when available, while others formally include a juvenile record in the criminal history score. Some states' sentencing guidelines weight juvenile prior offenses somewhat less heavily than adult convictions and only include juvenile felonies committed after age sixteen or for fewer points than adult convictions. However, a few states do not distinguish qualitatively between juvenile and adult convictions and include both equally in an offender's criminal history score. E.g., Kan. Stat. Ann. § 21–4170(a) (1995).

In Apprendi v. New Jersey, 530 U.S. 466 (2000), the Supreme Court held that the Constitution requires the state to prove to a jury beyond a reasonable doubt any fact that increases the penalty for a crime beyond the statutory maximum, "other than the fact of a prior conviction." Because most states deny delinquents the right to a jury trial, see McKeiver v. Pennsylvania, 403 U.S. 528 (1971), Chapter 7, several courts have considered the implications of Apprendi for the use of juvenile convictions that enhance criminal sentences. In United States v. Tighe, 266 F.3d 1187 (9th Cir. 2001), the Ninth Circuit held that "Apprendi's narrow 'prior conviction' exception is limited to prior convictions resulting from proceedings that afforded the procedural necessities of a jury trial and proof beyond a reasonable doubt. Thus, the 'prior conviction' exception does not include non-jury juvenile adjudications." By contrast, the Eight Circuit in United States v. Smalley, 294 F.2d 1030 (8th Cir. 2002), upheld an enhanced sentence which included a prior juvenile adjudication. See also United States v. Jones, 332 F.3d 688 (3rd Cir. 2003); Barry C. Feld, "The Constitutional Tension Between Apprendi and McKeiver, Sentence Enhancements Based on Delinquency Convictions and the Quality of Justice in Juvenile Courts," 38 Wake Forest L. Rev. 1111 (2003). Both federal and state courts are divided on whether juvenile adjudications fall under Apprendi's "prior conviction" exception. The majority of courts allow judges to enhance criminal sentences based on prior delinquency adjudications because juvenile proceedings provide sufficient procedural safeguards to qualify under the "prior conviction" exception. E.g. United States v. Burge, 407 F.3d 1183 (11th Cir. 2005); People v. Superior Court, 113 Cal. App. 4th 817, 7 Cal. Rptr.3d 73 (200). A minority of jurisdiction conclude that juvenile adjudications obtained without a jury trial lack the procedural quality to meet the "prior conviction" exception or do not constitute "convictions" under state law. E.g. United States v. Tighe, 266 F.3d 1187 (9th Cir. 2001); State v. Brown, 879 So.2d 1276 (La. 2004); State v. Harris, 118 P. 3d 236 (Or. 2005).

2. SENTENCING JUVENILE AS ADULTS

Waiver of youths to criminal courts for sentencing as adults implicates legal and cultural understandings of juveniles' criminal responsibility. Transfer of young juveniles for very serious crimes may expose them to lengthy terms of years and life without parole (LWOP) sentences for crimes they committed at thirteen or fourteen years of age. Questions about young people's criminal responsibility arise in the broader context of culpability and deserved punishments, the tension between retributive and utilitarian sentencing policies, and the social and legal construction of childhood. Laws that expose children to life terms constitute a political and cultural judgment that young people may be just as blameworthy and culpable as their somewhat older counterparts.

The federal sentencing guidelines explicitly reject "youthfulness" as a justification to mitigate young offenders' sentences outside of the guidelines range. U.S. Sentencing Guidelines Manual § 5H.1 (1995). Several states' sentencing laws do recognize "youthfulness" as a mitigating factor. E.g., Ariz. Rev. Stat. § 13–702(D)(1) (1996); Fla. Stat. ch. 921.0016(4)(k) (1996) ("the defendant was too young to appreciate the consequences of the offense"); La. Rev. Stat. Ann. § 905.5(f) (West 1997) ("the youth of the offender at the time of the offense"); N.C. Gen. Stat. § 15A–134.D.16(e)(4) (1996) ("The defendant's age, immaturity, or limited mental capacity"). Under such aggravating-mitigating sentencing laws, trial court judges regularly consider youthfulness of defendants both de jure and de facto and appellate courts remand them for resentencing if they do not. E.g., State v. Adams, 864 S.W.2d 31, 33 (Tenn.1993); State v. Strunk, 846 P.2d 1297, 1300–02 (Utah 1993). However, states that recognize youthfulness as a mitigating factor simply treat it as one element to weigh with other factors when a judge imposes a sentence. In most jurisdictions, it remains a matter of trial court discretion whether a judge treats youthfulness as a mitigating factor and failure to exercise leniency does not constitute reversible error or an abuse of discretion.

As states send more youths to prisons, correctional options for handling juveniles include straight adult incarceration with minimal differentiation between juveniles and adults; graduated incarceration in which youths begin their sentences in a juvenile or separate adult facility and then serve the remainder of their sentence in the adult facility; or age-segregated incarceration either in separate facilities within the prison or in separate youth facilities for younger adults. Nearly all states confine juveniles-sentenced-as-adults in adult correctional facilities either with younger adult offenders or in the general population if the juvenile is of a certain age, for example, sixteen. Barry C. Feld, "Juvenile and Criminal Justice Systems' Responses to Youth Violence," 24 *Crime & Justice* 189 (1998).

3.   "CHILDREN ARE DIFFERENT"

In a recent trilogy of cases, the Supreme Court applied the Eighth Amendment to the entire category of juvenile offenders, repudiated its "death is different" jurisprudence, and required states to consider youthfulness as a mitigating factor in sentencing. Roper v. Simmons, 543 U.S. 551 (2005), prohibited states from executing offenders for murder they committed when younger than eighteen years of age. Roper reasoned that immature judgment, susceptibility to negative influences, and transitory personalities reduced youths' culpability and barred the most severe sentence. Graham v. Florida, 130 S.Ct. 2011, 2026 (2010), extended Roper's diminished responsibility rationale and prohibited states from imposing life without parole (LWOP) sentences on youths convicted of non-homicide offenses, *and* repudiated the Court's earlier Eighth Amendment position that "death is different." Miller v. Alabama, 132 S. Ct. 2455 (2012) used Roper and Graham's diminished responsibility rationale and employed another strand of death penalty jurisprudence to bar *mandatory* LWOP sentences for youths convicted of murder, required judges to make individualized sentencing decisions, and emphasized the importance of youthfulness as a mitigating factor.

Historically, some states executed offenders for the crimes they committed as children. Before the Court in Roper v. Simmons, 543 U.S. 5451 (2005), abolished the death penalty for juveniles, states had executed nearly 300 youths for crimes they

committed before they were eighteen years of age
and about two percent of death row inmates were
convicted of crimes they committed as children. For
two decades prior to Roper v. Simmons, the Court
considered several cases posing the question of
whether the Eighth Amendment prohibited states
from executing offenders for crimes they committed
as juveniles. In Eddings v. Oklahoma, 455 U.S. 104
(1982), the Court reversed the death penalty of a
sixteen-year-old because the trial court failed to
consider his emotional development and family
background as mitigating factors. In 1988, a
plurality of justices in Thompson v. Oklahoma, 487
U.S. 815 (1988), concluded that all fifteen-year-old
offenders lacked the culpability necessary to impose
the death penalty. The following year, the Court in
Stanford v. Kentucky, 492 U.S. 361 (1989), upheld
the death penalty for offenders who were sixteen or
seventeen years of age when they committed a
capital offense. Although Stanford acknowledged
that juveniles generally were less culpable than
adults, the Court rejected a categorical ban and
instead allowed juries to decide on a case-by-case
basis whether a particular youth possessed
sufficient culpability to warrant execution.

In 2005, the Court in Roper v. Simmons, 543 U.S.
551 (2005), in a 5—4 decision, overruled Stanford
and categorically barred states from executing
youths for crimes committed prior to eighteen years
of age. Several years earlier, the Court in Atkins v.
Virginia, 536 U.S. 304 (2002), held that the Eighth
Amendment barred states from executing
defendants with mental retardation. In Atkins, the

Court found a national consensus against executions existed because thirty states barred the practice, legislative changes increasingly disfavored executing defendants with mental retardation, and few states actually executed mentally impaired offenders. The Atkins Justices also conducted a proportionality analysis and concluded that defendants suffering from mental retardation lacked the culpability necessary to warrant execution.

Like its Atkins analyses, empirical and normative factors informed the Roper majority's assessment of "the evolving standards of decency that mark the progress of a maturing society." State legislation and jury sentencing decisions provided corresponding evidence of a national consensus against executing juveniles. In addition to the objective indicators of a national consensus, the Justices conducted a proportionality analysis of adolescents' culpability to decide whether the death penalty ever could be an appropriate punishment for juveniles. Justice Kennedy, for the majority, offered three reasons based simply upon age, why states could not punish criminally responsible juveniles as severely as adult offenders. First, juveniles' culpability cannot be equated with that of adults. Juveniles' immature judgment and lesser self-control cause them to commit acts impulsively and without full appreciation of the consequences. Second, juveniles are more susceptible than adults to negative peer influences. Juveniles' greater dependence on parents and community spreads responsibility for their misdeeds more broadly. Third, juveniles' personalities are more transitory and less well-formed compared with adults' personalities and juveniles' crimes provide less reliable evidence of depraved character. Because juveniles' character is transitional, "[f]rom a moral standpoint it would be misguided to equate the failings of a minor with those of an adult, for a great possibility exists that a minor's character deficiencies will be reformed." The Court noted that juveniles' immature judgment, susceptibility to negative influence, and transitory character also negate the retributive and deterrent justifications for the death penalty.

Justice O'Connor, who provided the swing vote which produced the contradictory outcomes in Thompson and Stanford, dissented from the Court's ruling in Roper. While she conceded that adolescents, as a class, are less mature or culpable than adults, she objected that the majority provided no evidence to contradict state legislatures' judgments that "at least some seventeen-year-old murderers are sufficiently mature to deserve the death penalty in an appropriate case." She questioned whether the differences in culpability between a seventeen-year-old juvenile and an eighteen-year-old adult justify a categorical bright-line rule. She also disputed the majority's conclusion that capital sentencing juries could not adequately assess an individual youth's culpability or give appropriate weight to youthfulness as a mitigating factor.

In a separate dissent, Justice Scalia criticized the majority's calculus for finding a national consensus against executing juveniles. He also disparaged the majority's selective reliance on social science research to support its categorical conclusion that all juveniles lacked sufficient culpability ever to warrant execution. Finally, he condemned the majority's rejection of individualized jury consideration of a youth's culpability in favor of a categorical prohibition.

Although both the O'Connor and Scalia dissents argued for individualized culpability assessments, Justice Kennedy opted for a categorical ban:

> The differences between juvenile and adult offenders are too marked and well understood to risk allowing a youthful person to receive the death penalty despite insufficient culpability. An unacceptable likelihood exists that the brutality or cold-blooded nature of any particular crime would overpower mitigating arguments based on youth as a matter of course, even where the juvenile offender's objective immaturity, vulnerability, and lack of true depravity should require a sentence less severe than death.

Justice Kennedy feared that jurors would ignore the mitigating role of youthfulness when the circumstances of a brutal, cold-blooded murder aroused their passions. To avoid these risks, the Court used age as a conclusive proxy for culpability to align how the law treats youthful offenders with how the law and our culture believe we should treat them.

Roper analyzed youths' reduced culpability within a retributive sentencing framework. Retributive sentencing theory proportions punishment to a crime's seriousness. A crime's seriousness is defined by two elements—harm and culpability—which determine how much punishment an actor deserves. Barry C. Feld, "Adolescent Criminal Responsibility, Proportionality, and Sentencing Policy: Roper, Graham, Miller/Jackson, and the Youth Discount," 31 *Law & Inequality* 263 (2013). An offender's age has no bearing on the amount of harm caused— children and adults can inflict the same injuries. But youths' inability fully to appreciate wrongfulness or to control their behavior may reduce culpability and lessen blameworthiness for the harms they cause.

Developmental psychology and neuroscience research inform how children's thinking and behaving change and may influence criminal responsibility. By mid-adolescence, most youths can distinguish right from wrong and reason similarly to adults under controlled conditions. But the ability to make good choices under laboratory conditions differs from decisions made in stressful circumstances with incomplete information. Emotions, excitement, or stress contribute to riskier decisions by youth than by adults. Developmental psychologists distinguish between youths' cognitive abilities and their judgment and self-control. Elizabeth S. Scott and Laurence Steinberg, *Rethinking Juvenile Justice* (2008). Although mid-adolescents' cognitive abilities are comparable with adults, their judgment and impulse control does not emerge for several more years. Youths' immature judgment reflects differences in risk perception, appreciation of future consequences, and experience with autonomy. Youths' generic difference from adults in knowledge and experience, time perspective, risk proclivity, and impulsivity renders their bad choices categorically less blameworthy.

Adolescents underestimate risks and focus on short-term gains rather than possible long-term losses to a greater extent than do adults. They possess less information and consider fewer options than do adults. They weigh costs and benefits differently than adults and apply different subjective values to outcomes. Scott and Steinberg, *Rethinking Juvenile Justice*. Youths crave sensation and excitement—the adrenaline rush—which increases their propensity to engage in risky behaviors. Risk-taking and sensation-seeking peak around sixteen or seventeen and then decline in adulthood—the ages when youths' involvement in criminal activity also increases.

The differences that social scientists observe between youths' and adults' thinking and behavior correspond with human brain development. Terry A. Maroney, "The False Promise of Adolescent Brain Science in Juvenile Justice," 85 *Notre Dame L. Rev.* 89 (2009). Two neurobiological systems—the prefrontal cortex (PFC) and the limbic system— influence youths' ability to exercise judgment and to control impulses. The PFC controls executive functions such as reasoning, planning, and impulse control. During late-adolescence, increased myelination and synaptic pruning improve reasoning ability and impulse control. By contrast, the limbic system controls instinctual behavior, such as the fight-or-flight response. During adolescence, the two systems are out of balance and teen-agers rely more heavily on the limbic system and less heavily on the PFC than do adults. Scott and Steinberg, *Rethinking Juvenile Justice*. Youths' heightened quest for pleasure and emotional rewards develops more rapidly than does the system for self-control and self-regulation.

The language and history of the Eighth Amendment does not dictate different tests for capital and non-capital sentences. But the Court has used different proportionality analyses based on its view that "death is different." Harmelin v. Michigan, 501 U.S. 957 (1991). Apart from Roper, the Court had not applied proportionality principles to juveniles as a class, prohibited lengthy sentences for them, or established a minimum age for LWOP sentences. As a result, lengthy mandatory minimum or LWOP sentences imposed on juveniles did not elicit close judicial scrutiny.

Graham v. Florida, 130 S.Ct. 2011 (2010), considered whether Roper's diminished responsibility rationale would apply to a nonhomicide juvenile offender sentenced to life without parole. Graham arose at the intersection of two lines of Eighth Amendment proportionality cases. One line of cases raised "gross disproportionality" claims and challenged term-of-year sentences that greatly exceeded the seriousness of the crime. The other line of cases made "categorical disproportionality" claims and challenged imposition of the death penalty on categories of offenders or offenses—e.g., those with mental retardation, juveniles, and non-homicide offenses.

Challenges to length-of-years sentences required the Court to consider whether the Eighth Amendment contains a "narrow proportionality principle" that "applies to non-capital sentences." Solem v. Helms, 463 U.S. 277 (1983), held that a sentence of life without possibility of parole for a property crime violated the Constitution. Solem's proportionality analyses focused on three factors: "(i) the gravity of the offense and the harshness of the penalty; (ii) the sentences imposed on other criminals in the same jurisdiction; and (iii) the sentences imposed for commission of the same crime in other jurisdictions." By contrast, Harmelin v. Michigan, 501 U.S. 957 (1991), upheld a life without parole sentence imposed on a first-time drug dealer. After Harmelin, courts only review length-of-years sentences that cross some ill-defined "grossly disproportionate" threshold.

Categorical challenges to the death penalty involved entire classes of offenses or offenders. Some decisions barred execution for non-homicide crimes and some felony-murderers. Others prohibited states from executing less culpable offenders— juveniles and the mental retarded. Graham posed "a categorical challenge to a term-of-years-sentence." It required the Court to decide the validity of a sentence—life without parole—applied to "an entire class of offenders who have committed a range of crimes," rather than whether it was grossly disproportionate as applied to the individual. Graham repudiated the Court's historical "death is different" distinction, extended Roper's reduced culpability rationale, and "declare[d] an entire class of offenders immune from a noncapital sentence . . ."

Once the Court framed Graham as a categorical challenge to a sentencing practice, it replicated Roper's proportionality analyses and found a national consensus against imposing an LWOP sentence on nonhomicide juvenile offenders. Graham rested on three features—the offender, the offense, and the sentence. It reiterated Roper's rationale that juveniles' reduced culpability warranted less severe penalties than those imposed on adults convicted of the same crime. Graham explicitly based young offenders' diminished responsibility on social science and neuroscience research.

> [D]evelopments in psychology and brain science continue to show fundamental differences between juvenile and adult minds. For example, parts of the brain involved in behavior control continue to mature through late adolescence.

Graham invoked the Court's felony-murder death-penalty decisions and concluded that even the most serious nonhomicide crimes "cannot be compared to murder in their severity and irrevocability." Because the criminal responsibility of juveniles who did not murder was "doubly diminished," an LWOP sentence was "grossly disproportionate."

Although execution differs from life imprisonment, the Court equated the death penalty with LWOP sentences for juveniles as similarly ultimate sanctions—"the sentence alters the offender's life by a forfeiture that is irrevocable." No penal rationale—retribution, deterrence, incapacitation, and rehabilitation—justified the penultimate sanction for nonhomicide juvenile offenders. As a result of "the limited culpability of juvenile nonhomicide offenders and the severity of life without parole sentences," Graham prohibited states from impose a life without parole sentence on youths who did not commit murder.

Graham ruled categorically and denied trial courts the option to impose LWOP sentences on a case-by-case basis. Graham reiterated clinicians' inability to distinguish between most juveniles who have the capacity to change and the few who might be incorrigible. Moreover, the same immaturity that diminished youths' responsibility increased the risk of error in assessing their culpability. Developmental immaturity impairs youths' ability to understand legal proceedings, to communicate with counsel, and to make legal decisions.

As in Roper, the principal difference among the Graham Justices focused on whether to apply a categorical rule and bar LWOP for all non-homicide juveniles or to impose the sentence on a case-by-case basis. Chief Justice Roberts agreed that Graham's sentence was disproportionate, but argued that sentences should be individualized, rather than applied categorically. Chief Justice Roberts included the "culpability of the offender" in his proportionality analyses, a departure from previous non-capital proportionality decisions that defined crime seriousness on the basis of harm alone. Although he characterized Graham's LWOP sentence as grossly disproportional, he did not identify what factors distinguish it from other youths' non-homicide crimes in which an LWOP might be imposed.

Justice Thomas' dissent criticized the Graham majority for repudiating the Court's "death is different" jurisprudence and for adopting a categorical prohibition of a non-capital sentence. He rejected the conclusion that all youths always lack the culpability to warrant an LWOP sentence and argued that trial courts could individualize and balance the seriousness of a crime with a youth's diminished responsibility. He noted the anomaly of barring juvenile LWOPs for nonhomicide crimes, but leaving "intact state and federal laws that permit life-without-parole sentences for juveniles who commit murder." He characterized this as disproportionality based on categories of crimes rather than characteristics of offenders, an inconsistency the Court addressed in Miller v. Alabama,132 S. Ct. 2455 (2012).

When the Court decided Miller, forty-two states permitted judges to impose LWOP sentences on adults or juveniles convicted of murder and in twenty-nine states, the LWOP sentence is mandatory. Feld, "Adolescent Criminal Responsibility, Proportionality, and Sentencing Policy." Mandatory sentences preclude individualized culpability evaluations and equate the criminal responsibility of juveniles with adults. Courts rarely invalidate juvenile LWOP sentences and most reject juveniles' pleas to consider youthfulness as a mitigating factor. Although Roper treated youthfulness as a categorical mitigating factor, many trial judges treated it as an aggravating factor when they sentence juvenile murderers. In 2009, more than 2,500 people were serving LWOP sentences for crimes they committed as children. The number of juveniles serving life sentences and lengthy consecutive terms is much larger. Most juveniles who received an LWOP sentence had no prior adult or juvenile convictions. Amnesty International & Human Rights Watch, *The Rest of Their Lives* (2005). Although states may not execute a felony-murderer who did not kill or intend to kill, more than one-quarter of LWOP sentence imposed on juveniles were for a felony-murder.

The Court in Miller v. Alabama and a companion case, Jackson v. Hobbs, extended Roper and Graham to their logical conclusion and banned *mandatory* LWOP sentences for youths convicted of murder. Justice Kagan responded to Justice Thomas' Graham dissent that that decision rested on categories of crimes rather than characteristics of offenders and emphasized that "none of what it said about children—about their distinctive (and transitory) mental traits and environmental vulnerabilities—is crime specific."

Miller/Jackson invoked another line of death penalty cases that barred mandatory capital sentences and required individualized culpability assessments. Woodson v. North Carolina, 428 U.S. 280, 304 (1976). Mandatory death sentences precluded consideration of the crime, the offender, and relevant mitigating circumstances. Miller/Jackson invoked those precedents to require individualized culpability assessments prior imposing an LWOP sentence. Mandatory LWOP sentences prevent the sentencing judge from considering youthfulness or other mitigating factors and thereby disproportionally equate juveniles' and adults' culpability. Miller/Jackson asserted that once judges conducted an individualized culpability assessment and properly considered youths' generic diminished responsibility, there would be very few occasions in which to impose an LWOP sentence even for homicide.

Justice Thomas' dissent argued that Harmelin v. Michigan had upheld a mandatory LWOP sentence for an adult drug-dealer without requiring individualized sentencing. Justice Kagan responded that a sentencing scheme that was valid for adults could still violate the constitution when applied to children. "We have by now held on multiple occasions that a sentencing rule permissible for adults may not be so for children. . . . So if (as Harmelin recognized) 'death is different,' children are different too." Chief Justice Roberts' argued that no national consensus against mandatory LWOP sentences existed because the majority of states approved the practice for adults and juveniles convicted of murder. Justice Kagan asserted that Miller/Jackson did not absolutely preclude an LWOP sentence for a juvenile murderer, but only required its individualized application after taking into account the youthfulness of the offender. Individualized assessment avoided the danger that juvenile waiver statutes and criminal sentencing provisions could produce more severe outcomes than the legislature intended.

Justice Breyer filed a separate concurrence in Jackson because fourteen-year-old Jackson was convicted of felony-murder and received a mandatory LWOP sentence as an accomplice rather than as the shooter. The Court's felony-murder decisions limited the death penalty to those who killed or intended to kill. Because Graham recognized the "twice diminished" moral culpability of youths "who do not kill, intend to kill, or foresee that life will be taken," Justice Breyer reasoned that a juvenile who neither killed nor intended to kill is no more culpable than a youth convicted of a nonhomicide felony.

Despite the Court's recognition of adolescents' reduced criminal responsibility, Graham provided non-homicide offenders very limited relief—"some meaningful opportunity to obtain release." Justice Thomas' dissent properly asked, "But what, exactly, does such a 'meaningful' opportunity entail? When must it occur? And what Eighth Amendment principles will govern review by the parole boards that the Court now demands that States empanel?" Similarly, Miller only required an individualized evaluation of culpability and consideration of the mitigating qualities of youthfulness, but did not preclude an LWOP sentence for juveniles who murder. However, Miller does not provide legislatures, judges, or parole boards with any practical guidance how to incorporate the mitigating qualities of youth into sentencing or release decisions.

State courts are divided whether to apply Miller retroactively to the thousands of youths who previously received mandatory LWOP sentences for murder. Compare e.g., Geter v. State, 2012 WL 4448860 (Fla. 3d DCA Sept. 27, 2012) (holding that Miller "was not of fundamental significance" but, instead, was "a procedural change in law" regarding criminal sentencing, and, thus, could not be applied retroactively); People v. Carp, 2012 WL 5846553 (Mich. Ct. Ap. 2012) (holding that Michigan law does not apply retroactively to cases on collateral review because the decision is procedural and does not comprise a watershed ruling), with State v. Simmons, 99 So.3d 28 (La. 2012) (remanding mandatory LWOP juvenile for reconsideration and resentencing based on Miller); State v. Lockheart, 820 N.W.2d 769 (Iowa Ct. App. 2012) (Remanding for resentencing in accordance with Miller in which the sentencing court shall "have the opportunity to consider mitigating circumstances before imposing the harshest possible penalty for juveniles."); People v. Williams, 982 N.E.2d 181 (Ill. App. 1st, 2012) (holding that "[U]nder the proportionate punishment analysis in Miller, defendant was denied a "basic 'precept of justice' " by not receiving any consideration of his age from the circuit court in sentencing," and finding that a new rule applies retroactively "where it has made a substantial or substantive change in the law. . . . Miller not only changed procedures, but also made a substantial change in the law in holding under the Eighth Amendment that the government cannot constitutionally apply a mandatory sentence of life without parole for homicides committed by juveniles."). State legislatures are revising sentencing laws to convert mandatory LWOP statutes to life with the possibility of parole, to impose minimum terms of years, or to specify mitigating factors in sentencing guidelines. Feld, "Adolescent Criminal Responsibility, Proportionality, and Sentencing Policy."

CHAPTER 7

ADJUDICATION OF DELINQUENCY: PROCEDURAL RIGHTS AT TRIAL

Procedure and substance intertwine in juvenile courts. Progressive reformers assumed juveniles lacked competence to exercise procedural rights and envisioned an informal court that decided cases in the child's "best interests." The Supreme Court in Gault emphasized the disjunctions between juvenile courts' "rehabilitative rhetoric" and their "punitive reality" and required greater procedural safeguards for delinquents charged for criminal violations. Although Gault provided the impetus for the procedural convergence between juvenile and criminal courts, a substantial gulf remains between theory and reality, between the "law on the books" and the "law in action." More than four decades ago, the Court in Kent v. United States observed that "the child receives the worst of both worlds: he gets neither the protections accorded to adults nor the solicitous care and regenerative treatment postulated for children." Theoretically, the Constitution and state laws entitle delinquents to formal, adversarial trials and the effective assistance of counsel. In reality, juvenile courts try youths using a procedural regime under which few adults charged with crimes and facing the prospects of confinement would consent to be tried.

Despite the increasing convergence of juvenile and criminal courts, most states provide neither special procedures to protect juveniles from their own immaturity nor the full panoply of adult criminal procedural rights. In some instances, states treat delinquents just like adult criminal defendants when formal equality redounds to their disadvantage, for example, as we saw in Chapter 3 where juveniles waive their Miranda rights under the adult standard—"knowing, intelligent, and voluntary." Most states allow delinquents to waive their right to an attorney at trial under the same standard and without consultation with counsel. In other instances, states use less adequate juvenile court safeguards when those deficient procedures provide a comparative advantage to the state, for example denying them a right to a jury trial. As a matter of logic and consistency, either young offenders possess the competency of adults or they do not. If they do, then presumably they deserve the same legal rights as adults, for better or worse. If they do not, then they require special procedural protections to compensate for their immaturity and developmental limitations. In the "worst of both worlds" of juvenile court procedural justice, appellate courts and legislators pick and choose between competing liberationist and protectionist policies. They manipulate competing constructions of adolescents as autonomous and responsible or as immature and incompetent to maximize social control and to reinforce legal paternalism.

As in Chapter 3, this Chapter does not review all criminal defendants' procedural trial rights and then contrast them with juvenile courts' procedural analogs. Rather, it examines how courts and legislators use the fluid concepts of childhood or rehabilitation—e.g., McKeiver's denial of a constitutional right to a jury trial—to rebuff young peoples' claims for procedural parity with adult criminal defendants. Despite the formal procedural convergence between juvenile and criminal courts, the question remains whether youths continue to receive the "worst of both worlds" in delinquency proceedings.

A.   CONSTITUTIONAL DOMESTICATION OF THE JUVENILE COURT

The Warren Court undertook the "constitutional domestication of the juvenile court" as part of its "Due Process Revolution" in the 1960s. During the 1960s, the Warren Court interpreted the Fourteenth Amendment of the Constitution and the Bill of Rights to restrict governmental intervention in citizens' lives, to extend equality to minorities and the disenfranchised, and to regularize administrative and criminal justice decision making. The Court's criminal procedure decisions followed closely upon its civil rights opinions because those accused of crimes consisted disproportionately of the poor, minorities, and the young.

During the 1960s, the Supreme Court used three interrelated strategies to provide constitutional procedural safeguards to state criminal defendants: incorporation, reinterpretation, and equal protection. LaFave, *Criminal Procedure*. First, the Court incorporated most sections of the Fourth, Fifth, and Sixth Amendments into the Fourteenth

Amendment's due process clause and applied those provisions of the Bill of Rights to the states. Second, it reinterpreted those provisions, redefined and expanded the meanings of those constitutional rights, and exercised greater judicial oversight over state law enforcement and criminal justice officials. Third, it expanded greatly the principles of equal protection of law and extended constitutional safeguards to administrative officials previously immune from judicial scrutiny. The leading Supreme Court juvenile justice decisions of the era—Gault, Winship, and McKeiver—involved issues of constitutional methodology, federalism, and jurisprudence as well as the specific details of the procedural rights available to delinquents state juvenile court proceedings.

1.   GAULT AND PROCEDURAL DUE PROCESS

Authorities took fifteen-year-old Gerald Gault into custody for making an obscene phone call, detained him overnight without notice to his parents, and held a hearing the next day at which a probation officer alleged he was a delinquent. The judge did not advise Gault or his parents of any rights, appoint an attorney, hear any witnesses, create a record, or make any findings. The judge found Gault delinquent after he questioned him about the phone call and he admitted dialing the number. At a dispositional hearing a week later, the judge committed Gault to the State Industrial School "for the period of his minority [that is, until 21], unless sooner discharged by due process of law." An adult convicted of the same offense could have been sentenced to a $50 fine or two months' imprisonment. The Gault appeal raised the question of what procedural safeguards, if any, the Constitution required at the adjudicatory hearing— the trial—of a delinquent charged with conduct that would be a crime if committed by an adult and whom the judge could commit to an institution. By emphasizing procedural regularity, the Court shifted juvenile courts' focus from a juvenile's "real needs" to criminal deeds. It modified delinquency hearings from a social welfare inquiry into a quasi-criminal prosecution. Justice Stewart's dissent in Gault objected to any constitutional safeguards in delinquency proceedings and argued that juvenile courts did not conduct adversary hearings but acted as *parens patriae* to help children.

Recall from Chapter 1, Gault was an empirical decision based on the "law in action" rather than the "law on the books." Gault confronted the reality of a juvenile court quite different from the rhetoric of its Progressive creators. The Court's decision reflected contemporaneous empirical studies of juvenile courts as well as changes in attitudes about the importance of procedural safeguards. See *President's Crime Commission.* The Court observed that juvenile courts' failure to provide procedural safeguards sometimes resulted in unfair and inaccurate fact-finding. It noted that high adolescent crime rates and delinquents' recidivism contradicted juvenile court proponents' claims of successful intervention. Gault saw no significant constitutional difference between commitment to an industrial school for delinquents and to a reformatory for criminals. Although the Court accepted juvenile courts' rehabilitative goals, it insisted that they must provide some procedural safeguards to achieve those objectives.

The separate Gault opinions by Justice Fortas, for the majority, and the separate concurring opinions by Justices Black and Harlan echoed the historic divisions within the Court about the incorporation of the Bill of Rights into the Fourteenth Amendment and its application to state criminal and delinquency proceedings. LaFave, *Criminal Procedure.* Justice Fortas concluded that state delinquency trials must provide sufficient procedural safeguards to comport with Fourteenth Amendment due process notions of fundamental fairness. Justice Black's concurrence argued that because delinquency proceedings effectively are trials for youths accused of crimes which could lead to confinement, juveniles should enjoy the same procedural safeguards as adult defendants. Reflecting a total incorporation position, Black based delinquents' procedural rights on provisions of the Fifth and Sixth Amendments—self-incrimination, counsel, confrontation and cross-examination—rather than general notions of due process. By contrast, Justice Harlan based his decision exclusively on the Fourteenth Amendment due process clause. In deciding which rights were necessary to provide a constitutionally adequate proceeding, Harlan declined simply to transplant adult criminal procedures into juvenile court as would Black. Rather, Harlan sought fundamentally fair proceedings which would not thwart juvenile courts' rehabilitative goals.

Gault held that as a matter of procedural due process states must provide delinquents with notice, the right to counsel, the right to confront and cross-examine witnesses, and the privilege against self-incrimination. The Warren Court's due process jurisprudence emphasized the dual functions that constitutional procedures serve—to assure accurate fact-finding *and* to protect against governmental oppression. The right to notice, counsel, confrontation, and the privilege against self-incrimination further both interests.

The Court required timely notice in order to enable the juvenile to prepare a defense and to limit the bases of delinquency adjudications. "Notice, to comply with due process requirements, must be given sufficiently in advance of scheduled court proceedings so that reasonable opportunity to prepare will be afforded, and it must 'set forth the alleged misconduct with particularity'." Because the Court simply required advanced written notice to the juvenile and her parents "that would be deemed constitutionally adequate in a civil or criminal proceeding," questions remained about the degree of factual specificity required and whether parental notification is a constitutional requirement. The Court also concluded that "confrontation and sworn testimony by witnesses available for cross-examination were essential for a finding of 'delinquency'."

Gault's holding on the right to counsel simultaneously made juvenile courts more like criminal courts and limited the scope of the right. The Court found that representation by counsel was a fundamental right. It concluded that a juvenile court judge, probation officer, or parent could not adequately substitute for an attorney to protect a delinquent's rights at trial. Although lawyers could make delinquency trials more adversarial, the Court viewed that consequence positively. "A proceeding where the issue is whether the child will be found to be 'delinquent' and subjected to the loss of his liberty for years is comparable in seriousness to a felony prosecution." Because delinquency adjudications hinged on technical legal issues and affected a child's liberty interests, only an attorney could provide an effective legal defense.

In many procedural contexts, the Warren Court found a right to counsel in order to monitor the operation of justice systems and to assure compliance with other procedural requirements. Although the Court cited the President's Crime Commission, which recommended mandatory appointment of counsel, Gault only held that due process required a juvenile court judge to notify the child and parent of the right to counsel and to appoint counsel if they could not afford one. Gault also acknowledged that juveniles could waive the right to counsel. The Court based juveniles' right to counsel on the Fourteenth Amendment due process clause rather than the specific provision of the Sixth Amendment. It also allowed delinquents to waive counsel which adversely affected the availability

and performance of lawyers in juvenile courts. See
Ch. 7. D. infra.

Gault's holding that the Constitution granted
juveniles the Fifth Amendment privilege against
self-incrimination was the most important part of
its rulings, because it contradicted to the traditional
theory of a *parens patriae* juvenile court. Unlike the
other constitutional rights which Gault granted as a
matter of Fourteenth Amendment due process, the
Court based its holding explicitly on the Fifth
Amendment. Despite the historic insistence that
delinquency proceedings were civil matters, the
Court's   Fifth   Amendment   holding   clearly
established the quasi-criminal and adversary nature
of delinquency trials. The Court already used the
Fourteenth Amendment due process clause to
evaluate the voluntariness and reliability of
juveniles' confessions. See Chapter 3 C. While
Fourteenth Amendment voluntariness focuses on
factual accuracy and the unreliability of coerced
confessions, the privilege against self-incrimination
is the bulwark of an adversarial system, defines the
relationship between the individual and the state as
one of equals, and prevents governmental
oppression. The Court incorporated the privilege in
juvenile courts because delinquents faced criminal
charges and possible institutional confinement.
Justice Harlan dissented from the decision to
incorporate the privilege against self-incrimination
because he recognized that it was an essential
element of the adversary process. He feared that it
might radically alter the character of juvenile courts
and create a criminal trial atmosphere.

2.   WINSHIP AND BURDEN OF PROOF

In re Winship, 397 U.S. 358 (S.Ct.1970), followed Gault chronologically and analytically. Winship presented the question whether Fourteenth Amendment due process required proof beyond a reasonable doubt in delinquency proceedings. Because the Court had not previously decided the question, it first ruled that due process required proof beyond a reasonable doubt in criminal cases. Justice Brennan offered several justifications to require proof beyond a reasonable doubt in criminal proceedings. It reduced the risk of factual error. It protected defendants' liberty interests and freedom from the stigma of an unjustified conviction. By placing the risks of factual error on the state, proof beyond a reasonable doubt legitimates the outcomes of the criminal process and prevents governmental oppression.

The Court then held that the standard of proof beyond a reasonable applied in delinquency proceedings for the same reasons. Winship rejected the civil versus criminal distinctions and the treatment versus punishment rationale argued by the state and held that the stigma of a criminal conviction and the possibility of institutional confinement required the highest standard of proof in delinquency proceedings. Winship balanced the values of the safeguard against the impact it would have on court proceedings and concluded that proof beyond a reasonable doubt would not adversely affect juvenile court proceedings. Justice Harlan's concurring opinion elaborated on the role that burdens of proof play in adjudications. Fact-finding entails the weighing of the probability of reconstructed facts and burdens of proof reflect confidence in the likely existence of those facts and the dangers of errors favoring or penalizing the individual or the state. Harlan opined that "we do not view the social disutility of convicting an innocent man as equivalent to the disutility of acquitting someone who is guilty" because it is far worse to convict an innocent person than to free a guilty person. Applying that same principle to delinquency cases, he observed that "a factual error here, as in a criminal case, exposes the accused [delinquent] to a complete loss of his personal liberty through a state-imposed confinement away from his home . . . [and] stigmatizes a youth . . . bottomed on a finding that the accused committed a crime."

Chief Justice Burger dissented and objected that the Winship majority's decision would straight-jacket already overloaded juvenile courts with additional constitutional procedures. He proposed greater flexibility to adjudicate delinquents rather than additional criminal procedural safeguards. Later, in Addington v. Texas, 441 U.S. 418 (S.Ct.1979), which involved the burden of proof in involuntary civil commitment proceedings, Burger equated delinquency hearings with criminal trials. "Winship recognized that the basic issue—whether the individual in fact committed a criminal act— was the same in both [criminal and delinquency] proceedings. There being no meaningful distinctions between the two proceedings, we required the state to prove the juvenile's act and intent beyond a reasonable doubt." In Addington, Burger noted that proof beyond a reasonable doubt is a critical component of criminal cases because it helps to preserve the moral force of criminal law and should not be applied too broadly or in non-criminal cases.

3.   McKEIVER AND THE JURY AND PUBLIC TRIAL

McKeiver v. Pennsylvania, 403 U.S. 528 (S.Ct.1971), was the Supreme Court's third decision affecting trial procedures for delinquents. It provides the constitutional basis and jurisprudential rationale for most of the remaining procedural differences between juvenile and criminal proceedings. McKeiver posed the question whether Fourteenth Amendment due process and fundamental fairness required states to provide delinquents with a jury trial in state proceedings. The Court denied juveniles a constitutional right to a jury. McKeiver represents the Court's most significant decision to maintain a juvenile justice system that differs procedurally and philosophically from the criminal justice system. The denial of a jury trial, in turn, affects many other procedural aspects of delinquency trials: evidentiary admissibility, the timing of suppression hearings, the quality of fact-finding, and the nature of post-adjudication dispositions.

The year prior to McKeiver, the Court in Duncan v. Louisiana, 391 U.S. 145 (S.Ct.1968), granted adult criminal defendants a Sixth Amendment constitutional right to a jury trial in state criminal proceedings because fundamental fairness required both factual accuracy *and* protection against governmental oppression:

> Providing an accused with the right to be tried by a jury of his peers gave him an inestimable safeguard against the corrupt or overzealous prosecutor and against the compliant, biased, or eccentric judge. If the defendant preferred the common-sense judgment of a jury to the more tutored but perhaps less sympathetic reaction of the single judge, he was to have it. Beyond this, the jury trial provisions in the Federal and State Constitutions reflect a fundamental decision about the exercise of official power—a reluctance to entrust plenary powers over the life and liberty of the citizen to one judge or to a group of judges. Fear of unchecked power, so typical of our State and Federal Governments in other respects, found expression in the criminal law in this insistence upon community participation in the determination of guilt or innocence.

Justice Blackmun's plurality opinion in McKeiver used the Fourteenth Amendment due process clause, rather than the Sixth Amendment provision for juries relied on in Duncan, to decide the constitutional question. He asserted that due process and fundamental fairness concerned only accurate fact-finding, even though Gault provided the privilege against self-incrimination to prevent governmental oppression as well. McKeiver envisioned "alternative guarantees and protections" and noted that concerns about procedural safeguards, such as the jury trial, ignore "every aspect of fairness, of concern, of sympathy, and of paternal attention that the juvenile court system contemplates."

Rather than a systematic analysis, McKeiver simply listed reasons why judges provided an adequate alternative to a jury's fact-finding capabilities, why a jury would disrupt or impair informal juvenile proceedings, and why a jury would not affirmatively improve the operations of juvenile courts. The Court balanced the function of the jury right against its impact on the juvenile system. It also considered whether jury trials were less critical in the juvenile than in the criminal justice system. The McKeiver plurality and Justice White's concurrence noted that juvenile courts' intake process and judges' rehabilitative ideology protected against governmental oppression. The Court re-affirmed its commitment to the "rehabilitative ideal," emphasized the desirability of maintaining informal and flexible juvenile courts, and asserted that judges could find facts as readily and fairly as juries. In addition, the Court emphasized the adverse impact that a jury trial could have on the juvenile court: it could make proceedings more adversarial and foster greater convergence with the criminal process; it would introduce greater formality; and it could abridge confidentiality and lead to public trials. Granting juveniles the right to a jury trial would eliminate virtually all procedural differences between juvenile and criminal courts and might provide the impetus to eliminate a separate juvenile court.

Blackmun asserted that jury trials could lead to public trials, although he did not analyze why that would be detrimental. By contrast, Justice Brennan's concurring and dissenting opinion in McKeiver is consistent with the broader two-fold rationale of Gault—factual-accuracy and preventing government oppression—and responded to Blackmun's concerns about public trials. Brennan balanced the function of the jury against its impact on juvenile courts and saw a public trial as an alternative method to assure the same protections. Unlike Blackmun, Brennan recognized that Gault was not concerned solely with accurate fact-finding. For Brennan, due process does not command a particular procedure but a result—protecting the individual from the government. Although in adult proceedings, the jury functions to prevent governmental oppression, Brennan felt that a public trial in juvenile courts could perform that function because of the community's greater concern for younger offenders.

Justice White's McKeiver concurrence highlighted some important distinctions between treatment in juvenile courts and punishment in criminal proceedings. White, more than Blackmun, developed the treatment rationale to justify denying delinquents all adult criminal procedural safeguards. Whereas the criminal law punishes morally responsible actors for making blameworthy choices, the juvenile system regards delinquents as less culpable for their criminal misdeeds and imposes less severe sanctions. White emphasized jurisprudential distinctions between juvenile and criminal courts—determinism versus free will and treatment versus punishment. He asserted that real differences remained between criminal and juvenile courts because of the indeterminate and non-proportional length of juvenile dispositions and the rejection of punishment for blameworthy choices.

Three dissenting McKeiver Justices continued the incorporation debate and argued that if the state accused a juvenile of a crime that could result in institutional confinement, then the proceeding was effectively a criminal trial in all but name and required adult criminal procedural protections. In such a de facto criminal proceeding, Duncan v. Louisiana already had decided the question of the right to a jury trial as a Sixth Amendment matter.

If McKeiver had held that juveniles enjoyed a constitutional right to a jury trial, then virtually every delinquent would enjoy that right. In Baldwin v. New York, 399 U.S. 66 (S.Ct.1970), the Court held that in adult criminal prosecutions, "no offense can be deemed 'petty' for purposes of the right to trial by jury where imprisonment of more than six months is authorized." Under Baldwin, the penalty authorized by statute, rather than the actual sentence a judge imposed, determined whether a defendant enjoyed a Sixth Amendment right to a jury trial. Most states' delinquency disposition statutes authorize sentences for longer than six months even for misdemeanors, and may extend for the duration of minority, for a term of years, or even beyond the age of majority. See Chapter 8. If juveniles had a constitutional right to a jury trial, then no delinquency proceeding would be deemed "petty" under Baldwin.

a. Judge and Jury Reasonable Doubt

The Supreme Court has emphasized that the criminal standard of proof beyond a reasonable doubt and the right to have a jury apply it are interrelated. E.g. Sullivan v. Louisiana, 508 U.S. 275 (S.Ct.1993). Thus, even if Blackmun was correct that due process and fundamental fairness only require accurate fact-finding, one may question whether judges and juries decide cases similarly and produce comparable factual outcomes and verdicts. Juries decide cases differently than do judges, provide special protections to assure factual accuracy, use a higher evidentiary threshold when they apply Winship's proof beyond a reasonable doubt standard, and acquit defendants more readily than do judges. See e.g., Barry C. Feld, "The Constitutional Tension Between *Apprendi* and *McKeiver*: Sentence Enhancements Based on Delinquency Convictions and the Quality of Justice in Juvenile Courts," 38 Wake Forest L. Rev. 1111 (2003).

Fact-finding by judges and juries differs intrinsically because the former may try dozens of cases a year while the latter may hear only one or two cases in a lifetime. As a result of hearing many cases routinely, judges may become less meticulous in considering evidence, may evaluate facts more casually, and may apply less stringently than jurors the concepts of reasonable doubt and presumption of innocence. The personal characteristics of judges differ from those of jurors, but defendants cannot assess how those factors might affect their decisions. Through voir dire, litigants examine jurors about their attitudes, beliefs, and experiences. No comparable opportunity exists to explore judges' backgrounds, attitudes, or biases. Juries and judges also evaluate testimony differently. Judges more readily convict on the basis of insufficient evidence than do jurors. Analysts attribute this tendency to judges' exposure to inadmissible evidence from which jurors are sheltered, to judges' familiarity with the police and probations officers who regularly testify before them, and to judges' greater skepticism about the testimony of the accused. E.g., Feld, Constitutional Tension Between Apprendi and McKeiver. Juvenile court judges hear testimony from the same police and probation officers on a recurring basis and develop settled opinions about their credibility. As a result of hearing earlier charges against a juvenile, presiding over a detention hearing, or deciding a pretrial motion to suppress evidence, a judge already may have a predetermined view of a youth's credibility, character, and guilt. Fact-finding by a judge differs from that by a jury because an individual fact-finder does not have to discuss either the law or the evidence with members of a group before reaching a conclusion. Although a judge must instruct a jury explicitly about the law it applies to a case, in a bench trial a judge does not state the law, so it is more difficult to determine whether she correctly understood and applied it.

b. Right to a Jury Trial in the States

McKeiver noted that the Court's reading of the federal Constitution did not prevent states from providing delinquents with a jury trial either by statute or by interpretation of state constitutional provisions. Prior to McKeiver, several state courts construed Gault and Duncan v. Louisiana to require jury trials in juvenile courts. These opinions did not use McKeiver's balancing process to weigh the advantages of a jury against their impact on juvenile courts. They reasoned that Gault required procedural safeguards because crime and delinquency are similar, the constitution required a jury for crimes, and mandated a jury for delinquency trials. Several others states long had granted delinquents a statutory right to a jury trial.

In R.L.R. v. State, 487 P.2d 27 (Alaska 1971), the court considered juveniles' rights to a jury trial and to a public trial under the Alaska state constitution. The court critically analyzed "the benevolent social theory" undergirding the juvenile court act and concluded that the state's commitment to the rehabilitative ideal did not justify depriving juveniles of their constitutional rights. For R.L.R., like the dissenters in McKeiver, the fact that the state charged a juvenile with a criminal offense that could result in incarceration established the state right to a jury trial. Moreover, under state

constitutional law, the right to a jury trial was co-
extensive with the right to counsel which attached
for any offense carrying the possibility of
imprisonment. As a matter of judicial decision or
statutory enactment, about ten states provide
juveniles with a right to a jury trial in juvenile court
for some or all criminal charges. E.g. Colo. Rev.
Stat. § 19–2–107(1)(a) (2000); Mich. Comp. Laws
Ann. § 712A.17 (West 1993); N.M. Stat. Ann. § 32A–
2–16A (Michie 1988); Tex. Fam. Code Ann.
§ 54.03(c) (Vernon 2000). Even jurisdictions that
provide a statutory right to a jury trial may restrict
its availability to youths charged with more serious
offenses, such as an aggravated juvenile offense or
crimes of violence. E.g. A.C., IV v. People, 16 P.3d
240 (Colo.2001). Although McKeiver and opponents
of jury trials in juvenile court contend that they
substantially disrupt delinquency proceedings, the
experience of states that provide juveniles with a
jury and empirical studies of their use do not
support those fears. E.g. Feld, Constitutional
Tension Between Apprendi and McKeiver. Like
adult criminal defendants, the vast majorities of
delinquents plead guilty rather than go to trial.

The differences between punishment and
treatment remain central to the contemporary
vitality of the Court's rationale in McKeiver. During
the 1990s, every state revised its juvenile code to
make it easier to transfer some youths to criminal
court for prosecution as adults and to enable
juvenile court judges to impose longer and more
restrictive sanctions on those delinquents who
remain within the juvenile court's jurisdiction. E.g.

Torbet, *State Responses*; Chapter 6. As states adopted "get tough" policies, juveniles renewed requests for a constitutional right to a jury trial, state supreme courts re-evaluated differences between juvenile treatment and criminal punishment, and reconsidered the continuing vitality of McKeiver.

The Supreme Court uses several criteria to analyze whether a state treats or punishes a person when state agencies use coercive controls. E.g. Allen v. Illinois, 478 U.S. 364 (S.Ct.1986). Courts consider juvenile courts' legislative preambles or purpose clauses, delinquency sentencing statutes, judges' sentencing practices, conditions of confinement, and evaluations of treatment effectiveness to determine whether juvenile court dispositions are therapeutic or punitive. State courts use these factors to evaluate delinquents' requests for a jury trial in light of punitive legislative changes.

Several states have considered whether McKeiver's denial of a constitutional right to a jury trial remains valid after recent "get tough" legislative changes. Several juveniles in Wisconsin challenged 1995 amendments to the state's juvenile code that simultaneously repealed a statutory right to a jury trial and increased the severity of delinquency sanctions. State v. Hezzie R., 219 Wis.2d 848, 580 N.W.2d 660 (Wis.1998). The Hezzie R. majority surveyed the shift in philosophical emphases from rehabilitation to accountability and community protection, the symbolic renaming of the Children's Code as the Juvenile Justice Code, its statutory placement next to the criminal code, and the increased penalties and collateral consequences associated with convictions for serious offenses. The juveniles argued that the amendments effectively converted a delinquency proceeding into a criminal trial in all but name. The majority rejected their claims and insisted that rehabilitation remained an objective of the juvenile code because judges made individualized sentencing decisions. Even though conviction of certain offenses could lead to commitment in a secure facility until age 25, the court concluded that the state confined youths to treat them and segregated them from adults. Despite a quarter-century of substantial changes in sentencing policies, Hezzie R. regarded McKeiver as controlling authority. A strong dissent in Hezzie R. concluded that the purpose and effect of delinquency proceedings had become criminal in nature and required a jury trial. Revisions of the purpose clause, sentencing structure, and collateral consequences of convictions effectively had converted delinquency proceedings into de facto criminal proceedings. Accordingly, McKeiver provided no precedent for a system that differed radically from the one the Court reviewed in 1971.

The Pennsylvania Superior Court in In the Interest of J.F. and G.G., 714 A.2d 467 (Pa.Super.Ct.1998), reviewed similar get tough changes in the Pennsylvania juvenile code and reached the same conclusion as Hezzie R. Again, juveniles argued that statutory amendments transformed the juvenile court into a punitive system akin to the criminal justice system and requested a jury trial. The Court analyzed the history of the juvenile court, amendments to the purpose clause, sentencing provisions, subsequent uses of delinquency convictions to enhance sentences, and collateral consequences of adjudication. The court concluded that rehabilitation remained a goal of the juvenile system and reaffirmed the validity of McKeiver. The Court in In the Interest of D.J., 817 So. 2d 26 (La. 2002), concluded that notwithstanding legislative enactment of "get tough" law," differences in the severity of penalties imposed on delinquents and adults justified procedural differences between the two systems and reaffirmed denial of a jury trial. Even when a state includes delinquency convictions as a "strike" to enhance sentences under a "three-strike" laws, courts deny youths the right to a jury trial. E.g. People v. Fowler, 72 Cal.App.4th 581, 84 Cal.Rptr.2d 874 (Cal.App.1999).

By contrast, the Kansas Supreme Court in In re L.M., 286 Kan.460, 186 P.3d 164 (Kan. 2008), overruled an earlier precedent, Findlay v. State, 681 P.2d 20 (1984), and held that juveniles have a constitutional right to a jury trial under the Sixth and Fourteenth Amendments and under the State Constitution. The Court reasoned that two decades of legislative changes to the state's juvenile code had eroded the benevolent, rehabilitative, and parens patriae character of Kansas' juvenile courts that distinguished them from the criminal justice system. As evidence of the erosion of juvenile courts' rehabilitative goals, the Court noted changes in the purpose clause to emphasize public protection and juvenile accountability, replacement of non-punitive juvenile justice rhetoric with terminology similar to that contained in the criminal code, adoption of a matrix that used the same principles as the adult sentencing guidelines and based juveniles' sentences on their present offense and prior record, and removal of protections such as closed and confidential proceedings on which McKeiver relied to distinguish juvenile and criminal courts. "[B]ecause the juvenile justice system is now patterned after the adult criminal system, we conclude that the changes have superseded the McKeiver and Findlay Courts' reasoning and those decisions are no longer binding precedent for us to follow . . . [T]he Kansas juvenile justice system has become more akin to an adult criminal prosecution, [and] we hold that juveniles have a constitutional right to a jury trial under the Sixth and Fourteenth Amendments." The dissent in L.M. acknowledged that the juvenile system had become more punitive, but objected that the majority overemphasized those changes and failed to recognize the remaining protective and rehabilitative features that continued to distinguish it from the punitive, retributive adult criminal system.

In a multi-purpose system like the juvenile court, at what point on a continuum from a purely rehabilitative juvenile court to an explicitly punitive one, do legislative changes "cross the line" and create the functional equivalent of a criminal court? The Louisiana Supreme Court in In re C.B., 708 So.2d 391 (La.1998), concluded that the legislature crossed the line when it denied juveniles confined in adult correctional institutions the right to a jury trial. In In re C.B., the legislation provided for delinquents' transfer to adult correctional facilities at age seventeen to complete their remaining juvenile sentences. The court concluded that once the juvenile code allowed judges to sentence juveniles to the same institutions as adults convicted of crimes, then no differences existed between juvenile and criminal proceedings to justify dispensing with a jury trial. The court in Hezzie R. struck down a provision of the Wisconsin juvenile code that allowed the state to transfer juveniles convicted without a jury trial to the adult correctional system. If a state sentences juveniles to adult correctional institution, then it clearly punishes them and must provide a right a jury as a constitutional prerequisite. E.g. In re Jeffrey C., 781 A.2d 4 (N.H.2001) (juvenile entitled to jury trial prior to commitment to adult facility).

Because the vast majority of states deny delinquents the right to a jury trial, youths sometimes ask the juvenile court judge to waive them to criminal court so that they may to have a jury trial. Unless the waiver statute expressly allows juveniles to file a waiver motion, state courts consistently rebuff youths' efforts to obtain a jury trial. E.g. In re K.A.A., 410 N.W.2d 836 (Minn.1987) (allowing a juvenile to waive juvenile court jurisdiction ignores juvenile's and state's interest in treating youth); In re Anna Marie S., 99 Cal.App.3d 869, 872, 160 Cal.Rptr. 495, 497 (Cal.Ct.App.1979) (state has a compelling interest to treat all juveniles who are amenable to treatment); In re D.B., 187

Ga.App. 3, 4, 369 S.E.2d 498, 499 (Ga.Ct.App.1988) (juvenile must abide by the determination of others as to his best interests).

c. Right to a Public Trial in the States

The Sixth Amendment guarantees adult criminal defendants the right to a public trial. E.g. Estes v. Texas, 381 U.S. 532 (S.Ct.1965). In In re Oliver, 333 U.S. 257 (S.Ct.1948), the Court noted that public trials bring the matters at issue to the attention of unknown witnesses who then may come forward to provide testimony, they provide citizens with information about the administration of justice, they promote confidence in the judiciary, and provide a check on potential abuses of judicial power. Traditionally, juvenile courts conducted confidential proceedings that were closed to the public, although the judge had discretion to allow people with a special interest to attend. The practice of allowing students, social workers, lawyers, social scientists, and other to observe the court without any specific interest in the child or case vitiates the promise of confidentiality without affording the benefits of a public hearing. American Bar Association, *Juvenile Justice Standards Relating to Adjudication* (1980).

The McKeiver plurality denied delinquents a jury trial because it feared that it would introduce into the juvenile system the "delay, the formality, and the clamor of the adversary system and, possibly, the public trial." By contrast, Justice Brennan's concurring and dissenting opinion in McKeiver regarded a public trial as the functional equivalent of a jury trial to prevent governmental oppression. The court in R.L.R. identified other interests that a public trial protected—reducing governmental oppression through visibility and accountability of proceedings, bringing the case to the attention of potential unknown witnesses, providing the public with knowledge about justice administration, and securing confidence in the judiciary. The R.L.R. court observed that juvenile court judges allowed many observers into nominally closed delinquency proceedings, thereby compromising confidentiality concerns but without affording the benefits of public hearings. R.L.R. noted that these protections were especially crucial in the low-visibility juvenile justice system. "We cannot help but notice that children's cases appealed to this court have often shown much more extensive and fundamental error than is generally found in adult criminal cases and wonder whether secrecy is not fostering a judicial attitude of casualness toward the law in children's proceedings." The court gave short-shrift to the state's interests in limiting public trials—protecting youthful indiscretions from publicity, protecting a youth from stigma that might interfere with her rehabilitation, protecting a youth's family from embarrassment or loss of employment, and discouraging youths from engaging in further anti-social acts in order to gain attention. The court in In the Interest of Dino, 359 So.2d 586 (La.1978), also found a state constitutional right to a public trial in delinquency proceedings. About half of the states have opened delinquency proceedings to the public either for specified serious crimes or more broadly.

E.g. Torbet, *State Responses*. For example, Minnesota opens to the public all delinquency proceedings of youths sixteen- or seventeen-years of age and charged with a felony. E.g. Minn. Stat. § 260B.155 (West 2000).

Closed delinquency proceedings create conflict when juvenile court confidentiality restrictions collide with First Amendment press access. The Supreme Court has held that the press enjoys a First Amendment right of access to criminal trials to foster an appearance of fairness, to heighten public respect for the process, and to enhance the "quality and safeguard the integrity of the fact-finding process, with benefits to both the defendant and to society as a whole." Globe Newspaper Co. v. Superior Court, 457 U.S. 596 (S.Ct.1982). Similarly, the Court in Smith v. Daily Mail Publishing, 443 U.S. 97 (S.Ct.1979), held that if a newspaper lawfully obtains accurate information about a delinquency matter from an independent source, then the state cannot prohibit or sanction the paper for publishing that information. In the absence of a statutory right of press access, state courts decline to permit newspapers to attend and report on closed juvenile court proceedings. The court in In re J.S., 438 A.2d 1125 (Vt.1981), emphasized the traditional confidentiality, the protective and welfare nature of the proceedings, and the non-punitive goals of the juvenile court to deny press access. Other states' statutes provide that delinquency proceedings are "closed unless the court finds compelling reasons to require otherwise" and places the burden on the newspaper to establish the "compelling reasons" that require open proceedings. E.g. Matter of M.C., 527 N.W.2d 290 (S.D.1995).

In other jurisdictions, juvenile courts have discretion whether or not to exclude the public and the press. The court in State ex rel. Plain Dealer Publishing Company v. Geauga County Court of Common Pleas, 734 N.E.2d 1214 (Ohio 2000), balanced juveniles' interests in confidential and rehabilitative proceedings against increased visibility and accountability of justice administration and offenders. It concluded that a juvenile court may restrict public access to delinquency proceedings after a public hearing in which the court finds that: public access could harm the child or endanger the fairness of the trial, the potential for harm outweighs the benefits of public access, and no reasonable alternatives to closure exist.

B. NOTICE OF CHARGES

Recall from Chapter 4, if court intake staff or prosecutors decide to refer a case for formal court intervention, then they file a delinquency petition. State statutes vary as to whether the prosecutor or the probation officer must sign the petition. E.g. Fla. Stat. Ann. § 985.21 (2001) (juvenile probation officer recommends to state attorney whether or not to file petition). The petition is the formal charging document that asserts the grounds for court jurisdiction—delinquency, status offense, child in need of supervision, or the like—and the factual bases to support that conclusion. A petition is the juvenile court equivalent of a complaint, information, or indictment in a criminal prosecution or a complaint in a civil matter.

The Supreme Court in Gault required states to give the child and her parent timely written notice of charges sufficiently in advance to allow the child to prepare a defense—"notice which would be deemed constitutionally adequate in a civil or criminal proceeding." Statutes govern the specific contents of petitions and the timeliness with which the state must give notice. E.g. Minn. Stat. § 260B.141 (West 2000); Tex. Fam. Code § 53.01 (Vernon 2000). Because Gault relied on the Fourteenth Amendment due process clause, rather than the Sixth Amendment, several questions remained unanswered. Does the language "adequate in a civil or criminal proceeding" require the state to file a petition alleging probable cause as in a criminal charging document? Does the language that "the child and his parents or guardian [must] be notified" give parents a constitutional right to notice as well as the child? If so, then what are the consequences if the state fails to notify them? May the state amend its petition during the trial if the facts and offense proven vary from those initially charged?

State statutes authorize juvenile courts to provide notice by personal service or by mail and allow greater time for the latter. E.g. Minn. Stat. Ann. § 260B.141 (West 2000); N.D. Cent. Code § 27–2–23 (2000). Statutes also provide for a period of time between the filing of a petition and an arraignment hearing in order to allow a youth's attorney to prepare. E.g. Tex. Fam. Code Ann. § 53.05 (Vernon 2000) (10 days).

Some jurisdictions require the same specificity in a petition as in an indictment or complaint including reference to the criminal statute. E.g. In re Dennis, 291 So.2d 731 (Miss.1974); In re D.S.H., 549 P.2d 826 (Okla.Crim.App.1976) (delinquency allegation requires same particularity and specificity as in criminal cases). Others require the petition to state "with reasonable particularity, the time, place, and manner of the acts alleged and the penal law or standard of conduct allegedly violated by the acts," e.g. Tex. Fam. Code Ann. § 53.04(d) (Vernon 2000), but do not require the particularity of a criminal indictment. E.g. In re M.A.V., Jr., v. Webb County Court, 842 S.W.2d 739 (Tex.Ct.App.1992). Some statutes require the allegations in the petition to provide a criminal probable cause statement. E.g. N.Y. Fam. Ct. §§ 311.1 and 311.2 (McKinney 2000).

While some states require the petition to include a statement of probable cause either in its allegations or by supplemental reports, most states do not require a probable cause statement in the petition unless the state detains the youth. E.g., Cal. Welf. & Inst. Code § 656(f) (1999) ("A concise statement of facts . . . to support the conclusion that the minor . . . is a person within the definition [of the jurisdiction of juvenile court]"); In re Jesse P., 3 Cal.App.4th 1177, 5 Cal.Rptr.2d 321 (Cal.Ct.App.1992); Md. R. Proc. Juv. Causes 11–

103(2)(c) (1998) ("The facts, in clear and simple language, on which the allegations are based"); Minn. R. Juv. Proc. 6.03 Subd. 3(A) and (B) (1999) ("a concise statement alleging the child is delinquent" and "a description of the alleged offense and reference to the statute or ordinance which was violated"). Most statutes and court rule simply require a delinquency petition to contain a "plain and concise statement, without allegations of an evidentiary nature, asserting facts supporting every element of a criminal offense and the juvenile's commission thereof with sufficient precision clearly to apprise the juvenile of the conduct which is the subject of the accusation." N.C. Gen. Stat. § 7A–560 (1998); In the Interest of A.W., 438 N.W.2d 557, 559 (S.D.1989) ("the test of the sufficiency of a petition of delinquency is whether it apprises a juvenile with reasonable certainty of the nature of the accusation against him so that he may prepare his defense and plead the judgment as a bar to any subsequent prosecution for the same offense.").

Gault required notice to parents as well as to the juvenile. Courts divide on whether failure to notify a parent violates the Constitution and, if so, what the appropriate remedy is. In United States v. Watts, 513 F.2d 5 (10th Cir.1975), the court found that failure to notify the parents did not require automatic reversal of the juvenile's delinquency adjudication. The court reasoned that the purpose of the notification statute was to provide the juvenile an opportunity to consult with those people most concerned with her best interests, to make aware of the charges, and to provide a reasonable opportunity for her to prepare a defense. The court concluded that the parents' function seemed to be similar to that of counsel. Despite the technical violation of the notice requirement, the juvenile was not denied due process and the court declined to adopt a per se rule requiring reversal. Other jurisdictions have construed statutes that require parental notification as mandatory provisions. Failure to comply with the statutory mandate requires reversal of a juvenile's adjudication or waiver to criminal court. E.g., Karim v. Commonwealth, 21 Va. App. 652, 466 S.E.2d 772 (Va.Ct.App.1996) (mandatory provision and failure to comply renders proceedings invalid); Baker v. Commonwealth, 28 Va.App. 306, 504 S.E.2d 394 (Va.Ct.App.1998); In re C.R.H., 163 Ill.2d 263, 644 N.E.2d 1153, 206 Ill.Dec. 100 (Ill. 1994) (constitutional right to parental notice and court lacks jurisdiction to adjudicate delinquent in the absence of compliance).

State charging practices for juveniles differ from those for adults in other respects. For example, under the California penal code, once a court dismisses a misdemeanor charge against an adult defendant, the prosecutor may not refile the charge. For less serious offenses, the state only gets "one bite at the apple." By contrast, the court in In re Nan P., 230 Cal.App.3d 751, 281 Cal.Rptr. 468 (Cal.Ct.App.1991), held that the adult practice does not apply to delinquency cases because rehabilitation remains the primary purpose of the juvenile system and the state has a stronger interest to establish jurisdiction to "nip budding character defects before they blossom into adult criminal behavior."

Because most jurisdiction encourage plain and concise petitions without technical criminal pleading, prosecutors often discover variance between the allegations of the petition and the proof they present at trial. State statutes typically authorize amendment of petitions prior to the attachment of jeopardy. "With leave of court, prior to the adjudication hearing, the petitioner may amend the petition to include new allegations of fact or requests for adjudication. However, if such leave is granted, the child may request a continuance of the adjudication hearing." La. Code Juv. Proc. Ann. § 846 (2000); State v. R.W., 721 So.2d 943 (La.Ct.App.1998) (amendment prior to adjudication and case held open to allow juvenile opportunity to prepare defense to amended petition).

The court in In re Steven G., 556 A.2d 131 (Conn.1989), confronted the more difficult question whether the state's attorney could amend the petition after it began the delinquency hearing. Although in adult criminal proceeding, the state may not amend a complaint in mid-trial to add different charges without violating due process, the court in Steven G. approved the practice in delinquency proceedings. The court noted that because the state conducts delinquency hearings without a jury, they remain more informal than criminal trials. Juvenile court practice allows the prosecutor to amend the petition provided she notifies the parties and provides sufficient time to prepare to meet the new charges. E.g. In re Isaac G., 189 Ariz. 634, 944 P.2d 1248 (Ariz.Ct.App.1997) (court may amend petition and give juvenile opportunity to prepare defense to amended charges); In re Victoria K., 11 P.3d 1066 (Ariz.Ct.App.2000) (as a result of changes in juvenile rules, courts no longer have authority sua sponte to amend petition). Other courts prohibit amendment if the substituted charges would require a different defense from that originally charged. E.g. State ex rel. Juvenile Department v. Henson, 97 Or.App. 26, 775 P.2d 325 (Or.App.1989); In the Interest of M.W., 218 Ga.App. 658, 462 S.E.2d 796 (Ga.Ct.App.1995) (state may not cure fatal variance between allegations and evidence introduced at trial). Even if the state amends the petition, the court must give a continuance to allow the defense to prepare to meet the new charges. A failure to do so violates due process. In re Roy C., 169 Cal.App.3d 912, 215 Cal.Rptr. 513 (Cal.Ct.App.1985).

Courts distinguish between amending a petition to charge a different offense and adjudicating a youth for lesser included offenses, all the elements of which are subsumed in the notice given for the higher offense charged. E.g. D.P. v. State, 200 S.E.2d 499 (Ga.Ct.App.1973) (state alleged burglary and proved receiving stolen property). The standard is whether the elements of the greater offense always and necessarily include those that comprise the lesser offense. Courts differ as to whether a status offense constitutes a "lesser included" element of a delinquency allegation. For example, the court in In re Felton, 124 Ohio App.3d 500, 706

N.E.2d 809 (Ohio Ct.App.1997), allowed the state to amend a petition charging delinquency and to convict a youth for "unruly conduct" which endangers his health or morals, a status offense.

C. HEARINGS AND EVIDENCE

Following Gault, Winship and McKeiver, delinquents theoretically enjoy most of the trial rights available to adult criminal defendants, except the right to a jury trial. Some state statutes succinctly provide that "All rights guaranteed to criminal defendants by the Constitution of the United States or the Constitution of Louisiana, except the right to jury trial, shall be applicable in juvenile court proceedings brought under this Title." La. Child. Code Art. 808 (West 1999); N.J. Stat. § 2A:4A–40 (2001) ("all rights guaranteed to criminal defendants ... except the right to indictment, the right to trial by jury and the right to bail . . ."). However, the right to a jury trial affects other procedural and evidentiary aspects of criminal or delinquency trials.

State statutes and juvenile court rules of procedure typically make separate provisions for delinquent and status offenders that govern the conduct of trials, appointment of counsel, burdens of proof, admissibility of evidence, presence of parents, and the like. E.g. Cal. Welf. & Inst. Code § 701 (West 2000). Following Winship, states must prove delinquency by "proof beyond a reasonable doubt supported by evidence legally admissible in the trial of criminal cases." Cal. Welf. & Inst. Code § 701

(West 2000). Juveniles' right to a jury trial depends on state constitutional or statutory law. E.g. Colo. Rev. Stat. Ann. § 19–2–107 (West 2000) (juvenile charged as "aggravated juvenile offender" or with violent offense may demand trial by a six person jury); Minn. Ann. Stat. § 260B.155 Subd. 1(a) (West 2000) (delinquency hearings shall be without a jury and conducted in an informal manner).

After the state file of a petition, the juvenile court arraigns the youth. At the arraignment, if the juvenile has not retained counsel, then the court will advise her of the right to counsel and to appointed counsel if the child qualifies as an indigent. See Section D, Right to Counsel, infra. At the arraignment, the juvenile must admit or deny the allegations in the petition. "An oral or written answer to the petition may be made at or before the commencement of the hearing. If there is no answer, a general denial of the alleged conduct is assumed." Tex. Fam. Code Ann. § 53.04 (Vernon 2000). In the vast majority of cases, juveniles admit the allegations of the petition, i.e. plead guilty. See Section G, Guilty Plea, infra. Most states' juvenile codes require the juvenile either to admit or to deny the allegations of the petition and do not include the option of pleading nolo contendere. E.g. In the Interest of B.P.Y., 712 A.2d 769 (Pa.Super.Ct.1998) (no nolo contedere plea); Fla. R. Juv. P. 8.080 ("Before accepting a plea of guilty or nolo contendere, the court shall determine that the plea is knowingly and voluntarily entered . . ."). If the juvenile denies the allegations of the petition, then the court sets the matter on the calendar for an adjudicatory hearing or trial.

1.   DISCOVERY

The Supreme Court in Kent v. United States held that the youth's lawyer must have access to the social history report on which the juvenile court judge based the waiver decision. As a constitutional matter, prosecutors have a due process obligation to furnish defendants with exculpatory evidence within their possession. Brady v. Maryland, 373 U.S. 83 (S.Ct.1963). Although criminal defendants have a Fifth Amendment privilege against self-incrimination, the Court has held that conditioning the admissibility of a defendant's evidence at trial on pretrial discovery only affects the timing of disclosure and required him to disclose earlier in the proceedings information he planned to use at trial. Williams v. Florida, 399 U.S. 78 (S.Ct.1970). Beginning in the 1970s, states broadened the scope of discovery in criminal cases both by defense and by prosecution. LaFave, *Criminal Procedure.*

State courts typically use criminal court rules of discovery in delinquency proceedings despite juvenile courts' nominally civil character. E.g. Joe Z. v. Superior Court, 3 Cal.3d 797, 478 P.2d 26, 91 Cal.Rptr. 594 (Cal.1970) (discovery practices in delinquency proceedings derived from those used in criminal cases); In re Robert S., 9 Cal.App.4th 1417, 12 Cal.Rptr.2d 489 (Cal.App.1992); People ex rel. Hanrahan v. Felt, 48 Ill.2d 171, 269 N.E.2d 1 (Ill.1971) (delinquency is distinct from other civil actions and inappropriate automatically to apply civil discovery provisions). As a result of Kent, discovery provisions apply in both transfer hearings and delinquency proceedings. E.g. In re A.M., 139 Ohio App.3d 303, 743 N.E.2d 937 (Ohio App.2000) (discovery to prepare for probable cause hearing in waiver process).

State statutes and court rules govern the scope of discovery and the processes juveniles and prosecutors use to obtain disclosures from the other party. E.g. Tex. Fam. Code Ann. § 51.17 (Vernon 2002) ("Discovery . . . is governed by the Code of Criminal Procedure and by case decisions in criminal cases"); Ark. Code Ann. § 9–27–325(f) (Michie 2000) (apply rules of criminal procedure to delinquency proceedings). States typically pattern their juvenile rules for discovery after the applicable rules of criminal procedure. E.g. Minn. R. Juv. Proc. 10; Ohio R. Juv. P. 24. Under such rules, prosecutors must disclose to juveniles evidence that may raise constitutional issues—evidence obtained as a result of search and seizure, confessions, identification procedures, and the like—to enable the juvenile to make an appropriate motion to suppress evidence. Jurisdictions require prosecutors to disclose to defense counsel witness lists, copies of witnesses' prior records and any written or recorded statements, papers, documents or tangible objects it intends to introduce, and any statements made by the child or accomplices.

Because discovery is reciprocal—"a two-way street"—juvenile defendants must disclose certain information to the prosecution as a prerequisite to its introduction at trial. Clinton K. v. Superior Court, 44 Cal.Rptr.2d 140, 37 Cal.App.4th 1244 (Cal.Ct.App.1995) (court's inherent authority to permit discovery by prosecution prior to waiver hearing). These include documents, tangible objects, and test results which the juvenile intends to introduce at trial as well as notice of certain defenses, such as alibi, and prospective witnesses. Minn. R. Juv. Proc. 10.

2.   SUPPRESSION HEARINGS AND EVIDENCE

If jurors are exposed to inadmissible evidence, it may prejudice their decisions. This concern underlies many rules of evidence and affects the timing and conduct of suppression hearings. The Court in Jackson v. Denno, 378 U.S. 368 (S.Ct.1964), established the procedure to determine the admissibility of constitutional evidence at trial. Jackson rejected the practice of admitting a confession into evidence without any preliminary judicial determination of its voluntariness. Jackson reasoned that an appellate court could not adequately determine from a general verdict of guilt whether a jury had properly disregarded a confession that it had found involuntary. It feared that a jury could not decide about the voluntariness of a confession and the separate question of a defendant's guilt. Evidence of guilt would affect its evaluations of voluntariness and involuntary confessions could affect assessments of guilt. The Court concluded that state procedures must provide a "reliable and clear-cut determination of the voluntariness of the confession. . . . Whether the trial judge, another judge or another jury, but not the convicting jury, fully resolves the issue of voluntariness is not a matter of concern here." As a result, judges determine the constitutional admissibility of evidence obtained by police from searches, interrogation, and the like, prior to their introduction at trial and out of the presence of the jury. LaFave, *Criminal Procedure*.

The Supreme Court in New Jersey v. T.L.O., 469 U.S. 325 (S.Ct.1985), never reached the question whether the exclusionary rule applied in delinquency proceedings because it concluded that the school search was reasonable. All state courts that have considered the issue have applied the rule in delinquency adjudications and exclude evidence obtained in violation of the constitution. E.g. In re Scott K., 24 Cal.3d 395, 155 Cal.Rptr. 671, 595 P.2d 105 (Cal.1979) (exclusion ensures fact-finding process conforms with due process); In re Marsh, 40 Ill.2d 53, 237 N.E.2d 529 (Ill.1968); S.A.F. v. State, 483 So.2d 110 (Fla.Ct.App.1986); In re Montrail M., 87 Md.App. 420, 589 A.2d 1318 (Md.Ct.App.1991). Courts employ the exclusionary rule in federal delinquency cases as well.

> The failure to adhere to the exclusionary rule in juvenile delinquency cases would reduce significantly the effectiveness of the rule's general deterrent powers. . . . A holding that there is no practical remedy for the violation of the Fourth Amendment rights of suspects who will be processed by the federal juvenile

delinquency system might be received by some members of the law enforcement community as tantamount to a declaration that all restraints on police behavior toward juveniles had been removed. United States v. Doe, 801 F.Supp. 1562 (E.D.Tex.1992).

Some states follow adult criminal procedures and determine the constitutional admissibility of evidence prior to trial. E.g. Cal. Welf. & Inst. Code § 700.1 (West 1999) ("Any motion to suppress as evidence any tangible or intangible thing obtained as a result of an unlawful search or seizure shall be heard prior to the attachment of jeopardy . . ."); In the Matter of the Welfare of J.P.L., 359 N.W.2d 622 (Minn.Ct.App.1985) (better procedure in juvenile cases would be to conduct suppression hearing separately and before trial). Unlike the adult practice, however, many states litigate suppression issues during a juvenile's trial rather than in a separate pretrial evidentiary hearing or before a different fact-finder. The reason for allowing judges, but not juries, to decide both admissibility and guilt in same proceeding rests on the assumption that judges' professional training, temperament, and experience enables them to compartmentalize inadmissible and admissible evidence, and to decide the case based only on admissible evidence. Appellate courts presume that inadmissible evidence that would prejudice a jury does not improperly influence a trial judge exposed to the same evidence. Many procedural and evidentiary rules rest on the assumption that judges in bench trials are not influenced by exposure to inadmissible or suppressed evidence. It could be administratively impractical and inconvenient to require one judge to rule on the admissibility of evidence and another to preside at trial.

States can avoid the risk of evidentiary contamination for delinquents by providing for jury trials or by requiring a different judge to rule on the admissibility of evidence prior to trial as some jurisdictions do. Conducting suppression hearings prior to the trial also protects the state's right to an interlocutory appeal. Once jeopardy has attached, a ruling that evidence is inadmissible may preclude either appellate review or retrial of an acquitted defendant. E.g., Breed v. Jones. In addition, a pretrial suppression hearing assures that a juvenile defendant who wants to testify only about the voluntariness of a confession or the admissibility of other evidence is able to do so without prejudice. Conducting suppression hearings prior to trial or before a different judge minimize a fact-finder's possible confusion by separating testimony about admissibility from testimony that bears on questions of guilt or innocence.

Under California's adult criminal procedure, Cal. Penal Code § 1538.5 (West 1999), either the defendant or the state may obtain pretrial appellate review of an adverse ruling on a suppression motion. However, in Abdullah B. vs. Superior Court of Solano County, 135 Cal.App.3d 838, 185 Cal.Rptr. 784 (Cal.Ct.App.1982), the court endorsed a different procedure for review of juvenile court judges' pretrial rulings on suppression motions brought by juveniles. Unlike an adult defendant, a juvenile may not obtain an interlocutory appellate ruling before the state introduces the evidence at trial. Abdullah B. concluded that the expedited appellate review juveniles receive if the juvenile court convicts them offset this procedural difference.

a. Evidence

Delinquency hearings effectively are criminal prosecutions and most states explicitly provide that "the law of evidence shall apply in adjudicatory proceedings." E.g. Minn. Stat. Ann. § 260B.155 Subd. 1(a) (West 2000); Ill. Juv. Ct. Act § 704–6 (2000) (rules of evidence in criminal proceedings apply in delinquency cases); Tex. Fam. Code Ann. § 54.03 (Vernon 2000) (adjudication based only on "material, relevant, and competent evidence" admissible in accordance with code of criminal procedure). Gault granted juveniles the right to a delinquency adjudication based on "confrontation and sworn testimony by witnesses available for cross-examination . . ." Accordingly, a juvenile court may violate the right to confrontation and cross examination if it considers hearsay evidence that does not satisfy one of the recognized hearsay rule exceptions. E.g. In re Dennis H., 96 Cal.Rptr. 791 (Cal.Ct.App.1971).

Many evidentiary restrictions exist because of concerns about jurors' inability to properly assess or to disregard inadmissible evidence. Although appellate courts generally presume judges' ability to distinguish between admissible and inadmissible evidence when they find facts, courts have reversed delinquency adjudications when the trial judge read the child's social history report prior to adjudication on the merits. E.g. In re Gladys R., 1 Cal.3d 855, 83 Cal.Rptr. 671, 464 P.2d 127 (Cal.1970). The information contained in a social history report does not bear on the juvenile's guilt or innocence, may unduly prejudice the judge against the child, may encourage the court to find the child delinquent to provide help, and may undermine the appellate court's ability to review the trial judge's fact-finding based on the record created at trial. Although Gladys R. found the judge's review of the social history prior to the trial was prejudicial, in many jurisdictions the same judge presides at a child's detention hearing and later at trial. This practice exposes judges to the same type of potentially prejudicial social information prior to the adjudication of the charges.

b. Impeachment

Parties may impeach the testimony of witnesses by prior inconsistent statements, by testimony of other witnesses, and by a record of criminal convictions. Because delinquency adjudications are not formally criminal convictions, their use for impeachment may be problematic. In juvenile courts, the most significant impeachment issue concerns the use of prior delinquency convictions to challenge the credibility of a witness. Using prior adjudications to impeach involves a balancing of juvenile courts' traditional commitment to confidentiality and minimizing stigma against a defendant's right effectively to cross-examine a witness.

In Davis v. Alaska, 415 U.S. 308 (S.Ct.1974), the Court held that the defendant's right to confront a juvenile probationer to demonstrate bias and impeach credibility took precedence over the state's confidentiality statute. "Serious damage to the strength of the State's case would have been a real possibility had petitioner been allowed to pursue this line of inquiry ..." Protecting a defendant's liberty interest took precedence over confidentiality policies and the Court required the state to disclose the witness' prior record of delinquency adjudications.

Unlike Davis, which involved impeachment of a prosecution witness, state courts differ over the prosecutor's right to use delinquency convictions to impeach defense witnesses. In State v. Wilkins, 215 Kan. 145, 523 P.2d 728 (Kan.1974), the court allowed the state to impeach a defense witness and reasoned that the rule applied either way. By contrast, the court in State v. Thomas, 536 S.W.2d 529 (Mo.Ct.App.1976), held that impeaching a defendant with his own juvenile prior record was improper because the state, unlike the defendant, had no Sixth Amendment right to confrontation that offset the state's interest in maintaining confidential proceedings. Because a delinquency conviction is not formally a criminal conviction, courts generally prohibit the state from impeaching a juvenile defendant's credibility with his own prior delinquency record. E.g. State ex rel. K.P., 167

N.J.Super. 290, 400 A.2d 840 (N.J.Super.1979); People v. Sanchez, 170 Cal.App.3d 216, 216 Cal.Rptr. 21 (Cal.App.1985); In re Anthony H., 994 P.2d 407 (Ariz.Ct.App.1999) ("evidence of juvenile adjudication is generally not admissible" for impeachment); In re S.S.E., 629 N.W.2d 456 (Minn.Ct.App.2001) (only evidence admissible in criminal trial may be admitted in delinquency adjudication and only may impeach credibility with conviction of a crime). However, where a defense witness testifies about a juvenile's good character, courts allow the state to cross-examine the character witness about her knowledge of the juvenile's prior convictions. E.g. Wilburn v. State, 289 Ark. 224, 711 S.W.2d 760 (Ark.1986); Rogers v. United States, 566 A.2d 69 (D.C.App.1989).

3. PRIVILEGE AGAINST SELF–INCRIMINATION

The Court in Gault held that the "constitutional privilege against self-incrimination is applicable in the case of juveniles as it is with respect to adults." Some states have codified the privilege and others require the juvenile court judge to advise the juvenile and her parents of the privilege at the start of the adjudicatory hearing. E.g. Ga. Code Ann. § 15–11–31(b) (1994); Tex. Fam. Code Ann. § 54.03(b)(3) (Vernon 2000). Moreover, the privilege against self-incrimination applies through the conclusion of the disposition hearing and use of incriminating information gathered during a pre-sentence interview may violate that right. E.g. In re J.S.S., 20 S.W.3d 837 (Tex.App.2000) (Fifth

Amendment applies to sentencing as well as guilt phase). In many jurisdictions, the state may not use compelled disclosures to psychiatrists or psychologists in contemplation of a waiver proceeding as evidence of guilt in subsequent delinquency or criminal prosecutions. See Chapter 6 A. 1. b.

The Court in Allen v. Illinois, 478 U.S. 364 (S.Ct.1986), considered the availability of the Fifth Amendment privilege against self incrimination in proceedings under the Illinois Sexually Dangerous Persons Act. The trial court ordered Allen to submit to psychiatric examinations and psychiatrists testified about the information they obtained from him in his involuntary civil commitment proceeding. The Court concluded that the state committed Allen to provide treatment, rather than to punish him, and denied him the protections of the privilege. The statute's avowed purpose was therapeutic rather than punitive. Just as Justice White emphasized in his McKeiver concurrence, the Allen Court noted that Allen's commitment was indeterminate, another indicator of therapeutic purpose. Although the state provided many criminal procedural safeguards in the commitment proceeding, the Court asserted that when the state proposed to treat a patient through civil commitment proceedings, criminal procedural safeguards were unnecessary. The Allen Court distinguished Gault's holding to grant delinquents the privilege against self-incrimination. Allen emphasized that a loss of liberty per se did not trigger the right, but rather the purpose of the commitment determined the availability of the privilege. Allen mischaracterized Gault's Fifth Amendment rationale primarily as a concern that juvenile courts punished delinquents by sentencing them to adult prisons. The Allen dissent objected to the Court's denial of the privilege against self-incrimination, noted that the stigma of commitment as a sexually dangerous person was at least comparable to that of delinquency, the loss of liberty the same as in Gault, and decried the majority's evisceration of procedural safeguards under the guise of the state's benevolent purpose.

a. Parent–Child Privilege

Some jurisdictions create by statute a parent-child privilege that protects confidential communication between a minor child and her parent. E.g. Minn. Stat. § 595.02 (2001) ("A parent . . . may not be examined as to any communication made in confidence by the minor to the minor's parent . . ."). In the absence of such statutory provisions, courts generally have refused to create a parent-child testimonial privilege to excuse a parent from testifying against her child in a delinquency or criminal proceeding about matters revealed by the child. E.g. In re Grand Jury Subpoena, 722 N.E.2d 450 (Mass.2000) (creation of an intra-family testimonial privilege is a legislative determination).

D.   RIGHT TO COUNSEL

Procedural justice hinges on access to and the effective assistance of counsel. Gault based juveniles' right to counsel on the Fourteenth

Amendment due process clause rather than the Sixth Amendment right to counsel. The Court asserted that as a matter of due process "the assistance of counsel is ... essential for the determination of delinquency, carrying with it the awesome prospect of incarceration in a state institution." While Gault recognized that lawyers would make juvenile proceedings more formal and adversarial, the Court asserted that their presence would impart "a healthy atmosphere of accountability." However, Gault did not require mandatory or automatic appointment of counsel when delinquents appeared in court, but only held that "the child and his parents must be notified of the child's right to be represented by counsel retained by them, or if they are unable to afford counsel, that counsel will be appointed to represent the child." Gault also recognized that juveniles could waive the right to counsel.

Gault reflected the Warren Court's beliefs that adversarial procedures protected constitutional rights, limited the coercive powers of the state, assured the regularity of law enforcement, and preserved individual liberty and autonomy. Several years prior to Gault, in Gideon v. Wainwright, 372 U.S. 335 (S.Ct.1963), the Court incorporated the Sixth Amendment's guarantee of counsel and required state judges to appoint counsel for indigent adult criminal defendants in felony proceedings. "[I]n our adversary system of criminal justice, any person haled into court, who is too poor to hire a lawyer, cannot be assured a fair trial unless counsel is provided for him." Because Gault relied on the

Fourteenth Amendment due process clause, rather than the Sixth Amendment and Gideon, some ambiguity remained about the scope of the constitutional right to appointed counsel in delinquency proceedings.

In Argersinger v. Hamlin, 407 U.S. 25 (S.Ct.1972), the Court considered whether the Sixth Amendment required states to appoint counsel for indigent adult defendants charged with and imprisoned for a minor offense and held that "absent a knowing and intelligent waiver, no person may be imprisoned for any offense, whether classified as petty, misdemeanor or felony unless he was represented by counsel." In Scott v. Illinois, 440 U.S. 367 (S.Ct.1979), the Court clarified Argersinger and limited adult misdemeanants' constitutional right to court-appointed counsel to cases in which a judge actually sentenced a defendant to some form of incarceration. Most states' juvenile codes provide delinquents with a statutory right to court-appointed counsel even in misdemeanor cases that potentially could result in confinement. See, Barry C. Feld, *Justice for Children: The Right to Counsel and Juvenile Courts* (1993); United States General Accounting Office, *Juvenile Justice: Representation Rates Varies As Did Counsel's Impact On Court Outcomes* (1995) (statutory summary in appendix).

In the immediate aftermath of Gault, evaluations of the decision's impact reported that many juvenile court judges neither adequately advised juveniles of their right to counsel nor appointed lawyers for them. Feld, *Justice for Children*. Several empirical studies of delivery of legal services in juvenile courts in the late–1980s reported that the promise of counsel remained unfulfilled for many juveniles in many states. In three of six states studied, half or more of juveniles appeared without counsel including many youths whom judges removed from home and placed in training schools. Feld, *Justice for Children*. In 1992, Congress re-authorized the Juvenile Justice and Delinquency Prevention Act, 42 U.S.C.A. § 5601(a) (1994), and mandated the General Accounting Office (G.A.O.) to evaluate the delivery and effectiveness of counsel in juvenile court. The G.A.O. study also reported variability among states and within states in rates of representation. G.A.O., *Representation*.

The American Bar Association reported that "Many children go through the juvenile justice system without the benefit of legal counsel. Among those who do have counsel, some are represented by counsel who are untrained in the complexities of representing juveniles and fail to provide 'competent' representation." American Bar Association, *America's Children at Risk* (1993). The A.B.A. concluded that providing competent counsel for every youth charged with a crime would alleviate some of the endemic problems of juvenile justice— overcrowded conditions of confinement, racial disparities in processing, and inappropriate adjudication or transfer of youths to adult courts. Another study reported that the conditions under which lawyers worked in juvenile courts often significantly compromised youths' interests and left many of them literally defenseless. American Bar

Association, *A Call for Justice* (1995). In the last decade, the American Bar Association and National Juvenile Defender Center have conducted assessments of the delivery and quality of legal services in juvenile courts in twenty states and paint a grim picture. http://www.njdc.info/ assessments.php They consistently find that many, if not most, juveniles waive representation by counsel and that lawyers who represent juveniles often provide substandard services due to lack of training, inadequate resources, and crushing caseloads. Moreover, regardless of how poorly lawyers perform, juvenile and appellate courts cannot correct their own errors. Mary Berkheiser, "The Fiction of Juvenile Right to Counsel: Waiver in the Juvenile Courts," 54 Florida Law Rev. 577 (2002). Juvenile defenders rarely, if ever, appeal adverse decisions and often lack a record with which to challenge an invalid waiver of counsel or trial errors. Donald J. Harris, "Due Process vs. Helping Kids in Trouble: Implementing the Right to Appeal from Adjudications of Delinquency in Pennsylvania," 98 Dickinson Law Review 209(1994).

1.   APPOINTMENT AND WAIVER OF COUNSEL

Statutory and court rules provisions vary widely on the delivery of legal services. Some provide that the right to counsel attaches when police take a juvenile into custody, at a detention hearing, and "at all stages of all court proceedings, unless the right to counsel is freely, knowingly, and intelligently waived by the child." E.g. Fla. Stat. Ann. § 985.203 (West 2000). As a result of Gault, a statutory right of representation and court-appointed counsel for indigent juveniles exists at least after the formal initiation of delinquency proceedings, i.e. the filing of a delinquency petition. E.g. Ga. Code Ann. § 15–11–30(b) (2000); Tex. Fam. Code Ann. § 51.10(a) (Vernon 2000). Unless validly waived, a juvenile's right to counsel "in all proceedings" extends to dispositional hearings as well as trials. E.g. Ohio R.C. § 2151.352 (2004); In re William B., 163 Ohio App.3d 201, 387 N.E.2d 414 (Ohio Ap. 2005) (reversing sentence imposed without counsel or valid waiver). Other states prohibit any waiver of counsel. E.g. Tex. Fam. Code Ann. § 51.10(b) (Vernon 2000) (no waiver of counsel at adjudicatory or dispositional hearing). In states that grant juveniles the right to counsel at "every stage of proceedings," e.g. Tex. Fam. Code § 51.10(a), courts have extended the right to counsel to youths who seek habeas corpus relief to challenge a sentence commenced in juvenile court and continued into the adult correctional facilities. E.g. In re Hall, 2008 WL 1826534 (Tex).

Some states require mandatory appointment of counsel or standby counsel for any juvenile charged with a felony or gross misdemeanor or if the state seeks an out-of-home placement. E.g. Minn. Stat. Ann. § 260B.155 Subd. 2 (West 2000). Even if a juvenile desires to waive counsel, court rules require the court to appoint stand-by counsel in felony cases and authorize the court to appoint stand-by counsel even in misdemeanors. E.g. Minn. Juv. Proc. Rule 3.02. Statutes and court rules prohibit out-of-home placement of any juvenile who is not represented at the disposition or at the earlier proceedings on which the court bases the disposition. E.g. Wisc. Stat. Ann. § 932.23(1m)(a) (2008) (court may not place a juvenile who waives counsel in a correctional or secure residential facility); Minn. Juv. Proc. Rule 3.02 Subd. 3. Finally, some states presume that juveniles lack the capacity to waive counsel and require appointment of an attorney and only allow the juvenile to waive counsel if she demonstrates by clear and convincing evidence that she understands the nature of the charges, possesses the maturity and intelligence necessary to conduct her own defense, and establishes that waiver serves her "best interests." N.Y. Fam. Ct. Law § 249–a (McKinney 2000). Research on the delivery of legal services reports that the ease or difficulty with which juveniles may waive counsel directly affects rates of representation in a state. Feld, *Justice for Children*.

In most jurisdictions, a juvenile may waive her right to counsel. E.g. In re Manuel R., 207 Conn. 725, 543 A.2d 719 (Conn. 1988). A few states require an attorney to be present and consult with a juvenile prior to any waiver. E.g. State ex rel. J.M. v. Taylor, 276 S.E.2d 199 (W.Va.1981) (consultation prior to waiver); D.R. v. Commonwealth, 64 S.W.3d 292 (Ky. Ct. App. 2001) ("a child may waive the right to counsel only if that child has first been appointed, and consulted with, counsel concerning the waiver."). The vast majority of states do not require juvenile court judges to appoint counsel or stand-by counsel. They do not require a delinquent to consult with a lawyer prior to waiver of counsel.

As with waivers of Miranda rights, the constitutional standard to relinquish counsel during court proceedings is whether the juvenile made a "knowing, intelligent, and voluntary" waiver under the "totality of the circumstances." See Fare v. Michael C., Chapter 3.C.1.; Minn. Juv. Proc. Rule 3.04; Fla. Stat. Ann. § 985.203(1) (West 2000) (waiver of counsel made freely, knowingly, and intelligently). In Faretta v. California, 422 U.S. 806 (S.Ct.1975), the Supreme Court allowed adult criminal defendants to waive counsel and appear pro se. Faretta emphasized that the Sixth Amendment envisioned counsel as an aid to the defendant and not as a constitutional straightjacket. Respect for individual autonomy, dignity, and freedom of choice required trial judges to allow defendants to waive counsel if they were competent and respected court decorum. LaFave, *Criminal Procedure.* However, Faretta cautioned judges to conduct a "penetrating and comprehensive inquiry" and to explore the factors bearing on a defendant's ability to understand and proceed pro se including age, education, background, prior experience with trials, understanding of the complexity of trials, advantages of representation, disadvantages of self-representation, possible defenses that might be lost if not timely asserted, and the like. The Court in Von Moltke v. Gillies, 332 U.S. 708 (S.Ct.1948), held that a knowing and intelligent waiver of counsel required the judge to conduct a thorough evaluation of the defendant's understanding of the charges, the range of punishments, possible defenses and mitigating circumstances, and other factors.

Appellate courts allow juveniles to waive counsel under the Faretta framework and review the record to determine whether the youth had an adequate background to understand and waive his rights. In re Christopher H., 259 S.C. 161, 596 S.E.2d 500 (S.C. App. 2004) (factors include age, education, mental health, prior court experience, understanding of charges, willingness to comply with court rules, and the like).

Even if valid reasons exist to allow adults to waive their right to counsel, should courts allow juveniles to waive their rights? Should they use the same waiver standard as they do for adults? The court in In re Manuel R., 207 Conn. 725, 543 A.2d 719 (Conn.1988), examined the policies behind allowing juveniles to waive counsel and the procedures a court should follow to assure a valid waiver. The court rejected the youth's request for a per se rule that juveniles lacked competence to waive counsel and instead remitted the validity of waivers to a case-by-case assessment of each juvenile's capacity to waive. The court offered several policy reasons why juveniles, like adults, should be allowed to waive counsel. It reasoned that waiver of counsel would enable the child to assume responsibility for her conduct, enable her to participate meaningfully in the process, and could constitute a first step toward rehabilitation. By contrast, requiring mandatory appointment of counsel could reduce her sense of involvement in the process and reduce her to a passive spectator to the proceedings.

In order to establish that a waiver of counsel was "knowing, intelligent, and voluntary," Manuel R. required a colloquy between the court and the juvenile in order to make a record and establish: an advisory of the right to counsel; the juvenile's capacity to appreciate the consequences of waiver; the juvenile's understanding of the proceedings and their consequences; and the juvenile's awareness of the dangers of self-representation. Such a colloquy includes a discussion of the nature of charges and lesser included offenses, the range of allowable punishments, the existence of possible defenses, the juvenile's right to appointed counsel, an explanation of the role of counsel, and the availability of other trial rights. The court required a full colloquy between the judge and the juvenile and "special care" to establish the bases of any waiver. Other courts emphasize that judges must conduct a detailed inquiry because it is "extremely doubtful that any child of limited experience can possibly comprehend the importance of counsel." State v. T.G., 800 So.2d 204 (Fla.2001) (courts should be more careful when accepting a waiver of counsel from juveniles than from adults); In re Christopher H., 259 S.C. 161, 596 S.E.2d 500 (S.C.App.2004) (requiring record to show juvenile had sufficient background to waive and received clear advice of rights). Moreover, if a juvenile waives counsel, the judge must renew the offer of counsel at each stage of the proceedings. E.g. Fla. R. Juv. P. 8.165. Despite detailed statutory and judicial requirements, many trial judges often ignore them, give delinquents cursory warnings, fail to conduct the searching colloquy envisioned, do not make an adequate record, and allow many juveniles to waive counsel. E.G. Mary Berkheiser, "The Fiction of Juvenile Right to Counsel: Waiver in the Juvenile Courts," 54 Fla.L.Rev. 577 (2002) (noting that neither presumption against waiver or detailed statutory procedures prevent juvenile court judges from exercising discretion to find waivers and deny counsel).

The court in State ex rel. J.M., G.E. v. Taylor, and A.H. v. Trent, 166 W.Va. 511, 276 S.E.2d 199 (W.Va.1981), discussed the standard for waivers of counsel in juvenile court. Although the court recognized that the statute contemplated that juveniles could waive counsel, it required that a juvenile first consult with counsel to assure that any subsequent waiver is knowing, intelligent, and voluntary. A policy of prior consultation would foster development of legal services delivery systems to assure the presence of counsel in juvenile court. Requiring a youth to consult with counsel prior any waiver recognizes that the decision is a tactical, strategic, and legal one, rather than simply an abstract awareness of the right. Some states compensate for juveniles' limited experience, judgment, and capacity by using a higher waiver standard, creating a presumption of incompetence to waive, and placing a higher burden of proof on the juvenile affirmatively to demonstrate her competence. E.g. N.Y. Fam. Ct. Act § 249–a (McKinney 2000).

Although Gault recognized that counsel might make delinquency proceedings more adversarial, the Court regarded that as desirable. However, empirical evaluations of the performance and impact of counsel in juvenile courts indicate that juveniles who appear with counsel may fare more poorly than those who appear without counsel. E.g. Feld, *Justice for Children*; G.A.O., *Representation.* After controlling for the effects of other legal variables such as offense seriousness, prior record, and pretrial detention status, youths who appeared in juvenile court with lawyers received more severe dispositions than did those who waived counsel. Several factors contribute to the consistent research finding that the presence of lawyers is an aggravating factor when judges sentence delinquents: defense attorney incompetence; judicial pre-judgment of sentences; or judges' hostility to youths' exercise of rights.

First, attorneys who represent delinquents in juvenile court may be incompetent and prejudice their clients' cases. Organizational and institutional pressures such as heavy caseloads and inadequate preparation may adversely affect counsels' performance. E.g. http://www.njdc.info/assessments. php Other factors also compromise attorneys' zealous performance—organizational pressures to cooperate and maintain stable relationships with court personnel, judicial hostility to adversarial litigants, and role ambiguity created by the dual goals of rehabilitation and punishment. Undesirable conditions of employment, long hours, low pay, inadequate resources, crushing caseloads, and difficult clients may undermine the quality of representation. Public defender offices may not appoint their best lawyers and may use assignment to juvenile court either as professional punishment or as a training ground to enable new lawyers to gain trial experience. Secondly, judges may appoint counsel if they anticipate imposing a more severe sentence later. Scott v. Illinois, 440 U.S. 367 [1979]), prohibited "incarceration without representation," and judges' efforts to comply with that requirement may explain the relationship between initial decisions to appoint counsel and subsequent decisions to remove youths from their homes. For example, judges may predetermine the eventual disposition prior to a juvenile's first appearance based on information learned from arraignment, detention, prior court proceedings, or other extra-judicial sources. Because judges appoint counsel at the earliest stages of proceedings—arraignment or detention hearing—why would they expect to incarcerate a youth later? Can an attorney provide an effective defense if the judge has already pre-judged the case? Thirdly, juvenile court judges may sanction youths whose lawyers invoke formal procedures, disrupt routine procedures, or question their discretion in ways similar to the harsher sentences imposed on adults who demand a jury trial rather than plead guilty. Finally, juveniles appeal their convictions far less often than do adult criminal defendants. Caseload pressures, the parens patriae ideology of juvenile courts, differences in juvenile attorneys' assumed roles, and difficulties of representing children contribute to lawyers' reluctance to file appeals. Donald J. Harris, "Due Process vs. Helping Kids in Trouble," 98 Dick.L.Rev. 209 (1998) (noting adult appeal rate is ten times greater than juvenile appeal rate and attributing difference to parens patriae ideology and professional culture).

2. ROLE OF COUNSEL

The perceived differences between juvenile court treatment and criminal court punishment, the difficulties of representing a presumptively incompetent child rather than a self-determining adult, the problem of balancing children and their parents' competing preferences, the hazards of practicing in a highly discretionary legal environment, and the need to play different roles at different stages of the proceeding all contribute to attorneys' role conflict. Historically, if a lawyer appeared at all in juvenile court, then the judge expected her to function as a guardian ad litem or social worker and to assist the court to impose appropriate treatment. Juvenile court judges expected counsel to participate in a non-adversarial, open, and cooperative manner to achieve the child's "best interests." While Gault anticipated a more complex and adversarial role for attorneys in juvenile courts, McKeiver's insistence on closed, confidential, and jury-free proceedings envisioned a juvenile system that differed from that for adults and which required corresponding differences in defense attorney roles.

Analysts have identified several roles for lawyers in juvenile court: an adversarial model transplanted from criminal court; a guardian ad litem acting in the child's "best interests"; and a social worker acting as an aid to the court. E.g. Feld, *Justice for Children.* Commentators suggest that attorneys may tailor their role depending upon what they perceive to be in the child's "best interests" and whether the court will serve those interests. Particularly at disposition, a lawyer has a broader role to explore placement options and to present them to the court. E.g. State ex rel. D.D.H. v. Dostert, 165 W.Va. 448, 269 S.E.2d 410 (W.Va. 1980). While a criminal defendant almost invariably prefers leniency, a juvenile defense attorney may experience greater qualms about remitting a youth to an intolerable home situation or to a life of chemical dependency if treatment options exist. Juvenile courts typically enjoy a greater array of dispositional alternatives than do criminal courts and identifying programs and arranging admission to them poses additional responsibilities for counsel. Effective advocacy requires an attorney to consult with clinicians, social services personnel, and others to devise an appropriate treatment plan for the client. E.g. Ellen Marrus, "Best Interests Equals Zealous Advocacy: A Not So Radical View of Holistic Representation for Children Accused of Crime," 62 Md. L. Rev. 288 (2003). These additional and non-legal social services roles may discourage lawyers from appearing at or taking an active role at dispositions.

The American Bar Association proposed a straightforward transplantation of the role of criminal defense counsel into juvenile court. A.B.A., *Juvenile Justice Standards Relating to Counsel for Private Parties* (1980). Gault itself provides the rationale for an adversarial role. To allow an attorney to substitute her judgment about a child's "best interests" instead of following the client's preferences simply substitutes the paternalism of a lawyer for that of a judge or social worker. However, the adversarial model assumes a competent client capable of making self-regarding decisions. Moreover, following a child's preferences may create conflicts between the attorney and the child's parents. The parent and child may seek different outcomes or their interests may actively conflict, for example, if they are the victim of their child's delinquency. Parents control their child and an attorney must enlist their cooperation to advocate effectively on the child's behalf, for example, a disposition to return a child home. This pressures the lawyer to accommodate the interests of parent and child. Despite these pressures, however, a lawyer ultimately only can act as counsel for the child. E.g. Minn. R. Proc. Juv. Ct. 3.01.

Regardless of the role a lawyer adopts, a juvenile enjoys the right to effective assistance of counsel. The test for ineffective assistance of counsel requires the juvenile to demonstrate that counsel's performance was deficient and the deficient performance caused actual prejudice. E.g. Strickland v. Washington, 466 U.S. 668 (S.Ct.1984). A lawyer's failure to provide "actual and substantial" assistance to a juvenile considering a guilty plea, such as evaluating the evidence and discussing the consequences of a plea, constitutes ineffective assistance. E.g. State v. S.M., 996 P.2d 1111 (Wash.App. Div.2, 2000). Failure to perform according to an "objective standard of reasonableness" constitutes ineffective assistance. In re A.V., 285 Ill.App.3d 470, 220 Ill.Dec. 847, 674 N.E.2d 118 (Ill.App.1996) (ignorance of applicable standard of proof in probation revocation proceeding). A juvenile court's refusal to allow an attorney to make a closing argument or to allow counsel to comment on alternative sentencing arrangements at disposition denied a youth of effective assistance of counsel. In re F., 11 Cal.3d 249, 113 Cal.Rptr. 170, 520 P.2d 986 (1974); State v. Kenneth Y., 217 W.Va. 167, 617 S.E.2d 517 (W.Va. 2005). And a juvenile has the same right as an adult to an attorney unencumbered by multiple-representations and a conflict of interests. E.g. Holloway v. Arkansas, 435 U.S. 475 (S.Ct.1978); In Interest of V.W., 112 Ill.App.3d 587, 67 Ill.Dec. 965, 445 N.E.2d 445 (Ill.App.1983); In re A.I.E., 120 F.Supp.2d 537 (D.Virgin Islands 2000) (actual conflict where public defender represented juvenile defendant and witness against him in another matter).

E.   GUILTY PLEA

As a corollary of the privilege against self-incrimination, juveniles enjoy the right to testify at a hearing and to admit their guilt. Delinquents plead guilty in the vast majority of cases. As with adult pleas of guilty, a plea of guilty constitutes a waiver of trial rights—hearing, confrontation, and cross-examination, privilege against self-incrimination, proof beyond a reasonable doubt—and an admission of factual guilt. E.g. Boykin v. Alabama, 395 U.S. 238 (S.Ct.1969); LaFave, *Criminal Procedure.* Accordingly, the crucial issues are whether the record shows both that the child made the plea knowingly, intelligently, and voluntarily, and that it contains an adequate factual basis to support the plea. Juvenile courts use the same standards as do criminal courts to determine the validity of waivers of rights and the factual basis for the plea. E.g. In re Michael M., 11 Cal.App.3d 741, 96 Cal.Rptr. 887 (Cal.Ct.App.1970); In re Chavis, 230 S.E.2d 198 (N.C.Ct.App.1976); A.E.K. v. State, 432 So.2d 720 (Fla.Ct.App.1983) (reversed delinquency plea where record lacked showing of knowing and intelligent waiver of constitutional trial rights); Fla. R. Juv. Proc. 8.080 (knowing and voluntary waiver and factual basis, details of court colloquy).

Statutes and court rules describe the procedures for taking a guilty plea. E.g. W. Va. Code § 49–5–11 (2000); State ex rel. J.M. v. Taylor, 166 W.Va. 511, 276 S.E.2d 199 (W.Va.1981). At the start of the hearing, the court asks the juvenile whether he or she wishes to admit or deny the allegations of the petition. If the juvenile admits the allegations, then the court must find that the child fully understands her rights, and knowingly, intelligently, and voluntarily waives them and admits all the facts necessary to support a conviction on the charges. As part of the plea colloquy, the court must address the juvenile directly and inform her of the nature of the charges, lesser included offenses, possible defenses, the constitutional and statutory rights that the plea waives, and the maximum penalty which the court may impose. Judicial failure to follow these procedures invalidates the plea and requires a remand for a proper colloquy or an adjudicatory hearing. E.g. In the Matter of Harry W., 204 W.Va. 583, 514 S.E.2d 814 (W.Va.1999).

F.   RECORD AND APPEAL

Because Gault reversed the Arizona Supreme Court on other procedural grounds, it did not decide whether he also enjoyed a constitutional right to appellate review and a transcript. However, the Court noted that "the consequences of failure to provide an appeal, to record the proceedings, or to make findings or state the grounds for the juvenile court's conclusion" posed numerous problems for appellate courts and sometimes required remand for new hearings in their absence. State statutes routinely provide for the creation of a record of judicial proceedings "by stenographic notes or by electronic, mechanical, or other appropriate means." Tex. Fam. Code Ann. § 54.09 (Vernon 2000); Wash. R. Juv. Ct. 10.2 (delinquency proceedings "shall be recorded verbatim by means which provide an accurate record and which can be subsequently reduced to written form"). At the conclusion of the fact finding hearing, the trial court must make written findings of fact and conclusions of law relating to the allegations of the petition. E.g. Wash.

Rev. Code § 13.34.110 (2000); Wis. Stat. § 938.31 (2000).

State laws differ dramatically on the scope and timing of appellate review. Some states have enacted comprehensive appellate legislation while others provide little statutory or case law guidance for appeals from juvenile court. Appellate statutes generally restrict juveniles' appeals to review of a "final order" or "final judgment." E.g. Colo. Rev. Stat. Ann. § 19–1–109 (2008) (an appeal "may be taken from any order, decree or judgment."). To avoid interlocutory, partial reviews, and delays in the disposition of a case, most states do not allow a juvenile to appeal from an adjudication of delinquency but only after the court imposes a final sentence. E.g. B.F. v. State, 550 P.2d 991 (Okla.Crim.App.1976). Statutes or case law define what constitutes a final order and as a result, juvenile court decisions to place youths on informal supervision or to defer judgment are not appealable. Ricki J. v. Superior Court, 128 Cal. App. 4th 783 (2005). State appeals statutes often give juveniles priority on the appellate docket and expedited review. For example, cases of California juveniles appealing from a final order as delinquents or status offenders "shall have precedence over all other cases in the court to which the appeal is taken." Cal. Welf. & Inst. Code § 800(a) (2008). Others provide that juveniles' appeals "shall take precedence over all other business of the court to which the appeal is taken." Ala. Code 1975 § 12–15–120(a) (2008). Even with expedited review, appeals by many delinquents may fail because their cases become moot when dispositional orders expire or they are released from custody. E.g. A.M. v. State, 653 P.2d 346 (AK. Ct. App. 1982). Other courts hear juveniles' appeals regardless of mootness. E.g. In re Jeremy M. 918 A.2d 944 (Conn. App. Ct. 2007) (delinquent's discharge "from further accountability to the court was not rendered moot on ground that no practical relief could be afforded to juvenile.")

G. PROCEDURAL RIGHTS OF STATUS OFFENDERS

Gault only ruled on the constitutional rights of delinquents charged with a crime and facing the possibility of institutional confinement. As a result, states may provide somewhat different and less extensive procedural rights for status offenders— e.g., youths who are "unruly," "ungovernable," "incorrigible," "runaway," "truant," "in need of supervision," or in possession of alcohol or tobacco— whom prosecutors do not charge with delinquency for crimes. These procedural differences, in turn, affect the types of dispositions that juvenile court judges may impose on status offenders and delinquents. See Chapter 8 D.

The court in In the Matter of Spalding, 273 Md. 690, 332 A.2d 246 (Md. Ct. Spec. App. 1975), considered whether status offenders enjoy the privilege against self-incrimination at their trial. While Gault granted delinquents the Fifth Amendment privilege, the Court in Allen v. Illinois distinguished Gault and denied it to persons subject to a "Sexually Dangerous Offender" civil commitment proceeding. Spalding posed the question whether a status adjudication is more like a delinquency-criminal trial or more like a parens patriae or civil commitment proceeding. Gault's rationale to extend the privilege to delinquents included the stigma associated with conviction of a crime, conditions of institutional confinement, the functional equivalency between delinquency and criminal proceedings, concern about the accuracy of self-incriminating statements, and a desire to maintain equality between the state and the individual.

The Spalding majority held that the Fifth Amendment did not apply to trials for status offenses—Children in Need of Supervision (CINS). The court distinguished Gault, which entailed criminal conduct and institutional commitment, from CINS adjudications which involved non-criminal misconduct and a statute that prohibited incarcerating status offenders with delinquents in institutions. The dissent in Spalding argued that the underlying conduct—drug use and sexual offenses—on which the court based its CINS jurisdiction constituted crimes and the child still faced a loss of liberty. The dissent argued that the availability of the privilege against self-incrimination depended upon the state's restraint of liberty rather than simply confinement in a delinquency institution. However, the Supreme Court's reinterpretation of Gault in Allen clearly envisioned a narrower scope for the privilege and one which rejected the contention that a liberty restriction alone sufficed to justify the privilege.

Some states extend the right to counsel to both delinquency and status proceedings. E.g. Ga. Code Ann. § 15–11–30(b) (2000); Nev. Rev. Stat. § 62.085 (2000); N.M. Stat. Ann. § 32A–2–14(H) (2000). Other jurisdictions authorize a judge to appoint counsel for an "incorrigible" status offender at the court's discretion and require the public defender to represent her. Haas v. Colosi, 40 P.3d 1249 (Ariz. App. 2002). In the absence of statutory authorization, a youth adjudicated for conduct that "endanger[s] his welfare" and whom the court could not commit to an institution would not enjoy Gault's right to counsel. E.g. In re K., 26 Or.App. 451, 554 P.2d 180 (Or.App.1976). The court in In re Walker, 282 N.C. 28, 191 S.E.2d 702 (N.C.1972), considered whether a juvenile enjoyed a right to counsel at her initial status offense adjudication. The juvenile court adjudged Walker an "undisciplined" child at an initial hearing conducted without counsel and placed her on probation. Following probation violations, she appeared with counsel at a subsequent revocation hearing at which the juvenile court found her delinquent and committed her to an institution. The court held that she did not have a right to counsel at her initial adjudication for being an "undisciplined" child because the state did not charge her with a crime and could not place her in an institution. Because the statute prohibited incarcerating status offenders with delinquents, the court held that she did not enjoy a right to counsel.

Walker's rationale is similar to the distinctions between Argersinger v. Hamlin and Scott v. Illinois, where the Supreme Court conditioned an adult misdemeanant's right to counsel on whether the trial court actually ordered a sentence of confinement. In Nichols v. United States, 511 U.S. 738 (S.Ct.1994), the Court upheld the use of prior uncounselled convictions to enhance a defendant's subsequent criminal sentence. Nichols reasoned that a conviction that was constitutionally valid at the time it was obtained could be used to enhance a subsequent sentence. Walker's defense lawyer argued that her earlier status offense adjudication constituted a "critical stage" at which the right to counsel should attach because the trial judge based her subsequent commitment on conditions imposed at her initial uncounselled adjudication. The Walker majority rejected defendant's "critical stage" argument and found that the procedural steps were separable. The court held that the former proceeding—adjudication as a status offender—did not necessarily determine her later institutional confinement because the commitment required separate action—subsequent violation of probation—and the court appointed counsel at the latter hearing to determine whether the violations occurred. The dissent in Walker argued that her adjudication as an "undisciplined" child provided the predicate for her subsequent institutional confinement and therefore she should have a right to counsel at that earlier proceeding. By contrast, the court in In re Hutchins, 345 So.2d 703 (Fla.1977), held that the adjudication for ungovernability provided the crucial predicate for subsequent confinement and thus constituted a "critical stage" for which the right to counsel attached. In the absence of such a limitation, juveniles face the prospect of "bootstrapping" of status offenses into delinquency adjudications and institutional commitments. Amendments in 1980 to the Juvenile Justice and Delinquency Prevention Act, 42 U.S.C. 5603(16)(a), provided that juvenile court judges may find status offenders in contempt of court for violating a valid court order, for example, a condition of probation, and place them in secure detention facilities. Juvenile courts may use their contempt power to incarcerate repeat status offenders as delinquents. See Chapter 8. However, they must appoint counsel for juveniles at the contempt proceedings that may lead to confinement. Arkansas Dept. of Human Services v. Mainard, 358 Ark. 204, 188 S.W.3 901 (Ark. 2004).

State laws differ on the burden of proof that the state must satisfy in a status offense proceeding. Winship applied the criminal standard of proof "beyond a reasonable doubt" when the state charged a juvenile with a crime. However, states may use a "preponderance of the evidence" standard, a "clear and convincing" evidence standard, or a "proof beyond a reasonable doubt" standard in the adjudication of status offenses. E.g. Cal. Welf. & Inst. Code § 701 (West 2000) ("a preponderance of evidence, legally admissible in the trial of civil cases must be adduced to support a finding that the minor is a [status offender]"); In re Henderson, 199 N.W.2d 111 (Iowa 1972) ("clear and convincing" evidence standard and distinguishing Winship which involved allegation of a crime and possibility of institutional confinement); In the Matter of Karen

Price, 94 Misc.2d 345, 404 N.Y.S.2d 821 (N.Y.Fam.Ct.1978) (dismissed a PINS petition because state failed to prove beyond a reasonable doubt that juvenile was "habitually disobedient" and "beyond lawful control").

CHAPTER 8

DISPOSITIONAL DECISION

Disposition refers to the process by which these people decide what to do with a child whose behavior brings her within the delinquency or status jurisdiction of the juvenile court. Several different justice system actors make decisions about the welfare, legal status, and custody of a youth. Disposition decisions cumulate and judgments that police or intake workers make initially affect the choices that subsequent personnel make. E.g. Feld, *Bad Kids,* McCord, *Juvenile Crime, Juvenile Justice.* As we saw in Chapters 3 and 4, police officers may adjust a case informally on the street or at the station-house, divert it, or refer it to court intake for formal processing. Intake social workers or probation staff, in turn, may dispose of the case through informal supervision or diversion or refer the youth to juvenile court for formal adjudication. They may initially decide whether to detain a juvenile pending subsequent court proceedings. Prosecutors exercise additional screening, diverting, and gate-keeping functions through their charging decisions. Judicial sentencing decisions culminate those of other actors who winnow the cases ultimately presented to the juvenile court judge for formal disposition.

A. INTRODUCTION

At a disposition hearing, statutes and court rules afford judges broad discretion to select from a wide array of sentencing alternatives—dismissal, continuance without a finding of delinquency, restitution, probation with or without additional conditions or supervision, out-of-home placement, or institutional confinement. Because juvenile courts find virtually all youths against whom the state files petitions to be either delinquents or status offenders, the disposition constitutes the crucial stage in the process.

This chapter focuses on the final actor in the process—the juvenile court judge—and the procedures she uses to select from the range of dispositions available. It is useful to think about dispositions as a relationship between ends and means. What are the goals of a delinquency disposition and what intervention strategies can achieve those goals? What procedures should a juvenile court use to identify the appropriate treatment or sanction to achieve those substantive purposes? How should an appellate court review the procedural means used, the interventions prescribed, and the goals sought by a trial judge?

Historically, juvenile court judges imposed indeterminate and non-proportional dispositions in the best interests of the child-offender.

> The problem for determination by the judge is not, Has this boy or girl committed a specific wrong, but What is he, how has he become what he is, and what had best be done in his interest and in the interests of the state to save him from a downward career. It is apparent at once that the ordinary legal evidence in a

criminal court is not the sort of evidence to be heard in such a proceeding. Julian W. Mack, *The Juvenile Court*, 23 Harv. L. Rev. 104 (1909).

According to the theory of the Rehabilitative Ideal, the judicial inquiry only focused on a youth's misconduct for its diagnostic significance. State ex rel. S.J.C. v. Fox, 165 W.Va. 314, 268 S.E.2d 56 (W.Va.1980) ("[T]he gravity of the offense and previous acts of delinquency, their frequency, seriousness and relationship to the present charge are relevant considerations in determining the rehabilitative prospects of the juvenile."). The court's role was to develop a program to alleviate the conditions that caused the youth's delinquency. A delinquency disposition assumes that judges and clinicians can identify the factors that caused the delinquency, make a prognosis about its likely course if left untreated, develop and deliver appropriate interventions to alter those causes, and assess the ultimate prospects of success. In short, dispositions entail diagnosis, prescription, intervention, and prognosis. Because one cannot accurately predict the length of time necessary to ensure successful treatment, juvenile courts traditionally imposed indeterminate and non-proportional sentences. A juvenile's offense did not limit either the intensity or the duration of therapy because each child's needs were unique.

Since Gault and McKeiver, judicial, legislative, and administrative changes have eroded the original rehabilitative premises of juvenile sentencing. As a result of negative evaluation studies of treatment programs, practical short-comings, inadequate resources, and changing penal policies, states' commitment to rehabilitative sentencing declined during the 1970s and 1980s. In the late–1980s and early–1990s, get tough politicians proposed to crack down on youth crime, greatly increased the punitive powers of juvenile courts, and fostered a jurisprudential and substantive convergence with criminal courts. Many states have abandoned a singular commitment to the rehabilitative ideal and adopted punitive sanctions—determinate sentences, mandatory minimum sentences, parole release guidelines—in addition to, or as alternatives for, traditional treatment policies. Delinquents' requests for a jury trial provide the procedural strategy by which to challenge these punitive substantive policies. See Chapter 7.A.3.c., supra.

What are the goals of a justice system for young people who violate the criminal law? Rehabilitation? Retribution? General or special deterrence? Selective incapacitation? Mitigating the severity of adult sanctions for younger offenders? Limiting the collateral consequences of criminal convictions? As juvenile courts increasingly pursue multiple goals—the best interests of the child and protection of the community—how should state laws and juvenile court judges balance social welfare and criminal social control if and when these goals conflict?

The court in State ex rel. D.D.H. v. Dostert, 165 W.Va. 448, 269 S.E.2d 401 (W.Va.1980), analyzed the conflicting goals of delinquency dispositions and described the roles of various participants at a dispositional hearing. D.D.H. observed that a delinquency disposition included both treatment and punitive goals: social control, protecting public safety, deterrence, accountability, love and forgiveness, rehabilitation, retribution, and responsibility. The court identified alternative purposes for intervention—to rehabilitate and change a child, to modify her social environment, or to provide a more lenient sanction than harsh adult punishment. D.D.H. also analyzed the means to achieve those goals, noted the tension between rules and discretion, and examined how formally to structure dispositional procedures. At disposition, a juvenile court judge must answer a series of questions: what should we do with this child? Why should we impose one disposition rather than another? How should we decide and based on what evidence that this is the appropriate disposition? How should an appellate court review trial judges' adherence to procedural rules and substantive decisions?

D.D.H. described how the role of counsel at disposition differs from her role at adjudication. To perform properly, defense counsel must evaluate the child's background, investigate the least restrictive alternatives available, and develop and present realistic alternative placements to the court. Armed with information presented by defense counsel and the probation officer, the judge must balance considerations of the offender and the offense to make an appropriate disposition. The court considers the child's need for treatment and assistance, the community's need for protection, and penal considerations like deterrence, responsibility, and accountability. This requires the court to assess whether the child's misconduct was determined or freely chosen and whether means exist to alter the conditions that caused the behavior. The paucity of adequate alternatives in the community, the lack of systematic evaluations of program effectiveness, the multiplicity of agencies offering some types of resources, and the desperate conditions of some children's lives often constrains the court's decision.

B. DISPOSITIONAL PROCEDURES

A dispositional hearing provides the procedural means to the substantive goals of the juvenile process. Although Gault did not address dispositional procedures, states' juvenile codes provide for some type of formal sentencing hearing. Statutes and court rules prescribe hearing procedures, dispositional criteria, and the evidence a judge may consider to impose an appropriate sanction.

1. BIFURCATED HEARING

The procedural rights that Gault granted delinquents only applied to the adjudicatory hearing. "The problems of pre-adjudication treatment of juveniles and of post-adjudication disposition are unique to the juvenile process; hence, what we hold in this opinion with regard to the procedural requirements at the adjudicatory stage has no necessary applicability to other steps of the juvenile process." Despite this limitation, one consequence of Gault was to bifurcate delinquency proceedings and separate adjudication—the question whether the youth committed a crime and the court has jurisdiction—from disposition—the question of how the court should exercise its authority and what sentence to impose. "The disposition hearing shall be separate, distinct, and subsequent to the adjudication hearing." Tex. Fam. Code Ann. § 54.04(a) (Vernon 2000); Cal. R. Court 1431; O.C.G.A. § 15–11–33(c) (1998). As long as a judge functionally separates the two hearings, she need not schedule them at separate times and may shift immediately from an adjudicatory to a dispositional hearing. E.g. People v. Hardin, 184 Mich.App. 107, 457 N.W.2d 347 (Mich.App.1990); O.C.G.A. § 15–11–65 (2001) (following delinquency adjudication, court "shall proceed immediately or at a later time to conduct a dispositional hearing"). However, the court must hold the dispositional hearing separately to enable the juvenile to present evidence relevant to the appropriate disposition. In re C.W., 227 Ga.App. 763, 490 S.E.2d 442 (Ga.Ct.App.1997).

The procedures mandated by Gault and Winship do not necessarily apply at sentencing. A delinquency trial focuses on whether or not the child committed an offense and the court may only consider legally admissible evidence. By contrast, the disposition hearing considers the best interest and needs of the child. In addition to the current offense, a disposition report may include non-adjudicated allegations of crime, evidence of family function or pathology, hearsay reports of teachers and neighbors, clinical evaluations, reports on physical and mental health, and police, school, and court records. Because of the differences between the evidence needed to establish legal guilt at trial and the social and psychological evidence necessary to craft an appropriate disposition, premature exposure to the latter evidence could prejudice the former determination. State laws and court decisions insist on strict separation to avoid evidentiary contamination. E.g. In re Gladys R. (reversing decision of juvenile judge who reviewed social history report prior to delinquency adjudication); In re L.H., 102 Ill.App.3d 169, 57 Ill.Dec. 714, 429 N.E.2d 612 (Ill.App.1981); N.Y. Fam. Ct. Law § 750(1) (McKinney 2000) (social report "shall not be furnished to the court prior to the completion of the fact-finding hearing."). Statutes give juveniles the right to notice of the proceedings and an opportunity to be heard and present evidence relevant to the court's disposition. E.g. In re D.L.W., 543 N.E.2d 542 (Ill.App.Ct.1989); In re J.L.P., 100 Cal.Rptr. 601 (Cal.Ct.App.1972).

a. Right to Counsel

The Supreme Court in Kent v. United States, 383 U.S. 541 (S.Ct.1966), held that juveniles enjoyed a constitutional right to counsel at a waiver hearing because of the critical nature of the transfer decision. A few courts have held that juveniles enjoy a due process right to counsel at delinquency and even status offense dispositions. E.g. A.A. v. State,

538 P.2d 1004 (Alaska 1975); D.H. v. State, 688 N.E.2d 221 (Ind.Ct.App.1997); In re Torrey B., 6 Neb.App. 658, 577 N.W.2d 310 (Neb.Ct.App.1998). There are few reported decisions because state statutes and court rules uniformly provide for counsel at delinquency dispositions or at "every stage of the proceedings." E.g. Tex. Fam. Code Ann. § 51.10(a), (b) (Vernon 2000); N.D. Cent. Code § 27–20–26 (2000). To effectuate the right, the juvenile must be present at the hearing at which the court makes its disposition. E.g. In re Cecilia R., 36 N.Y.2d 317, 327 N.E.2d 812, 367 N.Y.S.2d 770 (N.Y.1975). Like the right to counsel at trial, a juvenile may waive counsel at disposition, provided that she does so knowingly, intelligently, and voluntarily. E.g. In re D.L., 999 S.W.2d 291 (Mo.Ct.App.1999).

The Court in Kent granted defense counsel access to a child's social report and the right to challenge probation officers' findings and recommendations. "[I]f the staff's submissions include materials which are susceptible to challenge or impeachment, it is precisely the role of counsel to 'denigrate' such matters. There is no irrebuttable presumption of accuracy attaching to staff reports." State statutes guarantee counsel's access to the social report, although in some jurisdiction, the court may order counsel not to reveal sensitive information to the child or parents if disclosure could be harmful to the child. E.g. Fla. Stat. Ann. § 39.09 (2000) (social history "shall be made available to the child's legal counsel"); Tex. Fam. Code § 54.04(b) (Vernon 2000) (court "shall provide the attorney" access to all written material the court will consider at disposition, but court may order counsel not to disclose harmful information). Courts construe the right to cross-examine witnesses to include those appearing at a disposition hearing as well at the trial. E.g. In re G.S.J., 281 N.W.2d 511 (Minn.1979).

Juveniles are entitled to effective assistance of counsel at disposition. E.g. Strickland v. Washington, 466 U.S. 668 (S.Ct.1984). To prevail on such a claim, the juvenile must demonstrate actual deficient performance that affected the outcome of the proceedings. Thus, counsel's failure to request an updated psychological evaluation or to call a juvenile's treating physician at disposition did not constitute ineffective assistance without additional evidence about the testimony they would have given. In re S.P., 9 S.W.3d 304 (Tex.App.1999).

2. DISPOSITIONAL CRITERIA

Statutes describe with varying specificity the factors that judges should consider when they make a disposition. Some focus primarily on characteristics of the offender, such as the "best interest of the child" or why the disposition is "necessary to the rehabilitation of the child." Some states require a judge to make written findings explaining "why the best interests of the child are served by the disposition ordered." E.g. Minn. Stat. Ann. § 260B.185 (2000); Tex. Fam. Code § 54.04(c) and (f) (Vernon 2000) (no disposition unless the child is "in need of rehabilitation" or for "protection of the public" and court shall state specifically "reasons for the disposition"). Other statutes focus judges' attention on offense criteria, for example, the seriousness of the youth's offense, her degree of culpability in participating in the offense, aggravating or mitigating factors, prior record, and willingness to participate in available programs. E.g. Conn. Stat. § 46b–140 (2000); Iowa Code Ann. § 232.52(1) (West 2000).

To limit the severity of dispositions, many jurisdictions require a judge to impose the "least restrictive alternative" available to address the child's delinquency. E.g. Ark. Code Ann. § 9–27–329(c) (Michie 2000) ("give preference to the least restrictive disposition consistent with the best interests and welfare of the juvenile and the public"); Cal. Welf. & Inst. Code § 626 (West 2000); Alaska Stat. § 47.10.080 (2000). Institutional commitment is supposed to be a last resort and for courts to use only when less drastic alternatives will not serve the child's needs. For example, a court only may commit a youth to an institution when no less restrictive alternative is appropriate based on the child's threat to society, exhaustion of other correctional options, amenability to treatment, willingness to cooperate with a treatment program, and deservingness of punishment. E.g., State ex rel. R.S. v. Trent, 169 W.Va. 493, 289 S.E.2d 166 (W.Va.1982). The least restrictive alternative requires a judge to make an individualized assessment of the child's needs at the time of disposition and a judge may not sentence a youth more severely than his circumstances warrant just to maintain consistency with the disposition of co-defendants. E.g. State ex rel. S.J.C. v. Fox, 165 W.Va. 314, 268 S.E.2d 56 (W.Va.1980). However, the least restrictive alternative is a statutory right and courts only can use non-institutional treatment facilities if the state actually provides alternative community resources. In re B.B., 516 N.W.2d 874 (Iowa 1994) (state limitation on number of group home placements available did not violate right to least restrictive placement). Other courts hold that a judge may not commit a youth to an institution simply because no other suitable alternatives exist. E.g. In re B.S., 549 N.E.2d 695 (Ill.App.Ct.1989); In re Aline D., 536 P.2d 65 (Cal.1975).

Even though statutes give judges discretionary authority, some appellate courts may limit their discretion with a principle of proportionality. "To measure what is necessary, a trial court must assess two factors, the severity of the child's delinquency, and the severity of the proposed remedy. When the severity of intervention is disproportionate to the problem, the intervention is not necessary and cannot lawfully occur." In re L.K.W., 372 N.W.2d 392 (Minn.Ct.App.1985).

a. Social Report

A judge requires background information about the child's real needs to properly make an individualized disposition. Probation staff conducts an investigation and prepares a report known as a social history, social study, or dispositional report— the juvenile equivalent of a criminal pre-sentence investigation. "At the disposition hearing, the juvenile court may consider written reports from probation officers, professional court employees, or professional consultants in addition to the testimony of witnesses." Tex. Fam. Code Ann. § 54.04(b) (Vernon 2000).

A social report investigates the juvenile's prior record, the present offense, unadjudicated offenses, the family situation, school performance, previous services provided by public or private social agencies, previous clinical evaluations, and the youth's response to earlier treatment. E.g. Ind. Code Ann. § 31–34–18–1 (Michie 2000). Juvenile courts accumulate much of this information in juvenile court files, probation files, or in preparation for a detention hearing. In more difficult cases, probation staff may solicit evaluations and reports from psychologists or psychiatrists. For youths charged with more serious offenses, some statutes mandate preparation of a social study. E.g. N.Y. Fam. Ct. Act § 750 (McKinney 2000) (social report is mandatory for youths adjudicated for designated felony). A judge's failure to consider the social report prior to making a disposition constitutes reversible error. E.g. In re B.B., 647 So.2d 268 (Fla.Dist.Ct.App.1994).

b. Evidence

Unlike the adjudicatory hearing which allows only evidence admissible in criminal trials, at the disposition hearing, a judge may receive hearsay and other "relevant and competent" evidence. Courts typically consider "all information helpful in determining the question presented, including oral and written reports." E.g. O.C.G.A. § 15–11–65 (2001); Ky. Rev. Stat. Ann. § 610.110(2) (2001). The social report itself often contains hearsay evidence—statements by teachers, neighbors, caseworkers, treatment providers, or others familiar with the child. The constitutional exclusionary rule normally does not apply at dispositional hearings. E.g. In re Michael V., 223 Cal.Rptr. 503 (Cal.Ct.App.1986) (illegally obtained evidence suppressed at adjudicatory hearing admissible at disposition); In re Peter B., 84 Cal.App.3d 583, 148 Cal.Rptr. 762 (Cal.App.1978) (confession inadmissible at trial properly considered at disposition hearing). However, the privilege against self-incrimination applies to sentencing hearings as well as to trials. E.g. Mitchell v. United States, 526 U.S. 314 (S.Ct.1999); Estelle v. Smith, 451 U.S. 454 (S.Ct.1981). Despite concern that the privilege may unduly limit the information available to a judge, courts have held that juveniles should receive a Miranda warning prior to a pre-disposition interview and an advisory of their right not to testify at the disposition hearing. E.g. In re J.S.S., 20 S.W.3d 837 (Tex.Ct.App.2000).

c. Individualized Disposition

The court must tailor its individualized disposition to meet the juvenile's needs at the time the judge imposes it. Although juvenile sentencing statutes may allow graduated responses to youths' delinquencies, the court in In re Ronnie P., 10 Cal.App.4th 1079, 12 Cal.Rptr.2d 875

(Cal.App.1992), required the juvenile court to make individualized and particularized findings to support its dispositional decision and not simply to execute a previously stayed disposition.

3.   APPELLATE REVIEW OF DISPOSITIONAL DECISIONS

Statutes require judges to make written findings of fact to support the disposition ordered. Some also require the court to make findings about alternative dispositions that the judge considered and why those were less appropriate than the one ordered. E.g. Minn. Stat. § 260B.185 (2000).

States differ on the scope of appellate review of a judge's dispositional order. Some courts review juvenile court dispositions de novo on the record. E.g. In re B.B., 516 N.W.2d 874 (Iowa 1994). Even where the standard of review is de novo, appellate courts assign "appreciable weight" to the judge's findings of fact and the disposition based on those findings. E.g. In re S.J., 304 N.W.2d 685 (N.D.1981). More commonly, appellate courts defer to trial judges' dispositional decisions and reverse them only if they are "clearly erroneous" or an "abuse of discretion." E.g. In re J.M., 546 N.W.2d 383 (S.D.1996); In re L.K.W., 372 N.W.2d 392 (Minn.Ct.App.1985). A few courts grant trial judges absolute discretion to make dispositional decisions. E.g. In re J.A., 510 N.W.2d 68 (Neb.1994) (judge authorized to impose a range of dispositions, so no need to provide reasons to justify decision). Where the statute authorizes dispositions based on the "child's need for protection or rehabilitation," appellate courts have reversed institutional commitments designed to punish or deter other youths. E.g. In re Appeal No. 179, 327 A.2d 793 (Md.Ct.Spec. App.1974).

C. SENTENCING STATUTES

Legislative preambles, sentencing statutes, judges' sentencing practices, and the correctional programs employed provide indicators of the purpose of juvenile court dispositions. E.g. Feld, *Bad Kids*. Originally, juvenile court judges imposed indeterminate and non-proportional sentences to meet a child's "real needs." In theory, an offense constituted only a diagnostic symptom and treatment personnel released the offender once they determined that she was rehabilitated. By contrast, when courts punish offenders, they typically impose determinate or mandatory minimum sentences based on the seriousness of the past offense. "The distinction between indeterminate and determinate sentencing is not semantic, but indicates fundamentally different public policies. Indeterminate sentencing is based upon notions of rehabilitation, while determinate sentencing is based upon a desire for retribution or punishment." In re Felder, 93 Misc.2d 369, 402 N.Y.S.2d 528 (N.Y.Fam.Ct.1978). Contrasting indeterminate, non-proportional, and offender-oriented dispositions with determinate, proportional and offense-based sentences provides one indicator of juvenile courts' increasing emphases on punishment.

This Section describes juvenile court sentencing laws and recent legislative changes. Sentencing laws may emphasize characteristics of the *offender* or the seriousness of the *offense*, that is, a child's *future welfare* or her *past behavior*. If legislators or judges focus primarily on a youth's offense, then they may use mandatory minimum, or determinate and proportional sentences to punish, incapacitate, or deter. If judges focus predominantly on the offender, then they use indeterminate and non-proportional dispositions to provide wide latitude to rehabilitate. Historically, juvenile courts intervened to promote a child's "best interests." Most juvenile codes authorized indeterminate sentences because judges and correctional personnel could not predict the course or duration necessary for successful treatment. While some statutes instruct judges to consider the "least restrictive alternative," most allow the court to confine a delinquent for a period of years or until she reaches the age of majority or some other limit.

1. INDETERMINATE SENTENCES: TREATMENT IN JUVENILE COURTS

Rehabilitation is offender-oriented and future-oriented; punishment is offense-oriented and backward-looking. "Conceptually, rehabilitation and punishment may be mutually exclusive penal goals. Punishment is retrospective and imposes harsh consequences for past offenses. It has a goal of proportional punishment which accords great significance to the seriousness of the offense. Rehabilitation, however, is prospective and tries to improve the offender's future welfare. Rehabilitation assigns primary importance to the individual as its sentences are non-proportional and indeterminate." In re M.D.N., 493 N.W.2d 680 (N.D.1992). If rehabilitation is the goal, then courts consider a youth's the offense for what it indicates about treatment needs. Because each offender differs, dispositions are individualized and the sentence a judge imposes on one delinquent has no relevance to another juvenile's needs or sentence. Although a serious offense may indicate greater need for treatment, no necessary relationship exists between the offense and the need for and duration of treatment.

Juvenile courts exercise jurisdictional authority over youths below a certain age, generally eighteen years of age. However, dispositional statutes may authorize longer sentences that may continue for a term of years, for a period beyond the jurisdictional age or the age of majority, until age twenty one, or even until age twenty-four. E.g. Conn. Gen. Stat. § 46b–141 (2000) (indeterminate time up to eighteen months); Iowa Code § 232.53 (2002) (indeterminate until age 18); Ky. Rev. Stat. § 635.090 (2001) (jurisdiction until 19th birthday); Idaho Code § 20–507 (2001) (until age 21). For older youths near the maximum age of jurisdiction, juvenile courts need a longer dispositional authority in order to provide appropriate treatment. E.g. Iowa Code § 232.53(2) (2002) (jurisdiction for juveniles aged 17 years continues for one year and six months from date of disposition).

In most states, juvenile courts impose indeterminate dispositions which continue until the jurisdictional limit. E.g. Minn. Stat. § 260B.185 Subd. 4 (2000) (indeterminate until age nineteen); Ct. Stat. § 46b–141 (2000) (indeterminate time up to eighteen months). For youths committed for a limited period, rather than for the duration of minority, statutes authorize the custodial agency, such as the department of corrections, to apply to juvenile court to extend the original commitment. Statutes allow for one- or two-year extensions until a juvenile reaches the maximum jurisdictional age. E.g. Ct. Stat. § 46b–141 (2000) (eighteen month extensions). In granting an extension, the court holds another disposition hearing to determine whether an extension is in the "best interests of the child or the community" or "necessary to accomplish the purposes of the order extended." O.C.G.A. § 15–11–41(g) (2000). The court in In re T.B., 268 Ga. 149, 486 S.E.2d 177 (Ga.1997), upheld the judge's authority to extend a youth's sentence beyond the length initially imposed. Although T.B. claimed that the extension increased his punishment and violated the constitutional prohibition on double jeopardy, the court found that the statute authorized extension for treatment rather than punishment.

Because delinquency dispositions are indeterminate, non-proportional, and continue for the duration of minority, at least for minor offenses, delinquents theoretically may receive longer sentences than a criminal court judge could impose on an adult convicted of the same offense. In Gault, for example, the judge committed the fifteen-year-old boy to the State Industrial School "for the period of his minority [that is, until age twenty-one], unless sooner discharged by due process of law." A criminal court judge could have sentenced an adult convicted of the offense to a maximum fine of fifty dollars or imprisonment for up to two months.

Youths who receive delinquency dispositions that exceed the maximum adult sentence for the same offense have argued that their sentences violate equal protection. Courts characterize delinquency dispositions as protective or rehabilitative, rather than punitive, find that treatment may require a longer period of confinement, and reject these challenges. Other courts conclude that a legislature rationally could believe that children need a different type and length of disposition than adults because of their greater malleability and treatment responsiveness. E.g. In re Allison, 547 S.E.2d 169 (N.C.App.2001). Other courts reject juveniles' equal protection challenges based on differences between children's and adults' liberty interests. In Smith v. State, 444 S.W.2d 941 (Tex.Ct.Civ.App.1969), the judge committed the fifteen-year-old youth to an institution for "an indeterminate period not extending beyond his twenty-first birthday," i.e., nearly five years, for an offense for which a judge could confine an adult for no longer than one year. The court concluded that juvenile courts' rehabilitative purpose and treatment, rather than punishment, provided a rational basis for extended indeterminacy. In addition, it found that a legislature reasonably could classify children differently from adults for policy purposes. Although courts use strict scrutiny to assess classifications that affect suspect classes or intrude on fundamental liberties, Smith concluded that age is not a suspect class and a longer disposition did not adversely affect any fundamental liberties. The court declined to evaluate whether the benefits of confinement outweighed the burdens, declined to substitute its judgment for the legislature about costs and benefits, and upheld the reasonableness of the classification.

The California supreme court in In re Eric J., 159 Cal.Rptr. 317, 601 P.2d 549 (Cal.1979), considered whether the maximum adult sentence should limit a juvenile's disposition. Eric J. invoked an earlier decision, People v. Olivas, 17 Cal.3d 236, 551 P.2d 375, 131 Cal.Rptr. 55 (Cal.1976), which held that courts could not sentence youthful misdemeanants—juveniles tried as adults—to the California Youth Authority for a longer term than the maximum time they could impose on adults convicted of the same offense. The Eric J. court declined to use the Olivas limitation because it found that juveniles sentenced as juveniles and youths sentenced as adults were not similarly situated. Juveniles had lesser liberty interests which justified greater controls than the state could impose on adults. Unlike adults' determinate and punitive sentences, the court found that "[j]uvenile commitment proceedings are designed for the purposes of rehabilitation and treatment, not punishment." It concluded that the differences between punishment and treatment and between adults and children justified longer sentences.

In State v. Rice, 98 Wash.2d 384, 655 P.2d 1145 (Wash.1982), the juvenile court convicted a youth of an attempted misdemeanor. The judge departed from the juvenile dispositional guidelines, which called for only a modest local sanction and imposed a one-year "manifest injustice" sentence. A judge could sentence an adult convicted of a misdemeanor to a maximum term of ninety days. Again, the juvenile argued that extending his sentence beyond the adult maximum violated equal protection. The Rice court held that the maximum adult sentence did not limit juvenile dispositions because the latter did not simply mirror the penal policies of the criminal code. The court reviewed the purposes and policies of the juvenile code and found that the law required the juvenile court to rehabilitate as well as to punish. A delinquent's rehabilitation may require a longer term than the maximum allowed under a criminal sentence. It found that juveniles' need for treatment required greater flexibility. Although the court used a strict scrutiny analysis because confinement infringed on liberty, it found a compelling state interest in rehabilitating the juvenile.

Some states avoid the problem of different sentence lengths for juveniles and adults convicted of the same crime by limiting the term of a delinquency commitment to those authorized for adults. E.g. N.C. Gen. Stat. § 7A–652(c) (2000); Tenn. Code Ann. § 37–1–1378(a)(1)(B) (2000) (juvenile commitment no longer than that for adult convicted of same offense); W. Va. Code § 49–5–13(5) (2001) (commitments shall not exceed the adult maximum term for same offense).

The Supreme Court in United States v. R.L.C., 503 U.S. 291 (S.Ct.1992), considered whether a federal juvenile court judge should sentence a delinquent to the sentence an adult defendant would receive under the sentencing guidelines or the longer sentence authorized by the criminal statute. Unlike state court decisions like Rice, Eric J., and Smith that used rehabilitation to rationalize longer sentences for juveniles, R.L.C. found that the federal guidelines statute superseded the criminal statute as the basis to determine sentence lengths. The Court invoked the rule of lenity and resolved any statutory ambiguity by interpreting the statute to favor the defendant. The dissenting justices in R.L.C. objected that using the guidelines' maximum sentence imposed a burden on juvenile court judges to calculate delinquents' sentences.

2.   DETERMINATE, MANDATORY, AND EXTENDED SENTENCES IN JUVENILE COURT

Although indeterminate, rehabilitative dispositions remain the norm for most ordinary delinquents, get-tough legislation enacted in about half the states uses determinate or mandatory minimum sentences to regulate some delinquents' dispositions, institutional commitments, or release. E.g. Feld, *Bad Kids*; Torbet, *State Responses*.

Determinate sentencing provisions restrict judicial discretion. Mandatory minimum statutes reflect legislative sentencing decisions. Correctional or parole release guidelines enable the executive branch to determine length of confinement. Most of these legislative changes target serious and persistent offenders and provide indicators of juvenile courts' shift from treatment to punishment. These provisions use offense criteria to regulate sentences, to increase punitiveness, and to enable legislators symbolically to demonstrate their toughness.

a. Purpose Clauses

Treatment provides the rationale to reject equal protection challenges, to sentence juveniles for longer terms than adults, and to deny juveniles criminal procedural safeguards such as the jury trial. The Court in McKeiver v. Pennsylvania and Allen v. Illinois used purpose clauses, sentencing statutes, sentencing practices, and conditions of confinement to distinguish between treatment and punishment. Since the creation of the juvenile court in Cook County, Illinois, in 1899, the historical purpose of juvenile court law has been

> to secure for each minor subject hereto such care and guidance, preferably in his own home, as will serve the moral, emotional, mental, and physical welfare of the minor and the best interests of the community; to preserve and strengthen the minor's family ties whenever possible, removing him from the custody of his

> parents only when his welfare or safety or the
> protection of the public cannot be adequately
> safeguarded without removl; and, when the
> minor is removed from his own family, to
> secure for him custody, care, and discipline as
> nearly as possible equivalent to that which
> should be given by his parents. . . . Ill. Ann.
> Stat. ch. 37, ¶ 701–2 (Smith–Hurd 1972).

Many states adopted some version of the Illinois
juvenile court purpose clause as the preamble to
their juvenile codes. Some provided the additional
purpose of "remov[ing] from a minor committing a
delinquency offense the taint of criminality and the
penal consequences of criminal behavior, by
substituting therefore an individual program of
counseling, supervision, treatment, and
rehabilitation."

Beginning in the 1980s, state legislatures began
to amend purpose clauses to de-emphasize the
exclusively rehabilitative role of juvenile courts and
to emphasize accountability, responsibility, and
other penal goals. E.g. Feld, *Bad Kids*. In 1984,
California amended its purpose clause to include the
goal of punishment. "Minors under the jurisdiction
of the juvenile court as a consequence of delinquent
conduct shall, in conformity with the interests of
public safety and protection, receive care, treatment
and guidance which is consistent with their best
interest, which holds them accountable for their
behavior, and which is appropriate for their
circumstances. This guidance may include
punishment that is consistent with the

rehabilitative objectives of this chapter." Cal. Welf. & Inst. Code § 202(b) (2000). Rehabilitative punishments include fines, compulsory service, conditions of probation, and commitment to facilities or institutions, but "does not include retribution." Cal. Welf. & Inst. Code § 202(e) (2000).

The court of appeals in In re Charles C., 232 Cal.App.3d 952, 284 Cal.Rptr. 4 (Cal. Ct. App. 5th Dist.1991), analyzed the amendment and concluded that "the addition of punishment as an expressed purpose of the Juvenile Court Law [does not] change[ ] the overriding purpose or design of the juvenile justice system warranting the imposition of a jury trial requirement. . . . The fundamental . . . purpose of the juvenile justice system . . . is the treatment and rehabilitation of youths . . . The state's punishment of minors is a 'rehabilitative tool,' distinguishable from the criminal justice system for adults which has a purely punitive purpose separate from its rehabilitative goals." The court in In re Javier A.,159 Cal.App.3d 913, 206 Cal.Rptr. 386 (Cal. Ct. App.1984), examined the same statutory changes and reached the opposite conclusion. "[A] juvenile delinquency proceeding . . . asks a court to decide whether a child has violated a specified criminal law and whether this violation is a felony or misdemeanor. If the court decides beyond a reasonable doubt the child did commit the crime, it can, in order to 'protect the public from criminal conduct,' deprive the child of his liberty for the same period of time an adult would lose his liberty for violating the same criminal law."

Although promoting a child's best interests remains the predominant goal of juvenile courts, states balance treatment with protecting public safety and other goals. State correctional policies emphasize "accountability; community protection; and competency development . . . [T]he court shall impose a sentence that will protect the community, hold the juvenile accountable for his actions, and assist the juvenile in developing skills to become a contributing member of a diverse community." Idaho Code § 20–501 (2000). Other codes' purposes include "protection of the public and public safety" and promoting "punishment for criminal acts." Tex. Fam. Code § 51.10 (Vernon 2000).

Courts acknowledge that changes in purpose clauses signal changes in juvenile courts' philosophical direction, but insist that punishment may play a role in rehabilitative dispositions. In State v. Lawley, 91 Wash.2d 654, 591 P.2d 772 (Wash.1979), the Washington supreme court reasoned that "sometimes punishment is treatment," and upheld the legislature's conclusion that "accountability for criminal behavior, the prior criminal activity and punishment commensurate with age, crime, and criminal history does as much to rehabilitate, correct, and direct an errant youth as does the prior philosophy of focusing upon the particular characteristics of the individual juvenile." The Nevada Supreme Court endorsed punishment as an appropriate function of juvenile courts. "By formally recognizing the legitimacy of punitive and deterrent sanctions for criminal offenses juvenile courts will be properly and somewhat belatedly expressing society's firm disapproval of juvenile crime and will be clearly issuing a threat of punishment for criminal acts to the juvenile population." In re Seven Minors, 99 Nev. 427, 664 P.2d 947 (Nev.1983). Some courts approve incarcerating delinquents because it may deter other youths, because some youths deserve punishment, and to uphold the integrity of the criminal law. E.g. Scott L. v. State, 760 P.2d 134 (Nev.1988).

b. Determinate Sentencing Statutes

In 1977, Washington enacted sentencing guidelines for delinquents. The law used presumptive, determinate guidelines based on the seriousness and persistence of youths' offending. The guideline's goals include "accountability" and "punishment commensurate with the age, crime and criminal history of the juvenile offender," as well as "treatment, supervision, and custody." Wash. Rev. Code § 13.40.010 (2000). The dispositional guidelines prescribed a standard range of sanctions based on offense and criminal history. Wash. Rev. Code § 13.40.030 (2000). At the disposition hearing, the judge considers aggravating and mitigating factors that warrant a departure from the standard range disposition. The judge imposes a presumptive sentence within the standard range, unless that sentence would produce a "manifest injustice," i.e. excessively harsh or lenient. Wash. Rev. Code § 13.40.020 (2000). Either party may appeal from a sentence that deviates from the standard range. Based on the offense and prior record, the guidelines grid instructs a judge to impose either a sentence of confinement or a local sanction, e.g., a community-based probationary disposition. Wash. Rev. Code § 13.40.020(5) (2000).

McKeiver relied on the difference between punishment and treatment to deny delinquents a jury trial and juveniles may challenge penal delinquency sentencing provisions by demanding a jury trial. After Washington adopted its just deserts juvenile code, a youth argued that the amended purpose clause and determinate sentence law entitled him to a jury trial. State v. Lawley, 91 Wash. 2d 654, 591 P.2d 772 (Wash.1979). The Washington Supreme Court acknowledged that determinate sentences might seem to convert a delinquency proceeding into a criminal prosecution, but concluded that proportional punishment could be as rehabilitative as individualized treatment. A decade later, the Court reaffirmed its denial of a state constitutional right to a jury trial. State v. Schaaf, 109 Wash. 2d 1, 743 P.2d 240 (Wash.1987). Even though juvenile courts imposed determinate sentences for criminal behavior, Schaaf asserted that youths differed in their degree of accountability and therefore needed fewer procedural safeguards. By contrast, the Kansas Supreme Court in In re L.M. 286 Kan. 460, 186 P.3d 164 (2008), concluded that changes in the state's juvenile code preamble, adoption of juvenile sentencing guidelines based on present offense and prior record, and the like eroded its rehabilitative rationale, more closely resembled the adult criminal system, and required the protections of a jury trial.

Several jurisdictions use offense-based sentences in their juvenile courts. E.g. Feld, *Bad Kids*; Torbet, *State Responses*. New Jersey juvenile court judges consider offense, criminal history, and aggravating and mitigating factors to sentence juveniles. N.J. Stat.Ann. §§ 2A:4A–43(a), –44(a), (d) (West 2000). Oklahoma adopted a "serious and habitual juvenile offender" law for violent and persistent offenders and creates a mechanism to develop determinate sentencing guidelines Okla. Stat. Ann. tit. 10, § 7303.5.3 (West. 1995). Texas adopted "Progressive Sanctions Guidelines" to "ensure . . . uniform and consistent consequences and punishments that correspond to the seriousness of each offender's current offense, prior delinquent history . . . [and] balance public protection and rehabilitation while holding juvenile offenders accountable." Tex. Fam. Code Ann. § 59.001 (Vernon's 2000). The Texas guidelines assign youths to different security levels and consequences based on the seriousness of their offense.

c. Mandatory Minimum Sentences

About half the states use offense-based guidelines to regulate some aspects of judicial sentencing discretion. These statutes use age and offense criteria to define serious or persistent offenders and to prescribe their sentences. States allow or require judges to impose mandatory minimum sentences for certain serious crimes or designated felonies. E.g. Feld, *Bad Kids*; Torbet, *State Responses*. Under some laws, judges retain discretion whether to impose the mandatory sentence length, whereas others require a judge to commit convicted youths for the mandatory minimum period. In Delaware, for example, a judge must sentence a youth convicted of a second felony within one year to a minimum of six months confinement. Del. Code. tit. 10 § 1009 (2000). States' mandatory minimum sentences apply to "violent and repeat offenders," "mandatory sentence offenders," "aggravated juvenile offenders," "habitual offenders," "serious juvenile offenders," or "designated felons." E.g., Ala. Code § 12–15–71.1 (2000); Colo.Rev.Stat. § 19–1–103 (2000); La. Child. Code Art. 897.1 (2000). "Since 1992, fifteen states and the District of Columbia have added or modified statutes that provide for a mandatory minimum period of incarceration of juveniles committing certain violent or other serious crimes." Torbet, *State Responses*.

These mandatory sentencing statutes focus on somewhat less culpable, serious, or younger juveniles than those waived to criminal court. When juvenile courts retain jurisdiction, mandatory sentences assure that judges and corrections officials confine these youths for significant terms. The statutes prescribe terms of confinement that range from twelve to eighteen months, to age twenty-one, or to the adult sentence limit for youths convicted of serious offenses. For example, in Georgia, a juvenile court judge may sentence a youth convicted of a designated felony to the Department of Youth Services for a term of five years with a minimum period of confinement of twelve months or eighteen months. Ga. Code Ann. § 15–11–37(2) (2000). If a youth commits a second

designated felony or seriously injures an older
person, then a judge must impose a mandatory
eighteen-month minimum sentence. Alabama
enacted a "serious juvenile offender" law with a one-
year mandatory minimum sentence for youths
convicted of Class A felonies or crimes involving
physical injury or use of a firearm. Ala. Code § 12–
15–71.1(a) and (b) (2000). Louisiana enacted a
mandatory sentencing statute that required judges
to commit youths convicted of violent felonies to "a
secure detention facility until the child attains the
age of twenty-one years without benefit of parole,
probation, suspension of imposition or execution of
sentence." La. Child. Code Art. 897.1 (2000).
Although details vary, mandatory sentences based
on serious or persistent offending preclude
individualized consideration of youths' real needs.
The Court in Allen emphasized that the possibility
of "release after the briefest time in confinement"
provided one indicator of a therapeutic rather than
punitive sanction.

d. Correctional or Parole Release Guidelines

Several states' departments of corrections use
administrative guidelines to provide proportional or
minimum terms of institutional confinement. E.g.
Feld, *Bad Kids*. These guidelines represent another
form of offense-based sentencing. Unless
presumptive or mandatory minimum laws restrict
their discretion, judges retain control over the "in-
out" decision whether or not to commit a youth.
Parole release guidelines affect only those youths
whom judges commit to correctional agencies. For

example, the Arizona department of corrections' juvenile confinement and release guidelines specify mandatory minimum terms that range from three to eighteen months based on the seriousness of the offense. E.g. Ariz. Rev. Stat. Ann. § 8–241 (2000). Minnesota's department of corrections uses determinate "length of stay" guidelines based on present offense and risk factors such as prior record and probation or parole status. E.g. Feld, *Bad Kids*. California's Youthful Offender Parole Board decides to release juveniles committed to the Youth Authority based on a seven category scale of offense seriousness. Other states use similar offense classification systems to determine lengths of stay and security level placements of committed youths. Torbet, *State Responses*.

All of these *de jure* sentencing provisions— determinate and mandatory minimum laws and correctional and parole release guidelines—share the common feature of offense-based dispositions and link the length of time delinquents serve to the seriousness of the crime rather than to their real needs. They regulate judicial discretion and relate the duration and intensity of a youth's sentence to present offense and prior record.

D. DISPOSITIONAL OPTIONS

Juvenile court statutes give judges discretion to select from a range of dispositional options: dismissal; continuance without a finding of delinquency; probation; out of home placement; or institutional confinement. E.g. Fla. Stat. § 985.231

(2002). Judges answer the question "what should be done with this child?" in part, by reference to explicit statutory mandates. Sentencing guidelines and presumptive and mandatory sentencing provisions formally restrict their discretion. Despite recent statutory changes, juvenile court judges exercise greater sentencing discretion than do criminal court judges because they consider the "best interests of the child." Even in states with formal sentencing laws, the juvenile system uses more flexible processes because the ideology of rehabilitation fosters greater informality and discretion.

Research evaluating juvenile court judges' discretionary sentencing practices report two general findings. First, the Principle of Offense—present offense and prior record—accounts for most of the variance in delinquency sentences. Every methodologically rigorous study of juvenile sentencing practices reports that judges focus primarily on juveniles' present offense and prior record when they sentence delinquents. E.g. Feld, *Bad Kids*. In short, juvenile court judges attend to the same offense factors that criminal court judges do. Second, after controlling for offense variables, juvenile courts' individualized justice produces racial disparities in the sentencing of minority offenders. After controlling for a youth's age, gender, detention status, and offense, studies report that juvenile courts disproportionately sentence minority youths more severely than they do white juveniles with similar offenses and prior records. E.g. Feld, *Bad Kids*; McCord, *Juvenile Justice*; National

Research Council, *Reforming Juvenile Justice: A Developmental Approach* (2013).

Bureaucratic considerations encourage judges to give primacy to the seriousness of offense and prior record when they sentence delinquents. Analysts attribute judges' reliance on criminal sentencing criteria to juvenile court organizational imperatives—a desire to avoid scandal and unfavorable political and media attention. Avoiding scandals encourage judges to impose more restrictive sentences on delinquents with more serious offenses or extensive prior records. Internal and external organizational factors also constrain judges' sentencing autonomy. Juvenile courts develop bureaucratic strategies to reconcile their mandate to make decisions in a child's "best interests" with other, contradictory purposes like "protecting public safety," "punishing consistently with rehabilitative objectives," and "controlling the commission of unlawful acts by children." Because juvenile courts collect information about youths' present offense and prior record, these factors readily lend themselves to decisional rules, provide bases on which to classify and sentence youths, and enable courts to defend their decisions if necessary. The principle of offense dominates juvenile courts' dispositions because of the penal basis of delinquency jurisdiction and bureaucratic and administrative considerations.

Empirical research reports that racial disparities pervade juvenile court case processing and decision making. Inequalities occur at different stages in different jurisdictions and decisions amplify minority over-representation as youths penetrate more deeply into the system. E.g. McCord, *Juvenile Justice.* Quite apart from overt discrimination, juvenile justice personnel may view black youths as more threatening or likely to recidivate than white youths and process them differently. In part, minority youth over-representation reflects racial differences in rates of criminal activity. McCord, *Juvenile Justice.* Juvenile courts sentence youths on the basis of their social circumstances that mirror socioeconomic status and race inequality. Minority youths may receive more severe dispositions than do white youths because their social circumstances and needs differ. For example, racial differences in family composition and the ability of parents to sponsor and provide out-patient supervision of delinquent youths and to provide some assurance against re-offending may adversely affect dispositions of minority youths.

The structural context of juvenile court decision-making may also place minority juveniles at a disadvantage. For example, more formal urban courts tend to sentence all juveniles more severely than do suburban or rural courts. E.g. Feld, *Justice for Children.* Urban courts also have greater access to detention facilities and detained youths typically receive more severe sentences than do those who remain at liberty. A larger proportion of minority youths reside in urban than in rural settings and police disproportionately arrest and detain minority juveniles for violent and drug crimes. Snyder and Sickmund, *National Report.* Thus crime patterns, urbanism, socioeconomic status, and race interact to produce minority over-representation in detention facilities and institutions. E.g. Feld, *Bad Kids*.

The disproportionate over-representation of minority youths in juvenile detention and correctional institutions prompted Congress to amend the Juvenile Justice and Delinquency Prevention Act in 1988. The amendments require states receiving federal juvenile justice funds to assure equitable treatment on the basis, *inter alia*, of race, and to assess sources of minority over-representation in detention facilities and correctional institutions—the Disproportionate Minority Confinement (DMC) mandate. 42 U.S.C. § 5633(a)(16) (1993 Supp.). In response to the DMC mandate, states examined and found racial disparities in their juvenile justice systems in both secure pre-adjudication detention facilities and post-adjudication institutional commitments. E.g. McCord, *Juvenile Justice*; National Research Council, *Reforming Juvenile Justice*. Discretionary decisions at various stages of the justice process amplify racial disparities and result in more severe dispositions for minority than for comparable white youths. By 1991, juvenile courts confined less than one-third (31 percent) of non-Hispanic white juveniles in public long-term facilities; minority youths comprised more two-thirds (69 percent) of confined youths. Snyder and Sickmund, *National Report*.

1.   PROBATION

Three constellations of variables explain how juvenile court judges sentence youths. First, whether a judge places a delinquent on probation or sentences him to an institution depends on the risk of danger and scandal evident in the youth's current offense and prior record. Second, the willingness and ability of parents or surrogates to sponsor and supervise a child in the community conditions judges' assessments of the child's risk. Third, when the seriousness of the offense and parental supervision do not clearly dictate whether to confine a youth or place her on probation, available treatment facilities and institutional bed-space may tip judges' decisions one way or the other.

Sentencing statutes authorize judges to place youths on probation, the oldest and most commonly used juvenile disposition. Snyder and Sickmund, *National Report* (in 1996, judges imposed formal probation on 54% of adjudicated delinquents). Prior to a formal adjudication, the court may place a youth on informal probation in which the youth voluntarily agrees to comply with the conditions. Following delinquency adjudication, the court may order and the juvenile must comply with the terms and conditions of probation. Juvenile courts place about half the youths referred to them on informal probation without a formal finding of delinquency. Snyder and Sickmund, *National Report.* Some states limit the term of probation for delinquents to two years with an additional extension for one year under "exceptional circumstances." E.g. N.Y. Fam.

Ct. Act § 353.2(6) (McKinney 2000). Unless the statute explicitly limits the length of probation, courts have upheld probation orders that continue for the duration of minority, even for minor offenses. E.g. In re Westbrook, 288 S.E.2d 395 (S.C.1982) (shoplifting).

a. Conditions of Probation

Courts have wide discretion to specify conditions of probation tailored to the needs of the child. Probation officers maintain contact with a child to assure compliance with conditions of probation. If the child fails to follow conditions of probation, then the judge may revoke the probation and impose a more severe disposition.

During a period of probation, a youth typically remains at home or in the custody of another relative and continues normal activities such as school and work. Although a condition of probation typically requires a child to reside with a parent, courts have the authority place a child with a relative, guardian or in a suitable foster home or other residence as a condition of probation. E.g. Conn. Stat. Ann. § 46b–140(b) (2000); Cal. Welf. & Inst. Code § 727(a) (2000) (relative, group home, or foster care). The court may order the juvenile to meet regularly with a probation officer, observe curfews or other restrictions on liberty, complete community service orders, undergo medical or psychiatric evaluation, participate in out-patient counseling or treatment programs, undergo alcohol or drug abuse treatment, submit to random testing, make restitution to the victim, and the like. E.g. Conn. Stat. § 46b–140(c) (2000). When a judge imposes conditions of probation, the order must seek to rehabilitate, rather than simply to punish, the offending youth. Judicial orders may specify conditions of probation tailored to fit the needs of the child, to enable probation officers to monitor the child, to impose structure on the child's life, and to foster the delinquent's long-term prospects.

Courts have authority to impose conditions of probation "that are related to the needs of the juvenile and . . . reasonably necessary to ensure that the juvenile will lead a law-abiding life." N.C.Gen.Stat. § 7B–2510(a) (2004). As special probationary conditions, a juvenile court ordered a youth convicted of involuntary manslaughter to visit and place flowers on the victim's grave on the anniversary of his birth and death, to wear a necklace with a picture of the victim, and to refrain from participating in school activities such as football games and dances. In re J.B., 172 N.C.App. 747, 616 S.E.2d 385 (2005). Appellate courts uphold conditions of probation that require a juvenile to attend school, In re Gerald B., 164 Cal.Rptr. 193 (Cal.Ct.App.1980), to earn passing grades, In re Angel J. (Cal. Ct. App. 1992), and to obey all laws including curfews. Courts conditions may require a probationer to submit to suspicionless searches and to random testing for the presence of alcohol. E.g. In the Matter of the Interests of A.L.J. v. State, 836 P.2d 307 (Wyo.1992) (delinquent adjudicated for alcohol-related offense and testing-for-alcohol condition designed to avoid any future problems involving alcohol); In re Kacy S., 68 Cal.App.4th 704, 80 Cal.Rptr.2d 432 (Cal.Ct.App.1998) (urine testing). Where the juvenile court found that viewing television contributed to the child's delinquency, it properly prohibited her from watching it for a year. E.g. In re McDonald, 515 S.E.2d 719 (N.C.Ct.App.1999). Courts have invalidated conditions of probation that require youths to attend church or participate in religious training as First Amendment violations. E.g. L.M. v. State, 587 So.2d 648 (Fla.Ct.App.1991).

The California court of appeals articulated criteria to review juvenile court probation conditions: "A probation condition will not be held invalid unless it 1) has no relationship to the crime of which the offender was convicted, 2) related to conduct which is not in itself criminal, and 3) requires or forbids conduct which is not reasonable related to future criminality. All three requirements must be met before the condition is invalidated." In re Frank V., 285 Cal.Rptr. 16, 21 (Cal.Ct.App.1991). Thus, courts may impose conditions of probation which are not explicitly related to the violation that resulted in the delinquency adjudication. E.g. In the Interest of James P., 180 Wis.2d 677, 510 N.W.2d 730 (Wis.Ct.App.1993) (adjudicated for firearms offense and required to submit to blood test to determine paternity).

b. Restitution

Courts may impose conditions of probation to rehabilitate, but not to punish, a delinquent. In the absence of express statutory authority to impose a fine, for example, courts characterize fines payable to the state as an invalid penalty. E.g. In re Gardini, 243 Pa.Super. 338, 365 A.2d 1252 (Pa.Super.Ct.1976) (vacating dispositional order that included a fine because "court sought to punish the appellant for his actions by fining him"). However, many states' statutes authorize the juvenile court to impose fines. E.g. Cal. Welf. & Inst. Code § 731 (2000) (fine up to $250); Minn. Stat. § 260B.185 (2000) (fine up to $700). Such provisions require judges to determine fines and a payment schedule based on the child's ability to pay.

Virtually all disposition statutes include provisions to pay restitution to the victim either as a specific disposition or as a condition of probation. E.g. Neb. Rev. Stat. § 43–286(1)(a) (2000); N.Y. Fam. Ct. Act § 363.6(1)(a) (McKinney 2000). Restitution is appropriate when the juvenile's criminal conduct causes pecuniary damage. State ex rel. Juvenile Dep't v. Dickerson, 100 Or.App. 95, 784 P.2d 1121 (Or.App.1990); R.W.S. v. State, 162 Wis.2d 862, 471 N.W.2d 16 (Wis.1991). In instances of group offending, courts may impose joint and several liability on co-defendants for the loss or damages. E.g. State v. Blair, 56 Wash.App. 209, 783 P.2d 102 (Wash.App.1989); J.M. v. State, 786 P.2d 923 (Alaska Ct.App.1990). Juvenile court judges frequently order restitution for property damage or for personal injury as a condition of probation. E.g. Conn. Stat. Ann. § 46b–140(d) (2000) (restitution consists of "monetary reimbursement for the damage or injury"); Cal. Welf. & Inst. Code § 731 (West 2000).

Restitution orders may require a juvenile to "make the victim whole" and provide a connection between misconduct and consequences. Appellate courts require the juvenile court judge to design restitution to aid in the juvenile's rehabilitation. A restitution order may be part of a treatment program, but the amount of restitution must be reasonable in terms of the youth's ability to pay. E.g. State v. Kristopher G., 201 W.Va. 703, 500 S.E.2d 519 (W.Va.Sup.Ct.App.1997); Fla. Stat. Ann. § 985.231 (2001) (restitution order may not exceed amount child reasonably could be expected to pay). A court enters a restitution order in a disposition hearing and, unless validly waived, a child is entitled to assistance of counsel and the opportunity to present evidence to establish the proper amount. E.C.M. v. State, 835 So.2d 1280 (Fla. App. 2003) (court could not proceed with restitution hearing without advising juvenile or obtaining valid waiver of counsel); In re C.A.D., 11 Kan.App.2d 13, 711 P.2d 1336 (Kan.App.1985). The party aggrieved must provide a reasonable basis for the court to estimate the amount of damages which need not be established "beyond a reasonable doubt." E.g. State v. Fambrough, 66 Wash.App. 223, 831 P.2d 789 (Wash.Ct.App.1992) (proof of loss to impose restitution under juvenile code similar to that required to prove damages in tort). The amount of restitution a court orders must take account of a juvenile's ability to reasonably meet the obligation as well as to compensate the victim. In re J.J., 848

A.2d 1014 (Pa. Super. 2004). "It is an abuse of discretion to fail to take the following into consideration when fashioning a restitution order in a juvenile court case: 1) The financial resources and obligations of the juvenile; 2) the burden that payment of restitution will impose; 3) the juvenile's age, education, background, and all other relevant factors; and 4) the rehabilitative effect of the restitution order." D.J.W. v. State, 705 So.2d 521 (Ala. Crim. App. 1996).

c. Community Service

Judges may impose community service as part of a juvenile's conditions of probation. Judges commonly impose community service orders to benefit the community, to enable juveniles to accept responsibility for their actions, and to provide them with work experience. Community service work orders vary from cleaning parks or public grounds, performing maintenance or clerical work for public agencies, or helping in recreational programs for younger children under the supervision of probation officers or regular agency personnel. E.g. In re T.S., 144 Vt. 592, 481 A.2d 21 (Vt.1984) (45 hours of community service an appropriate condition of probation for juvenile to learn accountability and responsibility as a part of his rehabilitation); In re Shannon A., 60 Md.App. 399, 483 A.2d 363 (Md.Ct.Spec.App.1984) (1000 hours of community service, under the supervision of Juvenile Services, working with a brain-damaged child as part of rehabilitative effort).

d. Probation Revocation

The Supreme Court held that adult probationers enjoy a constitutional right to due process in probation revocation hearings. Gagnon v. Scarpelli, 411 U.S. 778 (S.Ct.1973). However, because the probationer already has been convicted of the crime, the procedures in a revocation hearing are more akin to a sentencing or dispositional hearing than to a criminal trial and requires notice, an opportunity to be heard, and to present evidence.

Once a judge places a delinquent on probation, if the juvenile subsequently commits a new offense or violates the conditions of probation, then court may revoke her probation. Probation officers or prosecutors initiate revocation proceedings when they have probable cause to believe a youth committed an offense or violated probation. The probation officer may take the child into custody and petition the court to continue the probation, to impose additional terms of probation, or to revoke the child's probation and impose a more restrictive disposition. E.g. Fla. Stat. § 985.231 (2001). A probation revocation proceeding affects a youth's liberty interests and requires basic due process protections such as notice and a hearing. Some states use the same revocation procedures for juveniles as those employed for adult probationers. Probation revocation hearings require notice of the alleged violation, an opportunity to admit or deny the allegations, and a hearing to determine whether the violation occurred and whether the court should revoke probation or impose another disposition. E.g.

Minn. R. Juv. Proc. 15.07. States differ in the burden of proof required in a revocation proceeding. Some require the probation officer or prosecutor to establish the violation by clear and convincing evidence. E.g. Minn. R. Juv. Proc. 15.07(D). Others use the adult standard of proof beyond a reasonable doubt in delinquency revocation proceedings when criminal conduct furnishes the basis for revocation. E.g. In the Interest of C.B., 196 Colo. 362, 585 P.2d 281 (Colo.1978). Other states use the preponderance of the evidence standard in delinquency revocation proceedings. E.g. People v. Belcher, 143 Mich.App. 68, 371 N.W.2d 474 (Mich.Ct.App.1985) (juvenile probationer analogous to adult and standard of proof in adult probation revocation is preponderance). If the court finds the youth violated probation, then the judge has discretion to continue the probation, to impose additional conditions, to impose short-term confinement, or to revoke probation and order a more severe disposition. E.g. Fla. Stat. § 985.231 (2001).

2. OUT-OF-HOME PLACEMENT

Disposition statutes authorize judges to place juveniles in community-based group homes or foster care facilities. Such placements occur when the parent is unable or unwilling to take custody of the child or cannot provide necessary supervision and control. E.g. W. Va. Code § 49–5–13(4) (2001). Such placements allow the child to remain in the community, provide an alternative to a dysfunctional family, and assure more structure and public security than in the home. Additional conditions of probation may accompany an out-of-home placement.

3.   INSTITUTIONAL CONFINEMENT

Confinement in secure facilities—"training schools" or "industrial schools"—constitutes the most restrictive disposition available to juvenile courts. State laws differ about the relationship between the judge who sentences a youth and the correctional agency that receives him. In most states, the court has the power to commit a youth to the department of corrections, but has no authority to control whether that agency places the youth in a particular facility or for how long. E.g. Idaho Code § 20–504 (2001). Once the court transfers legal custody to the department of corrections, it cannot review or overrule that agency's decision to confine or to release the youth. E.g., In re K.A., 879 A.2d 1 (D.C. 2005) (court lacks power to direct placement or treatment once it commits juvenile to custody of DHS); In re M.D.A., 306 Minn. 390, 237 N.W.2d 827 (Minn.1975); In re B.L.T., 853 P.2d 1226 (Mont.1993); In re L.A.J., 495 N.W.2d 128 (Iowa App.1992) (court lacks authority to direct a specific placement). In part, the department of corrections exercises plenary power over a child's care and placement to control expenditures for treatment and the judiciary may not control executive branch resource allocation decisions. E.g. State ex rel. T.A., 801 So.2d 351 (La.2001). For juveniles committed for more serious offenses, statutes may authorize the court to impose a mandatory minimum period of confinement in a residential facility. E.g. Ct. Stat.

§ 46b–140(i) (2000) ("court may set a minimum period of twelve months during which the child shall be placed in a residential facility . . ."). A few states' statutes authorize the judge to make facility-specific decisions about juvenile placements. W. Va. Code § 49–5–13(b) (2000); In re Harry W., 514 S.E.2d 814 (W.Va.1999).

Juveniles seldom spend the entire length of time authorized by a commitment in an institution. Less than half of juveniles committed to institutions remained in placement six months and only about fifteen percent remained in placement more than one year. Snyder and Sickmund, *National Report.* After an initial period of institutional confinement, the department of corrections normally releases juveniles under parole supervision or "after-care." If the juvenile violates the conditions of release or commits a new offense, following a parole revocation hearing, the child may be returned to the institution for the remainder of the original commitment. The Supreme Court held that adult parolees enjoyed certain procedural rights in revocation proceedings to address the charges of misconduct and whether the parole should be revoked. Morrissey v. Brewer, 408 U.S. 471 (S.Ct.1972). Parole revocation proceedings are similar to those used for probation revocation.

a. Conditions of Confinement

The Court in Gault recognized that confining delinquents for criminal misconduct bore characteristics of punishment.

The boy is committed to an institution where he may be restrained of liberty for years. It is of no constitutional consequence—and of limited practical meaning—that the institution to which he is committed is called an Industrial School. The fact of the matter is that, however euphemistic the title, a 'receiving home' or an 'industrial school' for juveniles is an institution of confinement in which the child is incarcerated for a greater or lesser time. His world becomes 'a building with whitewashed walls, regimented routine and institutional hours . . .' Instead of mother and father and sisters and brothers and friends and classmates, his world is peopled by guards, custodians, state employees, and 'delinquents' confined with him for anything from waywardness to rape and homicide.

The contradictions between the rhetoric of rehabilitation and the reality of institutional conditions motivated Gault to grant juveniles some procedural safeguards.

Evaluations of juvenile correctional facilities in the decades following Gault reveal a continuing gap between rehabilitative rhetoric and a more custodial and punitive reality. E.g. Barry C. Feld, *Neutralizing Inmate Violence: Juvenile Offenders in Institutions* (1977). A study sponsored by the Office of Juvenile Justice and Delinquency Prevention (O.J.J.D.P.) used nationally recognized professional standards to assess the quality of 984 juvenile detention centers and training schools that housed more than two-thirds (69 percent) of all delinquents. Dale G. Parent, et al., *Conditions of Confinement: Juvenile Detention and Corrections Facilities* (1994). It reported endemic institutional overcrowding. Almost half (44 percent) of all long-term public institutions housed inmate populations above design capacity, as did three-quarters (79 percent) of the largest facilities, those with more than 350 inmates. Nearly two-thirds (62 percent) of all inmates reside in overcrowded facilities. As states sentenced more youths to institutions, they increased their prison-like character, relied more extensively on fences and walls to maintain perimeter security, and used surveillance equipment to provide internal security. The OJJDP study classified nearly half (46 percent) the training schools as medium or maximum security facilities with perimeter fences, locked internal security, or both.

Recent changes in juvenile sentencing laws exacerbate institutional overcrowding. Youths confined for longer terms under get tough laws often comprise the most serious and chronic delinquent population. The institutions that house them suffer from over-crowding, limited physical mobility, and inadequate program resources. Overcrowding contributes to higher rates of inmate violence and suicide. Parent, *Conditions of Confinement*. These juvenile correctional facilities exhibit many negative features associated with adult prisons and sometimes function as little more than youth prisons. A number of lawsuits have challenged conditions of confinement in juvenile facilities, alleged that the conditions violated the Eight Amendment prohibition of cruel and unusual punishment, or denied inmates' Fourteenth Amendment due process right to treatment. Lower federal courts differ on the appropriate standard to evaluate conditions of confinement. Some apply the Eighth Amendment to prohibit guards beating juveniles with paddles. E.g. Nelson v. Heyne, 491 F.2d 352 (7th Cir.1974). Other courts apply the due process clause to prohibit abusive institutional practices. E.g., H.C. by Hewett v. Jarrard, 786 F.2d 1080 (11th Cir.1986) (applying due process clause to conditions of confinement); Santana v. Collazo, 714 F.2d 1172 (1st Cir.1983) (using Eighth Amendment as constitutional minimum, but applying due process clause to juveniles confined for status and minor offenses), cert. denied, 466 U.S. 974 (1984); Milonas v. Williams, 691 F.2d 931 (10th Cir.1982) (applying due process clause to conditions involving juveniles confined for discipline problems and crimes), cert. denied, 460 U.S. 1069 (1983); Gary H. v. Hegstrom, 831 F.2d 1430 (9th Cir.1987).

Courts use the Eight Amendment to prohibit certain practices and to prescribe the floor below which institutional conditions may not fall. Courts use either a "shock the conscience" test or a proportionality analysis to assess institutional conditions. E.g. Inmates of Boys' Training School v. Affleck, 346 F.Supp. 1354 (D.R.I.1972) ("evolving standards of decency"). The court asks whether the challenged practice shocks the conscience or is intolerable in a civilized society. The proportionality analyses focus on whether the challenged practices are unnecessarily cruel in light of their aims—i.e. the punishment is disproportionate to the offense or violation—and whether less severe methods could accomplish the same objective—i.e. a less restrictive alternative. E.g. Nelson v. Heyne, 355 F.Supp. 451 (N.D.Ind.1972), aff'd, 491 F.2d 352 (7th Cir.1974) (inmates beaten with a fraternity paddle, injected with psychotropic drugs for social control, and denied minimally adequate care and individualized treatment); Morales v. Turman, 383 F.Supp. 53 (E.D.Tex.1974), rev'd on other grounds, 535 F.2d 864 (5th Cir.1976) (physical brutality and abuse, staff administered beatings, sprayed with tear gas, extensive solitary confinement, degrading make-work, and minimal clinical services); Morgan v. Sproat, 432 F.Supp. 1130 (S.D.Miss.1977) (youths confined in cells with no windows or furnishings and flush holes for toilets and denied access to services, programs, or reading materials).

b. Right to Treatment

The right to treatment is a logical extension of the state's use of its parens patriae power to care for the individual. Institutions for the mentally ill and retarded confine individuals without providing procedural safeguards used for criminal confinement. It is the promise of benefit—a therapeutic "alternative purpose"—that justifies less rigorous procedural safeguards. Confinement without the promised treatment constitutes punishment and violates due process. The state only can justify incarceration without criminal procedural safeguards if it provides compensatory rehabilitative treatment. Donaldson v. O'Connor, 493 F.2d 507 (5th Cir.1974), vacated on other grounds, 422 U.S. 563 (1975); Rouse v. Cameron, 373 F.2d 451, 461 (D.C.Cir.1966).

Courts have found that confined juveniles enjoy a Fourteenth Amendment substantive due process right to treatment which imposes affirmative responsibilities on the state to confer benefits. When the state assumes the role of parens patriae, failure to fulfill those responsibilities violates due process. The quid pro quo rationale of the right to treatment is that the state denies delinquents certain procedural safeguards prior to confinement and in return must confer certain substantive benefits following commitment. Delinquents incarcerated in state training schools have invoked the quid pro quo rationale of civil commitment cases to obtain treatment rather than custodial confinement. E.g., Pena v. New York State Div. for Youth, 419 F.Supp. 203, 211 (S.D.N.Y.1976); Morales v. Turman, 383 F.Supp. 53, 64 (E.D.Tex.1974), rev'd on other grounds, 535 F.2d 864 (5th Cir.1976); Martarella v. Kelley, 349 F.Supp. 575, 602 (S.D.N.Y.1972).

The right to treatment is a controversial doctrine that raises issues of federalism and separation of powers. Juveniles typically sue state departments of corrections in federal courts and allege violations of the federal constitution. In addition to the ambiguity of the substantive due process right itself, their claims pit a federal court against a state executive agency. In most instances, implementation of the right requires a state to appropriate resources. Thus, satisfying the right to treatment may embroil federal judges in legislative judgments about resource allocations. Two cases reach opposite conclusions about the existence of the right and the remedies available to incarcerated delinquents. The court in Santana v. Collazo, 714 F.2d 1172 (1st Cir.1983), found other reasons to confine juveniles besides to deliver treatment—protection of society and protection of the juvenile from a dangerous and unhealthy environment. Conditions of confinement must bear a reasonable relationship to their purpose and the Santana court found that those other goals did not establish an affirmative right to rehabilitative treatment. The court concluded that the constitution guarantees juvenile offenders fewer procedural protections than criminal defendants and thus there is no constitutional *quid* for which treatment constitutes the necessary *quo*. The court found that practices such as solitary confinement may violate the Eighth Amendment prohibition of cruel and unusual punishments. By contrast, the court in Alexander v. Boyd, 876 F.Supp. 773 (D.S.C.1995), found that juveniles did enjoy a Fourteenth Amendment due process right to treatment which it defined as "minimally acceptable standards for treatment and rehabilitation." The court did not intend to create an affirmative duty to rehabilitate juveniles but only to assure minimally adequate conditions to provide juveniles with a reasonable opportunity to correct their behavior. Although the court defined the need for trained staff, minimally adequate levels of programming and services necessary to provide a reasonable opportunity to improve, it declined to specify the institutional policies and practices that the state must adopt to satisfy inmates' right to treatment. Appellate courts typically remand cases to the district court to implement appropriate institutional changes. E.g., Nelson v. Heyne. The district court judge appoints a special master who oversees negotiations between plaintiffs' attorneys and the department of corrections to fashion an acceptable remedy.

Although cases like Nelson v. Heyne reflect the ascendance of the right to treatment during the 1970s and early–1980s, the Court's decision in Youngberg v. Romeo, 457 U.S. 307 (S.Ct.1982), halted expansion of the doctrine. Youngberg considered the substantive due process rights of involuntarily committed, profoundly mentally retarded adults. The Court afforded institutionalized people conditions of confinement adequate to avoid harm and a right to minimally adequate training to protect inmates' safety, but declined to find an affirmative right to training that would lead to long-term improvement. Congress enacted the Prison Litigation Reform Act (PLRA), 18 U.S.C. § 3626 (1999) which restricts the power of state and federal courts to order prospective relief from conditions of confinement based on violation of federal rights. The PLRA applies to juvenile detention facilities and correctional institutions. It limits the prospective relief available to alleviate institutional conditions to that "necessary to correct the violation of the Federal right for a particular plaintiff or plaintiffs." In addition, any relief granted must be narrowly drawn, extend no further than necessary to correct the violation of the federal right, and must be the least intrusive means necessary.

State statutes provide an alternative basis on which juveniles challenge conditions of confinement and assert a right to treatment. Many states' laws contain provisions for the care, guidance and training, of committed delinquents. E.g. Ill. Comp. Stat. Ch. 705 ¶ 405 (Smith–Hurd 1997) ("right to services necessary to . . . proper development including health, education, and social services"); N.H. Rev. Stat. Ann. § 169–B:1 (2000) (purpose of juvenile court to provide "protection, care, treatment, counseling, supervision and rehabilitative resources"). State courts occasionally recognize a statutory "right to treatment." E.g. State v. S.H., 877 P.2d 205 (Wash.Ct.App.1994) (right to rehabilitative treatment under state juvenile code); State ex rel. J.D.W. v. Harris, 319 S.E.2d 815 (W.Va.1984) ("statutory right to rehabilitation and treatment"); State v. Trent, 289 S.E.2d 166 (W.Va.1982) ("constitutional and statutory right to treatment"). States' denial to juveniles of a jury trial and imposition of dispositions that exceed the adult sentence length bolster juveniles' claims for rehabilitative services. E.g. State v. Schaaf, 743 P.2d 240 (Wash.1987) (denial of jury trial); In re Eric J., 601 P.2d 549 (Cal.1979) (longer confinement than for adult in order to rehabilitate).

E.   DISPOSITION OF STATUS OFFENDERS

Juvenile court judges may impose the same dispositions on status offenders as on delinquent offenders, except for secure confinement in detention facilities and institutions. E.g. Miss. Code Ann. § 43–21–607 (2000); Neb. Rev. Stat. § 43–287 (2000). Gault formalized juvenile court delinquency procedures and during the 1970s and 1980s, delinquency dispositions became increasingly more punitive. States do not charge status offenders with criminal violations and non-criminal offenders enjoy fewer procedural safeguards even than do delinquents. See Chapter 7.G. One corollary of those procedural differences is that states may not confine status offenders in institutions with delinquents. The court in Harris v. Calendine, 160 W.Va. 172, 233 S.E.2d 318 (W.Va.1977), held that institutionalizing status offenders with delinquents violated equal protection, substantive due process, and constituted cruel and unusual punishment. The Harris court reasoned that because status offenders had committed no crime, the state only could provide dispositions consistent with its parens patriae authority to help. It required the state to exhaust every reasonable alternative to incarceration and if confinement were the only remaining option, to place status offenders only with other status offenders. If a judge placed a status offender in an institution, then Harris required the disposition record to include specific findings of the absence of other reasonable alternative placements. Harris concluded that the state's failure to provide reasonable alternative placements would not justify institutional confinement.

In 1974, Congress passed the Juvenile Justice and Delinquency Prevention Act which required deinstitutionalization of non-criminal status offenders (DSO). 42 U.S.C.A. §§ 5601, et seq. States that fail to comply with the federal DSO mandate risked reduction or loss of funds disbursed under the program. 42 U.S.C.A. § 5633(c). The JJDP Act discouraged institutional co-mingling of status offenders with delinquents, encouraged diversion of status offenders from juvenile court, and fostered alternatives to juvenile detention and correctional facilities. In order for states to be eligible to receive federal funds, the act required states to remove all status offenders from secure institutions. E.g. In re Michael G., 747 P.2d 1152 (Cal.1988) (segregation of status and delinquent offenders); Doe v. Norris, 751 S.W.2d 834 (Tenn.1988) (institutional commingling of status and delinquent offenders unconstitutionally punishes the former).

Deinstitutionalization restricted juvenile court judges' options to place status offenders and reduced their authority to enforce dispositional orders. If states could not confine status offenders in secure facilities, then it became more difficult to prevent them from running away from non-secure placements. Judges sometimes found a status offender who ran away from a non-secure placement in contempt for violating a valid court order or guilty of escape, a criminal offense. If youths repeatedly engaged in non-criminal behavior, then judges could "bootstrap" them into delinquents and place them in secure institutions. Although state policies about confining status offenders in institutions varied, amendments to the JJDP Act in 1980 weakened federal restrictions on secure confinement and allowed states to expand judges' contempt and incarceration authority. The amendments allowed judges to charge status offenders who ran away from community placements or who violated court orders with criminal contempt of court, a delinquent act, and to incarcerate them as delinquents in secure facilities. 42 USCA § 5603(16) ("other than an offense that constitutes a violation of a valid court order").

Following the federal DSO mandate, states differed over juvenile courts' authority to control status offenders who violated a valid court order. Most states approved juvenile courts' use of the contempt power to order secure confinement of contemptuous status offenders despite the legislative intent to ban detention. These jurisdictions authorized judges to incarcerate a status offender as a last resort if other, less-restrictive alternatives proved ineffective. E.g. In the Interest of D.L.D.,110 Wis.2d 168, 327 N.W.2d 682 (Wis.1983) (detention for contempt valid to uphold court's inherent authority to force status offender to comply with remedial court order); State ex rel. L.E.A. v. Hammergren, 294 N.W.2d 705 (Minn.1980) (record must show that child understood that failure to comply with court order could result in secure incarceration); In re J.E.S., 817 P.2d 508 (Colo.1991) (legislature violates separation of powers by prohibiting judges from using contempt power to enforce court orders by incarcerating status offender); Michael G. v. Superior Court, 44 Cal.3d 283, 747 P.2d 1152, 243 Cal.Rptr. 224 (Cal.1988) (approves secure confinement of status offender for contempt if minor had notice, violation was egregious, no adequate less restrictive alternative, and status offenders segregated from delinquents). A minority of states disapproved the use of courts' contempt power to place a status offender in a secure facility. W.M. v. State of Indiana, 437 N.E.2d 1028 (Ind.App.1982); Interest of Tasseing H., 281 Pa.Super. 400, 422 A.2d 530 (Pa.Super.1980).

The court in Harris v. Calendine, noted that "status offender legislation discriminates invidiously against females." Research on gender bias in juvenile courts reports that judges' use of their contempt power to bootstrap status offenders into delinquents and to place them in secure confinement remains a continuing source of gender inequality in juvenile courts. E.g. Donna M. Bishop and Charles E. Frazier, *Gender Bias in Juvenile Justice Processing: Implications of the JJDP Act*, 82 J. Crim. L. & Crim. 1162 (1992). As federal and state laws increasingly restricted institutional confinement of non-criminal offenders, juvenile courts and families sought alternative placements for troublesome youths. During the 1970s and 1980s, mental health facilities, adolescent psychiatric units, and chemical dependency treatment facilities provided private sector secure facilities to control some youths whom juvenile courts previously handled as status offenders. As DSO reduced access to public institutions, parents used private facilities to confine problematic, non-criminal youths in conflict with their families.

Legal regulation of parents' voluntary civil commitment of children for mental health treatment differs from the procedural safeguards that Gault granted delinquents. In Parham v. J.R., 442 U.S. 584 (S.Ct.1979), the Court considered the constitutional rights of juveniles in civil commitment proceedings. Parham used the Mathews v. Eldridge balancing test to weigh the private interests affected by the action, the risk of error those procedures entailed, and the probable value and burden of additional procedural safeguards. Although Parham recognized juveniles' liberty interests to avoid institutionalization, the Court asserted that the private interests at stake included both juveniles' liberty interests and parents' concern for their child's welfare and health. Parham presumed that parents act in their child's best interests and enjoy substantial authority to make decisions on their child's behalf, even if the child disagrees. Although the State has a substantial interest to avoid erroneous and unnecessary civil commitments, it also has an interest to allocate treatment resources to patients rather than to pre-hearing evaluations and hearings. In balancing these interests, the Court required a neutral fact-finder to evaluate the child to assess whether her condition satisfied commitment criteria. According to Parham, a staff physician who independently evaluates a child's mental condition and need for treatment constitutes a neutral fact-finder. Because civil commitment involves medical questions, it requires only competent staff to make evaluations. Parham feared that a formal hearing might exacerbate already strained parent-child relations. Parham's concurring-dissenting opinion acknowledged that a pre-commitment adversarial hearing might deter some parents from seeking medical attention for their children, delay the delivery of treatment, and exacerbate family conflict. However, it argued that a formal post-commitment hearing would pit a child's liberty interests against institutional staff and doctors who would be the adverse parties, rather than the parents.

Parham's decision to eschew either a pre-commitment hearing or post-commitment review poses significant dangers of erroneous confinement. It is difficult for physicians to accurately diagnose adolescents and their need for secure treatment. Although Parham relied on physicians as neutral fact-finders to evaluate juveniles for commitment, hospitals and doctors have fiscal incentives to fill under-utilized bed-space. Changes in insurance coverage and reimbursement policies encourage in-patient rather than out-patient treatment, even though the latter may be more appropriate for most youths. The confluence of Parham's minimal procedural safeguards, the economic interests of physicians, and the availability of third-party payers have coalesced to provide an economical and efficient alternative to the juvenile justice system to confine troubled and troublesome youths. E.g. Lois

Weithorn, *Mental Hospitalization of Troublesome Youth: An Analysis of Skyrocketing Admissions Rates*, 40 Stan. L. Rev. 773 (1988).

States may also evade the DSO mandate by relabeling status offenders as delinquents to obtain access to secure facilities. Status offenders are not a unique or discrete category of juveniles or conduct, and they share many of the same characteristics and behavioral versatility as delinquent offenders. As a result, the juvenile justice system could charge a status offender with a minor crime, adjudicate her as a delinquent, and commit her to an institution. Research reports that changing public attitudes and police practices toward domestic assaults may have lead states to charge girls with simple assault rather than with a status offense, such as incorrigibility or unruly conduct, and thereby evade the prohibitions of the JJDP Act. Analyses of girls' assault cases referred to juvenile court report that about half were family centered and involved conduct that parents and courts previously addressed as incorrigibility cases. Barry C. Feld, "Violent Girls or Relabeled Status Offenders? An Alternative Interpretation of the Data," 55 Crime & Delinquency 241 (2009).

INDEX

References are to Pages